THRESHOLD
EDITIONS

ALSO BY HERMAN J. OBERMAYER

Jews in the News:
British and American Newspaper Articles about Jews, 1665–1800

Soldiering for Freedom: A GI's Account of World War II

REHNQUIST

*A Personal Portrait of the
Distinguished Chief Justice of the U.S.*

HERMAN J. OBERMAYER

THRESHOLD
EDITIONS

New York   London   Toronto   Sydney

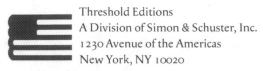

Threshold Editions
A Division of Simon & Schuster, Inc.
1230 Avenue of the Americas
New York, NY 10020

Note to Readers: This work is a memoir. It reflects the author's present recollections of his experiences over a period of years. Some dialogue and events have been re-created from memory and, in some cases, have been compressed to convey the substance of what was said and what occurred.

Photo credits:
Map of Rehnquist home (p. 53) produced by David Swanson Cartography, Hackensack, MN. Used with permission.

Photo of Passover Seder (p. 113) by Arthur S. Obermayer. Used with permission.

Photo of Herman Obermayer, Betty Nan Obermayer, and William H. Rehnquist, Ritz-Carlton Hotel, Arlington, VA, September 1999 (p. 207) by Warren Mattox, Mattox Photography. Used with permission.

Further permissions and copyright information can be found on page 267.

First Threshold Editions hardcover edition September 2009

THRESHOLD EDITIONS and colophon are trademarks of Simon & Schuster, Inc.

For information about special discounts for bulk purchases,
please contact Simon & Schuster Special Sales at
1-866-506-1949 or business@simonandschuster.com.

The Simon & Schuster Speakers Bureau can bring authors to your live event.
For more information or to book an event contact the Simon & Schuster Speakers Bureau at 1-866-248-3049 or visit our website at www.simonspeakers.com.

Manufactured in the United States of America

10   9   8   7   6   5   4   3   2   1

Library of Congress Cataloging-in-Publication Data is available.

ISBN 978-1-4767-4643-2

In Memory of

LEON J. OBERMAYER
1886–1984

and

JULIA SINSHEIMER OBERMAYER
1900–1996

Parenting exemplars

TABLE OF CONTENTS

TABLE OF CONTENTS

PART FOUR

PREFACE

I.

THE DEATH OF William H. Rehnquist, the sixteenth chief justice of the United States, on September 3, 2005, was a news event of worldwide importance. Around the globe it received front-page coverage. The president ordered that flags on all public buildings be flown at half-staff. For me, it was also an event of great importance. It meant the end of a profound friendship.

Editorial writers and commentators speculated on how the passing of Chief Justice Rehnquist, the Supreme Court's undisputed leader for almost two decades, would affect American life in the future, both near and distant. All agreed that history would remember him. He had made a difference. But there was wide disagreement as to whether he would be remembered favorably. While his judicial opinions were almost always scholarly and forceful, many also were controversial and provocative.

Still, virtually nothing was published about Bill Rehnquist the man. Obituary articles ranged from stereotyped and journalistic to scholarly and analytic. Many were generous and laudatory. They used superlatives to describe his intellect, his leadership skills, his memory and his legal reasoning. Yet, except for brief mentions of life-cycle-type events—births, marriages, graduations, public honors and promotions—virtually nothing was written about his personality or personal life. This was not attributable to sloppy reportage or poorly maintained archives. He had worked hard to keep his private life—including his friendship with me—out of the limelight. And media coverage following his death confirmed that he had succeeded.

The man who headed the federal judiciary under four presidents, and who served as a Supreme Court justice for a third of a century, was almost a nonperson, a historic figure about whom the general public knew little or nothing. This in itself is most unusual. It is truly remarkable in light of the highly visible role he played in two of the most important and contentious events in recent American history: the Supreme Court's decision that made George W. Bush the winner of the presidential election in 2000 and the impeachment trial of President Bill Clinton in 1999, when, for the second time in American history, a chief justice presided over the United States Senate. No other American played even a minor role in *both* of these historic occurrences.

Rehnquist's judicial opinions often inflamed passions. They aroused both ire and praise. But those feelings were rarely personalized. The underlying quirks and eccentricities were too well hidden. That is history's loss. In a small way, I will try to remedy that loss. Knowledge about the enthusiasms, biases, foibles and personal habits of the individuals who affect great events—including judicial events—contributes, often significantly, to understanding and evaluating them.

Among his contemporaries, curiosity about the late chief justice is not limited to the Clinton impeachment and the 2000 election. A broad swath of the public would like to know more about the man whose elegant and tightly reasoned dissent in *Roe v. Wade* has for almost thirty-five years provided the intellectual undergirding for right-to-life court briefs, and whose *Hustler* magazine opinion made it legal to tell small lies, as long as they were part of a satirical work in which the author was using them to make a larger point.

II.

From the late 1980s until his death, Bill and I enjoyed a warm, close, abiding friendship. When we were both at home, we were in touch by phone or in person nearly every week. Our friendship enhanced both our lives. We treasured it. Until his thyroid cancer operation in October 2004, both of us thought we were in excellent health and that we would continue to enjoy our friendship for many years. His death was a profound experience for me. An important chapter in my life had ended; a void was opened that will never be filled.

Today I am the survivor. Until now, I have kept the details of our relationship private—as we both preferred. But I believe I have been bequeathed a responsibility to write a factual and honest, yet personal and candid, book about my friend. Since one of us is now dead, exposing our relationship to public view cannot harm or compromise it. It can, however, enhance and facilitate the work of future historians and scholars who will study his opinions and the decisions of the court that he led.

Bill's judicial opinions should be appraised on their merits—legal, social, and ethical. That is someone else's job, an ongoing, evolving job. Yet, no product of the human brain was created in total isolation. Often those products can best be understood in the larger context of the life that created them.

III.

It is important that someone write a truly personal book about Bill because character matters—and I had a uniquely personal understanding of his character. While the roots of character are usually traced to family background and early childhood, a window into Bill's late-in-life tastes, habits, eccentricities and values can also cast light on its origins. I will unmask some of the traits that formed his character. He lived by a moral compass. In the course of a long life, he made many decisions, private as well as public. Many were foolish or wrong-headed. But his bad decisions cannot be traced back to venality or pettiness. I believe his chief ambition was to bequeath a judicial record that was the work product of a man who stood firm for what he perceived as right, a man who played the game straight with toughness and finesse. He stood at the apex of his profession. Within the federal judiciary he was the nominal CEO. His directions and instructions were not—and in real-world terms could not—be challenged. The restraint and discipline he showed during his workday, when he could have been an autocrat, carried over to his private life.

Bill had personal friends who knew him longer and differently, but none in the same way that I did. Court colleagues, former clerks, social friends, school chums and family all had meaningful special relationships. But each viewed him from a different perspective: their own. Hopefully, in the fullness of time, some of them will also write Rehnquist memoirs. Their writings will add texture and nuance to mine. Ours was a special relationship without encumbrances. We were close and devoted friends. Nothing more. But that is a great deal.

We met in the seventh decade of our lives. Our notions of right and wrong and good and bad were firmly in place. We knew who and what we liked and disliked—and we usually knew why. Almost by accident, we discovered that we had similar tastes and beliefs in matters as diverse as poetry and politics, movies and economics, TV sports and literary criticism.

IV.

FOR TWO HAPPILY married, well-established men to form an abiding friendship late in life is most unusual. It is different from the all-quality of a dessert or the waitress's coiffure or teeth would be considered pompous, inappropriate or just plain showing off.

We both entered the Army in 1943 as privates and, after serving overseas, we were discharged in 1946 as sergeants. Six of our seven children graduated from the same public high school in McLean, Virginia. Two were classmates. We even had a mutual teenage friend and classmate: Jim Heller graduated with Bill from Shorewood High School in June 1942 and three months later moved into Dartmouth's Streeter Hall with me.

When we met, we had both been married for more than thirty years to women with similar backgrounds. Both of our wives had given up careers to raise children, become involved in the community and in backing up the budding careers of their ambitious husbands. Nan Cornell and Bill were married in 1953 in a formal church wedding with a full retinue of bridesmaids and ushers in San Diego. Betty Nan Levy and I were married two years later in a large, formal synagogue ceremony in New Orleans.

While none of our offspring attended our alma maters and none became judges or daily newspaper publishers, most of the apples did not fall far from the tree. Bill's two oldest children, Jim and Jan, are practicing attorneys, and his youngest, Nancy, retired to raise children after a career as an editor. My middle two daughters, Roni and Adele, were TV journalists until they retired to raise families. My oldest, Helen, sells print advertising and my youngest, Elizabeth, is a social worker.

V.

SINCE 1971, WHEN President Richard Nixon surprised the nation by appointing an obscure forty-seven-year-old bureaucrat from Arizona to the Supreme Court, historians and political reporters have speculated about how Bill Rehnquist secured what is arguably the American republic's most coveted political appointment.

Extensive research then, as well as after his death, failed to disclose anything substantive beyond good luck, a first-rate intellect and a behind-the-scenes role in Barry Goldwater's unsuccessful run for the presidency. He was not a scion of great wealth. Nobody in the political firmament was indebted to him. He had no chits to cash. Bill's success has always been difficult to explain. Hopefully this book, by disclosing new details about a simple, nothing-to-hide life, will offer fresh insights into the real man behind the enigmatic persona.

In Arizona, where Bill lived for fifteen years, he was neither a joiner nor a recluse. He established several lifelong friendships there, but he failed to create a public record that could be praised or attacked. When he moved to the Washington area in 1969 to accept a post in the Nixon administration's Justice Department, his client list included some of Phoenix's more important businesses, but he never became active in bar association affairs beyond Maricopa County, where Phoenix is located.

Although an early member of the "Arizona Mafia" that managed Barry Goldwater's 1964 presidential campaign, Bill is only mentioned fleetingly in most political histories of the period. As the "house intellectual," he authored sophisticated position papers and wrote speeches for the candidate. He was a member of the "first team." But to the general public he was invisible.

Journalists have even searched the background of his wife, Nan, hoping to discover that she was an heiress, a political activist or the close relative of a prominent Republican. But this line of inquiry also turned out to be futile. Before her marriage, Nan was an analyst on the CIA's Austria desk with a "secret" clearance. Her father was a successful San Diego physician who had seven children and little interest in politics.

Bill's public demeanor and appearance are best described as unexceptional. Good-looking but not movie star handsome, he stood out in a crowd chiefly because of his height: six foot two. The wisps of hair surrounding his baldness never turned gray or white, and until the end they had a brownish-rusty hue. Always careful about his diet, he never became paunchy. He wore large-lens fashionable glasses, and his easy laugh showed a mouth full of old-fashioned gold crowns. He dressed appropriately but uninterestingly: button-down shirts, unobtrusive ties, Hush Puppy–type shoes, work pants (but never jeans) on weekends and off-the-rack suits that he usually bought from lower-end mall haberdashers.

A hearty greeting accompanied a weak handshake. At belly-laugh movies, he had no reticence about audibly guffawing. While his life-long back problems did not seriously compromise his posture, he was slightly pigeon-toed and walked with a discernible lope.

Bill welcomed gossip about mutual friends and colleagues. The social isolation forced on him by his exalted position meant that only rarely was he able to enjoy exchanging juicy tidbits about members of the judicial and social communities of which he was a part. While he was bored by trivia about athletes, entertainers and most players on the political stage, his awareness of social trivia's significance was confirmed in the history books he wrote. They were full of genealogical references and explanations of blood ties.

He lived modestly, far below his means. He had no interest in building an estate. Stock and bond investing bored him. His townhouse neighbors were law firm associates and middle-level civil servants. Ostentation offended him.

Those who were able to pierce the hard outside shell that hid Bill Rehnquist's character and personality discovered a quick-witted man who cherished abiding friendships, admired personal loyalty and empathized with other people's travails. He was obsessively frugal, annoyingly punctual, endlessly curious and addicted to cigarettes.

Conservatism was a core value. It was an essential part of the prism through which Bill viewed life. Its application to politics and government was only a small portion of a larger value system. He respected tradition and order, intellectual and social, as well as political and economic. He believed that the proven and established should not be rejected until there are substantial reasons to believe that the new is superior. While this is not a book about public policy, it is necessary to explain the role conservatism played in his thinking. Our friendship would never have developed as it did if we had not shared similar conservative approaches to politics, family life, economics and ethics.

Bill and I understood that candor and honesty are quite different from the granting of mutual access to all of a life's secrets. A respect for boundaries and limits is fundamental for most lasting human relationships. It is an essential component of successful marriages and parenting—as well as friendships. Early on we both acknowledged that our relationship had to be circumscribed by some ground rules. We never talked about his colleagues or cases before his court, unless, in an unusual circumstance, Bill initiated the discussion.

VI.

IN 1841, RALPH Waldo Emerson (1803–82), one of America's best-known poets and intellectuals, published an essay entitled "Friendship." Its enduring relevance is attested to by the fact that it has never been out of print since.

I am amazed at how accurately Emerson described the essence of Bill's and my relationship. He explained that true friendship could flourish only when certain preconditions were met. Bill and I met all of them.

They were:

- Friends must never be in a position to give each other anything beyond trust, warmth, candid conversation and comradeship. There must never be the potential for career or monetary benefit for either party.

- Friends must have symmetry. In the twenty-first century, as in the nineteenth century, "symmetry" describes a relationship that is proportional and balanced. In current usage the word is usually associated with art, decorating, landscaping and architecture. In Emerson's day it was usually applied to human interactions. It referred to individuals who shared philosophies, proximate birth dates and similar tastes in art, literature, friends and recreational activities. People with symmetry supported the same political candidates, belonged to the same organizations and had read many of the same classical texts.

- Friends must always be free to walk away from their association without notice, apology or penalty. To explain this, he contrasted a friendship with a marriage. Spouses often meet the first preconditions, but marriage is a contractual relationship. Neither partner can casually walk away.

It was only after several years of exploring each other's intellectual interests, lifestyle preferences and midlife reading habits that we realized how much we shared; how well we met Emerson's preconditions for true friendship.

VII.

I AM BOTH a saver and an inveterate note taker. Neatly filed at my home are college letters to and from my parents, correspondence about newspaper columns I wrote forty and fifty years ago, plus book reviews, annotated theater programs and unique Christmas cards going back to high school days.

My 2005 book about World War II, *Soldiering for Freedom*, puts on display my penchant for saving the trivia that cumulatively tends to document a life. That book is based on letters, photographs and certain artifacts of war that I had saved for more than sixty years. I fastidiously kept photographs as well as maps, labels, books, souvenirs, postcards and Nazi propaganda at a time when all of my earthly possessions had to fit into a barracks bag that was most often transported from place to place on my shoulder. Until after censorship was lifted in the European Theater of Operations, shortly after V-E Day (May 8, 1945), I had no idea how long I would have to keep my undeveloped rolls of film and war trivia in my barracks bag, where they occupied space that otherwise would have been used for an extra sweater or a pair of dry shoes.

It was inevitable—almost reflexive—that I would save small remembrances of my friendship with Bill. Through the years I regularly dropped "Rehnquist Items" into a red wallet folder. These included postcards, election bet picks, invitations and book reviews, plus occasional scribbled notes on the backs of envelopes, restaurant checks and theater programs.

A psychiatrist might search for the origins of my compulsive saving habit. It has been an important personality trait since early childhood. In varying circumstances my wife of fifty-three years still inquires about my fascination with the acquisition of memorabilia. I did not accumulate either World War II or Rehnquist mementos with the intent to write books.

Both Bill and I thought we were in robust health at the time of his eightieth birthday party two weeks before his surgery. We expected to share good times together for many more years. The day after the party, we discussed my dinner partners (two attractive women I had not previously known) like young men chatting about girls they had danced with at a ball. Writing a posthumous memoir was the furthest thing from my mind. If both of us had lived another five or six years— as we assumed—I doubt the survivor would have had the energy to write a book. Bill's untimely death made me curious about the contents of the "Rehnquist Items" in the red wallet folder. Notwithstanding the fact that it contained only unorganized trivia and an occasional note that I alone could decipher, a careful review of its contents helped convince me that writing this book was important.

VIII.

BIOGRAPHIES AND MEMOIRS are usually structured chronologically. In most circumstances it is natural, appropriate. The journey through life follows a divinely ordained time line. This book, however, will be somewhat different. It will acknowledge some of the more important personal, career and intellectual milestones in Bill's life in their natural order—before we met in 1986.

The two chapters that deal with his pre-Washington life are based on facts Bill told me about his boyhood in Wisconsin and his professional and political struggles in the frontier-like environment of Phoenix in the 1950s and 1960s. I did extensive library and archival research to supplement his recollections.

But the calendar will not ordain chapter sequence. As a matter of fact, there were only two calendar dates when our relationship took a turn: October 17, 1991, when Nan Rehnquist's death made Bill a lonely widower, and October 23, 2004, when thyroid cancer surgery made him an incurable invalid. An impressionistic approach allows me to portray a complex relationship more accurately than would a straight chronological narrative. It involves sifting through small details about movies, dinners, books, bets, tennis and casual conversations. Standing alone, no event in this book is significant. Yet cumulatively, they are meaningful, descriptive and revealing. They tell a story that has never been told before, one that could not be told any other way. In many ways they tell more about William Rehnquist than a chronological narrative would, or could.

Portrait painters are often able to probe complicated, hard-to-fathom persons. They are not concerned with chronology. They try to capture—and communicate to the viewer—a lifetime's experiences in the representation of a single moment in a subject's life. They often succeed. They illuminate the intangibles that form character. Artists evoke insights with juxtapositions, colors, forms, perspectives. So, too, do memoirists. Descriptions of a person's relationship with his friends, his literary and entertainment preferences, his approach to religious ritual and his attitude toward extravagance can often reveal more about that person than a scrupulously researched biography that emphasizes dates and momentous events.

A great painting can tell things that are beyond the scope of a historian. It can communicate emotions by its depiction of the eyes and mouth. In their own special way artists can often probe the true essence of a person. A subject's height, girth, scars, skin texture, posture and clothing preferences add context that often eludes an author. The artist's representation of the luster of the general's medals, the embossing on the cardinal's missal or the cut of the duchess's bodice add nuance, the aesthetic insight that distinguishes a great painting from a photograph.

Bill understood this. He carefully selected Tom Loepp, the artist who painted his portrait for the Supreme Court. Loepp, whose website, as well as his promotional brochure, says that cityscapes and nudes are his "personal oeuvre," appealed to Bill. Bill understood that serious painters of nudes view their art as a way to convey meaning and evoke responses from an unadorned face and form, without the distractions of clothing, jewelry, furniture or accoutrement. To the casual visitor, except for the signature gold stripes on his sleeve (which were added in 1994 after the original portrait was painted), Bill's portrait has little to distinguish it from the others that line the Supreme Court Building's corridors. Almost all the men are robed in black. You must look to the eyes and mouth to find the man. Loepp did that well. But there is more. There are other dimensions of Bill, the complex human being, that the artist did not—and could not—know.

With this book, I hope to complete the Rehnquist portrait. It only has two sources: my observations and recollections, plus written documents. There have been no interviews. All library and archive sources are fully identified in "Notes and Sources."

This book is a final act of posthumous loyalty. Without it, history will have an incomplete—and I believe unbalanced—picture of the remarkable man who was the sixteenth chief justice of the United States, a man I was proud to call my friend.

PART ONE

ONE

TENNIS AND LITERATURE

I.

IT IS UNLIKELY Bill and I would ever have met if a mutual acquaintance had not invited us to join a doubles tennis game he was organizing. If the players had not been terribly mismatched, we would not have become fast friends.

Ken Haggerty, a neighborhood dentist and a local Republican politician, invited Bill and me to join a "dream" tennis game he was organizing in the autumn of 1986. Since all of the players led active lives the "dream game" had five players, including a rotating substitute. The other players were Linwood Holton, the first Republican governor of Virginia since Reconstruction, and John (Dick) Hickey, the local Catholic bishop. We shared the same criteria: We were all political conservatives over fifty-five. We lived near one another in Northern Virginia and were members of the Washington Golf and Country Club. Plus, none of us had a regular weekend game. It all sounded like fun.

Haggerty had organized the game like a hostess planning a dinner party. A hostess assumes that if her guests share similar worldviews, the conversation will be lively and possibly stimulating. If their political perspectives are similar, there will be none of the bitter, nasty arguments that so often ruin social events in suburban Washington.

But athletic contests are not dinner parties. Tennis especially is fun only when the players are athletically well matched. Its demand for relatively equal skills is uncompromising. Conversation is incidental. Contestants usually know nothing about each other's politics or philosophical musings. On-court chatter is usually considered intrusive. Most players resent it.

After a few weeks it became clear that the "dream game" was hopelessly dysfunctional. Haggerty's notion on how to organize a weekly tennis game was totally wrong: even though our political and philosophical outlooks were similar, our tennis skills were not even close. Haggerty was a former all-American basketball player who had captained the Holy Cross College team that included NBA Hall of Famer Bob Cousy. None of the others could run around a backcourt half as fast as he could. Linwood Holton and I were never part of a sports team's starting lineup, not even at summer camp. Bill was a slightly better athlete than I was, but after high school his only competitive sports activity was social tennis. The Catholic bishop was a good athlete, but he knew so little about the game he had trouble keeping score. To compensate for an obviously awkward arrangement, Holton, always the politician, told jokes after bad points, particularly ones that were attributable to his own ineptitude.

Bill and I shared our disappointment with the way the game was evolving. We got up early on Sunday mornings to play tennis, not to listen to bad jokes. Haggerty and the bishop pretended they were having great fun; I found their upbeat chatter embarrassing. Nobody was having a good time.

While the "dream game" was becoming something of a weekly ordeal, Bill and I recognized that our athletic skills were similar. Further, we both felt that talk on the court should be limited to occasionally acknowledging a good shot by your opponent and, only when necessary, stating the score. One weekend, when Haggerty could not find four "dream game" members willing to rise early and participate in a game that was no fun, Bill and I decided to play singles together. We ended up having a good time. And for more than a dozen years, we continued to play singles every Sunday when we were both in town.

Bill, who played doubles weekly with his twentysomething law clerks, was a better doubles player than I was. The long reach that went along with the six-foot-two-inch frame made him formidable at the net. On the other hand, since I preferred playing singles, I could run around the backcourt better than he could. Neither of us had strong serves. Although both of our forehands were stronger than our backhands, neither of us scored points because of our forehands' overwhelming speed.

Although we were both in our sixties, we were in good enough shape that an hour of hard-fought tennis singles was exhilarating rather than exhausting. We were not serious athletes, but we were serious players. Once we decided who served first, there was no chitchat or trips to the water cooler. Our competitive natures precluded approaching a Sunday tennis game as casual exercise.

After we began playing singles together, we never again played in a "dream game." Although Justices Antonin Scalia and John Paul Stevens (both of whom were better players than we were) often played singles with nonjudicial friends at Washington Golf and Country Club at the same time, they never invited us to join their game, and vice versa.

We did, however, play mixed doubles a few times each year when Bill's daughter Nancy, who lived in Middlebury, Vermont, and his sister Jean Laurin, who lived in Grand Rapids, Michigan, came to visit. At least one mixed-doubles match with my wife, Betty Nan, and me was usually part of Bill's entertainment program for both. Jean played at about the same level as Betty Nan, and Nancy was younger and a better athlete. All three women were better tennis players than their male partners. Our matches were spirited and fun. Neither family won consistently.

Probably the most memorable match with Jean and Bill began at

7:00 a.m. on the day after Nan Rehnquist's funeral. When Bill suggested the game, I questioned whether he wanted to be seen at a country club less than twenty-four hours after his wife's funeral. But he brushed my inquiry aside. Two hours of vigorous exercise with his sister as his partner was as good a way as any to begin the next chapter in his life.

II.

WASHINGTON GOLF AND Country Club is a unique institution. Founded in 1894, it is Washington's oldest golf club and has listed on its membership roster Presidents Theodore Roosevelt, Taft, Wilson and Harding; the latter three were avid golfers who played the course regularly. Presidents Taft and Harding occasionally participated in club tournaments. Although there were no restrictions in its bylaws, blacks and Jews were not granted membership until the mid-1970s (I joined in 1978 and Bill in 1985).

Part of a country club's appeal is that within its confines the hierarchical distinctions that are part of everyday life in government and business are supposed to disappear. But country club ambience cannot always trump the real-world distinctions that exist outside its gates.

If, while waiting for our court or chatting after a match, another member stopped by, Bill usually jumped up, extended his hand and said, "Hi, I'm Bill Rehnquist." I always introduced him the same way. But only one in ten responded, "Hi, Bill." I estimate the remainder was evenly split: half continued the conversation without addressing him by name and the other half responded, "It's a pleasure to meet you, Mr. Chief Justice."

Still, I know of no activity in Washington in which rank and status mean less than in the contest for who gets to use Washington Golf's five indoor tennis courts on a midwinter Sunday morning. Court times are allocated on the basis of stringently enforced rules. Sunday between 8:00 a.m. and 10:00 a.m. is the preferred time to play tennis (before church and football). Often as many as fifty players vie for court times.

The tennis clerk begins accepting calls at 8:00 a.m. Saturday for Sunday court times. After 8:00:01 the tennis reservations telephone line is constantly busy. If a member does not slip through between busy signals until after 8:04 or 8:05, he or she probably missed the cut for the most desirable times. There are no exceptions. Everybody is on equal ground—even the chief justice of the United States and his fellow justices, who are often battling for the same time slot. In addition to me and Bill, Justices Stevens and Scalia, the president of the club, highly paid CEOs and prominent local citizens competed against twentysomethings who were skilled speed dialers. When two justices see each other on the court early Sunday morning, they likely jest, "Where did you learn speed dialing?" or "I was told nobody gets special treatment at this club." If we were both in town and we missed our regular Sunday morning game, it was almost always attributable to our getting beaten by overwhelmed phone lines.

III.

FOR MANY MONTHS, Bill's and my weekly tennis games were enjoyable, vigorous athletic contests. But little more. After our Sunday morning game, we usually relaxed and chatted for fifteen or twenty minutes. In the beginning we talked the universal language of small talk: sports, the weather and political trivia. It was enjoyable albeit superficial.

Then we began exploring what, if anything, we shared beyond evenly matched court skills. We were curious about each other. We were also reticent. Neither of us felt compelled to advance our relationship. Our pace was deliberate and hesitant. The most important element in our friendship, shared core values and intellectual interests, did not become apparent until after we had known each other on the tennis court for many months.

Then a period of obtuse inquiry began. It was reciprocal and unstructured. We knew that we shared certain core values. We wanted to know more about each other. But our objective was subtle, unstated.

IV.

ONE SUNDAY IN 1987, for no apparent reason, we began talking about the books that we were currently reading. For many years, discussion of our recreational reading became part of our routine. It continued long after we stopped playing tennis together.

When I visited Bill during his final days, we would almost always speak of our bedtime reading. It usually started a good conversation. Even if one of us was not knowledgeable about a particular work, we were often able to talk about the book's subject, its author or its literary genre. We soon learned that both of us had eclectic reading habits, as well as powers of recall that allowed us to make casual conversation about books we had read many years earlier.

The regular weekly commentary about our bedtime reading was substantive, challenging and enjoyable. It was also a self-revealing, almost confessional exercise. We disclosed to each other ideas, preferences and recollections that had remained dormant in our brains for a long time. Neither of us had friends with whom we could talk about books in the same wide-ranging manner.

These Sunday-morning talks added a new dimension to our lives. Our weekly book discussions confirmed that we shared ideals and values. But it would take several more months of book talk before we understood just how much.

During our last evening together in August 2005, when both of us knew Bill's death was imminent, we were still talking about our latest "for fun" read. David McCullough's *1776* led the *New York Times* Best Seller List during much of that summer, and I noticed the book was on the floor next to the recliner in front of the TV, where Bill spent most of his final days. He had just finished it. A few weeks earlier, by coincidence, I had also read it. I asked whether he had enjoyed it. His initial comment was dismissive. "Nothing really new there, just well-known events cleverly rearranged." But he continued, "I couldn't put it down once I started reading." My reaction had been similar. Then we talked about McCullough's remarkable narrative skills and how we envied him—and we were off once again.

V.

As our postgame conversations—particularly our book discussions—progressed, each of us began to gratuitously drop familiar quotations into our talks. With no one else present, it was just simple, uninhibited fun. The poems we quoted, as well as the lyrics from Hollywood and Broadway musicals, were well known. Almost all of the poems can be found in most standard anthologies of British and American verse. We were not trying to show off; we were searching for an intellectual bond. This was a prelude to the Sunday morning—almost a year after we began playing tennis—when we finally acknowledged that we were playing another kind of game, this one of wits. On that day another strong link was forged in our chain of friendship. I remember the circumstances clearly.

Throughout 1987, the *Washington Post* regularly reported on racial disturbances in the Deep South. Following a deadly riot in Tampa, there was unrest throughout the region. While we relaxed on a bench near an outdoor tennis court, we discussed how the most recent bouts of racial violence seemed to be concentrated in the booming, prosperous cities of the "New South." Cities with glistening glass towers that had been built over the remains of, or adjacent to, dirt-poor, unsanitary shantytowns were the focus of much of that year's civil unrest.

Without warning or prelude, Bill commented, "Ill fares the land, to hastening ills a prey, / where wealth accumulates, and men decay.' " I was familiar with Oliver Goldsmith's "The Deserted Village." It was obvious that he was commenting on the fact that the racial unrest at this particular time was concentrated in newly-affluent modern towns that were not so long ago part of "Dixie Land." Although I could not quote the lines that followed, I was able to respond quickly with a droll line from the same poem about the village schoolmaster: " 'And still they gaz'd, and still the wonder grew, / that one small head could carry all he knew.' " Bill recognized my response. And we both laughed. We had begun a game we would play for many years.

Bill followed with a verse about first- and second-generation post-slavery African-Americans, the parents of most of the urban citizens who were fomenting the unrest. It was from one of our favorite poems, Thomas Gray's "Elegy Written in a Country Churchyard":

> He gave to Misery all he had, a tear,
> He gained from Heaven ('twas all he wish'd) a friend.

Part of the fun of our game was juxtaposing quotations from different locales and genres. Gray's poem was about England's poor, uneducated and forsaken peasantry. But it was on target. I responded with lines from the same poem:

> Let not Ambition mock their useful toil,
> Their homely joys, and destiny obscure;
> Nor Grandeur hear with a disdainful smile
> The short and simple annals of the Poor.

Bill then took us back to the locale of the problem with a verse from Hammerstein and Kern's "Ol' Man River":

He don' plant taters
He don' plant cotton,
An 'dem dat plants 'em
Is soon forgotten . . .

I followed with the Civil Rights movement's theme song:

We shall overcome
We shall overcome some day

He kept us in an antidiscrimination mood by softly singing the *South Pacific* signature song "You've Got to Be Carefully Taught," the plaintive lament of an American naval lieutenant who discovers that differences in race, background and military rank make it impossible for him to marry his Polynesian girlfriend.

You've got to be taught to hate and fear
You've got to be taught from year to year
It's got to be drummed in your dear little ear
You've got to be carefully taught

Then I ratcheted up the game several notches when I quoted from one of the most famous speeches in American history, in which slavery is used as a metaphor. I recited from Patrick Henry's "War Is Inevitable" speech (the one that ends, "Give me liberty, or give me death"), which was delivered in the Virginia House of Burgesses, where virtually all the members owned slaves: "Is life so dear, or peace so sweet, as to be purchased at the price of chains and slavery? Forbid it, Almighty God!"

That was a hard one to top. Bill finished the game with a line from George and Ira Gershwin's "Porgy and Bess," an operetta about life in a black ghetto in South Carolina:

It ain't necessarily so
It ain't necessarily so.

Eventually our intellectual sporting event became more important than the athletic one that preceded it. Our poetry game was straightforward. But it was not simple or easy. While commenting on a newsworthy event during the preceding week, the initiator (we alternated each week) would work into our postgame conversation a few well-known lines from a 1930s or 1940s hit musical or a famous poem. The quotation had to be familiar to both of us. The other would respond by reciting lines from the same poem, a similar one or a related prose text. It was a game that was ours alone. We described the game to our spouses, but only the two participants fully understood its personal and intimate dynamic.

Our after-tennis exercise allowed us to explore the depth and breadth of each other's literary and entertainment tastes, as well as the paths we followed when making intellectual associations and connections. There were thousands of people in Washington who could recite more English poems and sing more show tunes than either of us, but only a few who could play in our game successfully. Our game survived for more than a decade because each of us understood the other and recognized that there were large gaps in each of our repertoires. The aim was to find quotations with which the other man was familiar and to which you could anticipate an appropriate response. If the game made either of us feel inadequate, we would have quit. If we had approached our poetry game with the same competitive zeal that we approached our tennis matches, the poetry game would have flopped. Like tennis, our intellectual game required closely matched skills and strengths. But unlike most sports contests, both players had to avoid exploiting the other's weaknesses. This was the trickiest part. After a few months we knew more about each other's thought processes than most friends learn in a lifetime.

From November to April we played tennis indoors, but during the rest of the year we played outside, even when the weather was a little chilly. During the outdoor months we had no trouble finding a bench or other facility so that we had enough privacy to play our game for fifteen or twenty minutes. In the winter we usually found enough privacy to play our poetry game indoors, but, if not, we retreated to one of our cars.

Over the years our subjects varied as widely as our interests. There was almost no subject we could not twist around so that we could find relevant quotes to respond to the initial proffer quote. For example, the week Bechtel Corporation, a worldwide engineering company, announced it was going to build a campuslike facility in nearby Frederick, Maryland, we began with alternating verses from Whittier's "Barbara Frietchie," which took place in Frederick. We followed with quotes that were both directly and indirectly applicable to the Civil War. They included Abraham Lincoln's Gettysburg Address and his Second Inaugural, Robert Frost's "The Gift Outright," Vachel Lindsay's "Abraham Lincoln Walks at Midnight," Tennyson's "Charge of the Light Brigade," "Battle Hymn of the Republic" and Whitman's "O Captain! My Captain!" The week following Irving Berlin's death we had no trouble recalling more than a dozen Berlin favorites including "God Bless America," "White Christmas," "Easter Parade," "The Girl That I Marry" and "There's No Business Like Show Business".

VI.

JUST BEFORE OUR sixty-fifth birthdays, at Bill's suggestion, we experimented with taking quotation gamesmanship to a higher level than I thought possible. At two luncheons, before and after the meal itself, we tried to conduct our entire conversation in quotations. It was an enjoyable, mind-stretching exercise. We had proved something to ourselves. But two times was enough.

We made up the rules as we went along. Neither of us had previously played a similar game. Bill, who enjoyed brain games of all sorts, admitted he had thought about it off and on through the years. But until he was in his middle sixties, he had been unable to find a willing playmate.

The rules were liberal. Any poem, song or rhyme that mentioned food, a meal or something edible was adequate for describing the simple luncheon fare on the table. There did not have to be direct connections with the meal we were eating or type of food we were being served. Although we often had a light beer with lunch, we ruled out drinking songs. As we saw it, wassailing ballads were special and different.

We would alternately recite familiar verses about food or eating until one of us ran dry. Then we would find a new topic, like the couple at the next table, the weather outside, the faux flowers on our table or maybe the waitress's décolletage. As in our post-tennis poetry game, the main objective was to keep the conversation going.

While waiting for our food to be served, I began with the Twenty-third Psalm, which may have been the first food quote either of us learned. Memorizing psalms was part of public school curriculums in both Philadelphia and Shorewood in the early 1930s:

> *Thou preparest a table before me in the presence of mine enemies;*
> *Thou anointest my head with oil; my cup runneth over.*

Bill followed with the soup song from *Alice in Wonderland*, a long leap from the psalmist's death contemplation.

> *Beautiful soup, so rich and green,*
> *Waiting in a hot tureen!*

When it was my turn I chose another non sequitur food reference from Rodgers and Hammerstein's *Oklahoma!*:

> *The corn is as high as an elephant's eye*
> *An' it looks like it's climbin' clear up to the sky*

Including short breaks to eat our lunch and sip our beers, we were able to sustain sequences about food for half an hour. Quotations about eating are part of every literary genre, including nursery rhymes like "Peter, Peter, pumpkin eater" and "Little Miss Muffet sat on her tuffet, eating her curds and whey."

Both times we played our game at the Two Quail, a small, unostentatious eatery near the Supreme Court. The proprietor always sat us in a nook at the rear of a back room. This meant that old friends did not stop by our table while we were playing our game.

One of our longest sequences also provided the most laughs. It focused on a uniformed naval officer and a fashionably dressed, obviously younger woman at a nearby table. I began with the opening lines of Coleridge's "Rime of the Ancient Mariner," and Bill followed with a complete stanza from Gilbert and Sullivan's *H.M.S. Pinafore,* and then I with "Anchors Aweigh," the Naval Academy fight song. Then we both focused on the officer's strikingly handsome companion. I started with the lines about the colonel's lady and Judy O'Grady being sisters under their skins from Kipling's "The Ladies." Bill countered with "The Lady Is a Tramp." We continued in this vein with Bill quoting a few lines from a Lutheran hymn about the "beautiful face of the Blessed Virgin," and my closing it with Ogden Nash's

Candy
Is dandy
But liquor
Is quicker.

After we had proven to ourselves that we could sustain a luncheon conversation with quotations, it was time to move on. Lunches were more fun if they were just casual guy talk.

VII.

WE HAD KNOWN each other less than a year when we made a very important nonliterary discovery while chatting after tennis. Friedrich Hayek's *The Road to Serfdom* had played a seminal role in both of our intellectual lives.

While discussing a *Washington Post* article about Arlington's powerful planning commission, and the orderly way our community had developed since it was first crisscrossed by subways, Bill made what appeared to be a casual, offhand remark. Arlington's experience with central planning was unique, he said. It would take more than a few decades to judge its success fairly. Friedrich Hayek, one of his favorite contemporary thinkers, thought most government planning was dangerous, he continued. (With the passage of time I have become convinced that Bill's reference to Hayek was not casual at all but carefully calculated.)

In any event, Bill's remark struck an immediate chord with me. After a few minutes of follow-up, we knew we shared another strong bond. Hayek's books undergird much of both Bill's and my economic and political philosophy. The significance of this discovery—for both of us—cannot be overstated.

Hayek's explanation of how a charismatic leader almost imperceptibly changed Germany's democratic government into a totalitarian dictatorship is rational, intellectually neat and appealing. In *The Road to Serfdom* he tells how Hitler's National Socialist Workers' Party (Nazis) and Mussolini's Fascist organization both came into power by winning legitimate elections in operating democracies. They sponsored programs of government largesse, palliatives for poverty and economic central planning. The program benefits were regularly enlarged and enhanced. They were popular. But, as Hayek perceived it, Hitler's and Mussolini's extravagant social welfare programs represented the first steps on the road to serfdom. Individuals had ceded to the state control over their economic well-being—in many instances total control—in exchange for handouts and financial security. Unintentionally and innocently, the Germans and Italians exchanged their personal freedom for doles from the public treasury. These generous and popular social welfare programs were fundamental factors in snuffing out nascent democracies, as Hayek saw it.

Perplexity about what happened to democracy in Europe in the 1930s and 1940s was an important part of the intellectual baggage we carried with us when we became soldiers in 1943. What went so terribly wrong in Germany in the 1930s and 1940s? Slightly more than six years separated Adolf Hitler's democratic election as chancellor of the Third Reich and the beginning of World War II. In that period, a country that epitomized the Enlightenment's culture and sophistication became a nation of monstrous barbarians. I have repeatedly asked myself that question. It will continue to bother me until my dying day.

Hayek did not attempt to assess the merits of particular government-funded social welfare regimes, many of which he believed were appropriate and beneficial, including subsidy for the aged and unemployment insurance. Rather, he attempted to show that there was a reciprocal relationship between the growth of taxpayer-funded social programs and the diminution of personal liberty.

VIII.

Bill and I first read *The Road to Serfdom* in 1945 when we were lonely soldier boys. I was a corporal assigned to an isolated gasoline pumping station near Verdun in the Ardennes region of France. Bill was a also a corporal. He was assigned to an isolated weather station in the Atlas Mountains near Marrakesh, Morocco. We were searching for ideas of the kind of world we wanted to come home to.

To fully appreciate Bill's and my abiding respect for *The Road to Serf-dom*, it is necessary to understand the circumstances that put us in desolate outposts at the edge of a French forest and in the foothills of a Moroccan mountain range. We were there because a federal statute, enacted in 1943, shortly after our eighteenth birthdays, required that all healthy eighteen-year-olds either volunteer for a particular branch of military or be conscripted into the Army. America's democratically elected government had arbitrarily taken away our liberty and incarcerated us behind barbed wire and guard towers. We had time to read books at dreary bivouacs in Europe and North Africa because the United States Army thought it could best use our talents there. At any time, without advance notice or explanation, a low-level military bureaucrat could have ordered us moved to another location where the odds favored our bodies being maimed or our lives being extinguished. These orders could not be questioned or challenged. There were no appeals.

Future generations will never fully understand the profound dread of government power that became part of the basic thought processes of boys who graduated from high school in 1942. We were patriotic. We loved our country. But we were scared. We had no control over our future. We knew that the selection process for dangerous missions was often irrational and/or random.

A book about how strong, powerful bureaucracies—military and civilian—can destroy electoral democracies found a natural audience in an army made up mostly of conscripted soldiers. Government power had turned our lives upside down—and we feared it.

The Road to Serfdom was one of the most popular books distributed to soldiers and sailors during World War II. The *Reader's Digest* condensed version went to more than one and a half million servicemen and -women in war zones outside the United States. Young men who had never before read a book about political philosophy read it—and talked about it. They developed an understanding of how democracies can be transformed into dictatorships. They knew that their own government could arbitrarily assign healthy men in the flower of youth to almost certain death.

Bill's and my admiration for the classical liberal philosophy of

Friedrich Hayek extended beyond *The Road to Serfdom*, but it remained one of the foundations on which our philosophy of government was built. Margaret Thatcher, who was born almost exactly one year after us (on October 13, 1925), was introduced to *The Road to Serfdom* when she was a student at Oxford, and the Luftwaffe brought the terrors of war directly to Britain. Throughout her public life she told audiences that Friedrich Hayek's slim volume was one of the cornerstones of her political philosophy.

It was not until I began writing this book that I learned that in 2001 Bill had told a national TV audience what an important role *The Road to Serfdom* had played in his intellectual development. During an interview on C-SPAN's *Booknotes*, Bill and Brian Lamb, the program's host, had this exchange:

BL: Can you remember when you began to form your own views of the world . . . ? Did you have an early ideology of any kind? A political following?

WHR: I don't think so. I remember feeling when I was in high school that a couple of the social science texts we had were what we would call today "brainwashing." They tended to be slanted in one way. But, you know, it was not a big item in my life at all.

BL: In those early years, when did you have somebody that you really followed, somebody that wrote or a founding father or somebody in history?

WHR: The first really controversial or advocacy book I ever read was when I was in the Air Force. [sic] And it was Friedrich Hayek's *The Road to Serfdom.* I was used to just textbooks that would set forth a bunch of facts, and you're supposed to memorize the facts and recite them back on the test. But this book was an advocacy book trying to show that state planning and socialism and that sort of a thing didn't work economically and was dangerous politically. And it made quite an impression on me.

IX.

WHILE THERE WAS nothing secret about our post-tennis poetry game, over time it forced us to disclose to each other a great deal about our intellectual interests, our preferences, our biases and the depth of our knowledge on a wide variety of subjects. What we had learned about each other cannot be easily articulated or neatly summarized. It was disorganized and random, revealing and penetrating. It also had a by-product: true friendship.

TWO

SHOREWOOD

I.

IN ORDER TO know and understand the real Bill Rehnquist, it is necessary to grasp how he viewed his youth, all of which was lived during the Great Depression in the tiny Village of Shorewood, Wisconsin. Shorewood's influence on him was profound and permanent. It was an atypical place at an unusual time in American history. Within its boundaries there were no soup kitchens or breadlines, no debutante balls or swanky country clubs. An independent municipality within an urban county, it was insulated and homogeneous.

When I first met Bill, thirty-four years had passed since he had graduated from Stanford Law School, and forty-four years since he had graduated from Shorewood High School. While he had been more successful at law school (first in his class versus one of the thirty-three students on the high school honor roll), he talked far more often about his high school days than he did about his university or law school experiences.

II.

FROM HIS BIRTH in 1924 until he became a soldier eighteen years later, Shorewood was Bill's entire life. Most Rehnquist biographical sketches identify his hometown as Milwaukee, Wisconsin. This is technically correct, but it is also somewhat misleading. Shorewood was an upper-middle-class, residential town of thirteen thousand inhabitants within Milwaukee County, a political subdivision that includes the City of Milwaukee, Shorewood and one other small village. The Village of Shorewood is an independent municipality in matters of zoning, education, police and library services. But it is just another part of Milwaukee County (like the City of Milwaukee) in matters of recording vital statistics, sheriff-jail operations and transportation, sewer, water and sanitation services.

With a total land area of approximately one thousand acres, the Village of Shorewood was—and still is—substantially smaller than many nearby dairy farms and baronial estates. Notwithstanding the fact that they share a common border and both receive essential municipal services from Milwaukee County, Shorewood in the 1930s and 1940s was worlds apart from its bustling, diverse, industrial neighbor, the City of Milwaukee.

Between the two world wars, Shorewood's quiet streets contrasted with Milwaukee's run-down row houses, tenements and raucous beer halls. It had the only large municipal government in America that was controlled by the Socialist Party. Most of the building lots in Shorewood were sold to thousands of individuals prior to its incorporation as a village in 1917. This precluded large-scale development at either end of the economic ladder.

Shorewood was a green ghetto where almost every family lived in a detached house with a neatly mowed lawn. Adjacent Milwaukee was also ghettoized in the 1930s, but in a vastly different way. Polish, German and Croatian immigrants, as well as native-born African-

Americans, formed their own structured, separate, homogeneous social areas. Neither the City of Milwaukee's nor the Village of Shorewood's segregation was the result of deed restrictions or racial laws.

In the 1930s the Village of Shorewood very nearly met the classic definition of a "classless society." Almost all of its residents were from the same economic class, lived in similar houses on lots of almost identical size and cheered for the same local high school football team, on which all the players were white (the U.S. Census of 1930 recorded two "Negro" residents of Shorewood, a household servant and her child). In the summer months they enjoyed a municipal beach facility on Lake Michigan with a lounge, dressing rooms and a snack bar, where only residents had unlimited free access. While Shorewood was truly a "classless" enclave within an urban municipality, its awareness of its uniqueness meant it was very class conscious. It had nothing in common with Karl Marx's utopian goal of a "classless society." Bill spent his youth in a community with safe streets and virtually no crime, where he, his sister Jean, and their parents were at ease as members of an established community.

III.

A LIFELONG MOVIE buff, Bill compared the Shorewood of the 1930s to Carvel, the fictional, near-perfect hometown of Andy Hardy and his family, the central characters in one of the era's most popular movie series (fourteen feature films between 1937 and 1946 starring Mickey Rooney, Judy Garland, Lewis Stone, Lionel Barrymore and Lana Turner before she became a sex symbol). Carvel was a tranquil, middle-American town of twenty-five thousand, with tree-lined streets, uncracked sidewalks, no talk of marital affairs and no underclass. It was a town where the teenagers in the all-white, classless high school sipped ice cream sodas in the local drugstore, danced to swing tunes in the high school gym, joined the Boy Scouts and Girl Scouts and attended church with their parents. The bouncy cheerleaders never got pregnant, and there were no neighborhood bars or pool halls.

The fictional Carvel, U.S.A., that was invented by MGM's studio staff writers often matched Bill's nostalgic recall of Shorewood. In the years just before World War II, a new Andy Hardy movie was released two or three times a year. Carvel for the Hardy family, like Shorewood for the Rehnquist family, was a way of life as well as a geographic site. The Hardy family was affluent enough to travel, but was made to look foolish by both New York debutantes and Parisian sophisticates. Judge Hardy, Andy's father, turned down his son's plea for a car at first, not because he could not afford to buy him one, but because he wanted him to understand the value of money (and the plight of the poor). He took his son on a charity tour before he gave him the money.

IV.

WILLIAM B. REHNQUIST (Bill's father was addressed as "Bill," while his son was addressed as "Billy") was unemployed for a brief period during the Depression. But he was always able to support his family in a manner that allowed them to participate fully in community activities. Financial problems forced the Rehnquists to move to three different homes during that decade, but they always found housing within the limits of Shorewood Village. At various times William B. was a regional sales manager for a printing equipment manufacturer, a paper company and a distributor of medical supplies and devices. He traveled throughout the Midwest, but his duties did not require him to spend long periods away from Shorewood.

While the Rehnquist family suffered its share of Depression woes, their middle-class lifestyle was never seriously disrupted. During his high school years Bill never held a full-time summer job. Between his junior and senior years at high school, he visited national parks while driving to California with a classmate. Between his graduation from high school and his entering the Army in the spring of 1943, he attended Kenyon College in Gambier, Ohio, with virtually all of his tuition and living expenses paid by his family. Kenyon College, Ohio's oldest institution of higher education, was considered one of the area's most elite schools. In 1942, it had a student body of six hundred men. Bill usually listed only Stanford and Harvard as his alma maters. Kenyon, on the other hand, usually lists Bill among its distinguished alumni.

V.

FOR ALMOST A century before Bill's birth, his mother's family was prominent and influential. While not wealthy, they were definitely "establishment." Margery Peck Rehnquist was the third generation of her family to graduate from high school in Berlin, Wisconsin, a small crossroads city approximately eighty miles north of Milwaukee. Her grandfather, who moved there with his parents in the 1840s, attended Ripon College and Wayland University before the Civil War. (Ripon College, during the period Covell A. Peck was a student there, became a footnote in America's political history. It is considered the birthplace of the Republican Party. The GOP was founded as a midwestern anti-slavery political organization.) Margery's father, Fred A. Peck, operated the family's hardware store, which was founded in 1863 and remained a family-owned business for more than fifty years. He was also an officer and director of a small property and casualty insurance company. Fred was such a prominent citizen that Berlin's mayor ordered all stores in the town to close the day of his funeral in 1911. Although Bill's parents spent virtually all of their adult lives in the Milwaukee County municipalities of Shorewood and Whitefish Bay, both were buried in the Peck family's cemetery plot in Berlin.

Intellectual achievement was held in high regard in the Rehnquist household. While Bill was something of an underachiever in high school, this cannot be attributed to lack of interest in academic excellence on his parents' part. Margery was an intellectual and she was proud of it. She read widely and enjoyed quoting poetry, an interest she encouraged in her son. During most of her married life, she earned a substantial income as the owner of a German-French translation business that served multinational companies based in greater Milwaukee.

Politics was a favored dinner-table topic. Margery served several terms as an officer of the local chapter of the American Association of University Women (AAUW), an advocacy organization that had worked in the public arena for the advancement of women's issues since shortly after the Civil War. Some of its major causes in the 1920s and 1930s were the legalization of the sale of birth control devices, particularly for women (the sale of female birth control devices was unlawful in many states and advertising them was unlawful in almost all states); granting women full access to government-funded colleges; establishing equal curriculums for boys and girls in metropolitan high schools; and, of course, full participation in the entire electoral process. She joined the Milwaukee Chapter of the AAUW shortly after she received her degree from the University of Wisconsin, which was two years before the ratification of the Nineteenth Amendment guaranteeing women the right to vote. In 1988 a special luncheon meeting of the Milwaukee Chapter of the AAUW was convened to celebrate Margery's ninetieth birthday and her more than fifty years of active membership. Bill, the featured speaker, was introduced as "Margery's son, Bill, the Chief Justice of the United States."

Bill's father, William B., was a prominent supporter of civic projects, particularly those that were promoted by the City Club of Milwaukee, of which he was president from 1955 to 1958. For more than a decade, he was an active member of the North Shore Republican organization. While there is no evidence that William B. ever held office in a Milwaukee area GOP organization, he apparently played a meaningful role in several local Republican clubs. Most newspaper articles about his civic activities, as well as his obituary in the *Milwaukee Journal,* mentioned his Republican affiliation.

Bill's parents encouraged his interest in politics and current events. In a TV interview, Brian Lamb, the host of C-SPAN's *Booknotes* program, asked Bill about his earliest exposure to serious reading outside of classrooms. He replied that he could not recall when he first became fascinated with learned discussions of politics and economics, but he was sure the interest was stimulated by books and magazines his parents sent him while he was posted at isolated weather stations in North Africa during World War II.

After Bill and his sister Jean graduated from college and moved away from Milwaukee, William B. found time to advance up the leadership ladder at Milwaukee's City Club. He joined the City Club during World War II, and in 1949 he was elected to its board of directors, a group that included the CEOs of some of Milwaukee's largest business and financial institutions.

With its own freestanding building in which it operated an upscale restaurant, a small auditorium and smaller conference and meeting rooms, the City Club was an important factor in Milwaukee's social life as well as that of the Rehnquists. A large and raucous rehearsal dinner was held at the City Club in 1952 before the wedding of Bill's only sibling, Jean. William B., whose friends joked about his frugality, was quoted in a spoof newspaper produced for the occasion: "So far the outlay for the wedding has exceeded the estimated retail value of the gifts by almost two. I can only hope that late returns will change this disheartening ratio." According to the rehearsal journal, Margery spoke glowingly about her daughter's skills as a cook and homemaker: "Jean was always a precocious child," the bride's mother reported. "She learned to boil water when she was only twenty-two years old. And now, a few days before her wedding, I can report that she has learned to bake water, fry water, and sauté water."

VI.

THE EXTENT AND pervasiveness of the social and economic dichotomy between the Village of Shorewood and its contiguous neighbor, the City of Milwaukee, during Bill's youth can probably be shown best by comparing how the two municipalities voted in the elections of 1932, 1936 and 1940, when all of America was in the midst of a deep economic depression. In 1932, Franklin D. Roosevelt won Shorewood by a mere 15 votes out of 6,539 cast. In the same year, FDR carried Milwaukee by a margin of better than 3 to 1 (135,711 for FDR to 39,059 for Herbert Hoover). While FDR's 1936 margin in Shorewood increased to 1.5 percent, or 104 votes out of 7,114 cast, in the City of Milwaukee his margin increased to more than 4 to 1. If the Socialist Party and Trade Union Party votes were added to the Democratic totals, the Republican candidate, Alf Landon, lost the City of Milwaukee by a 5-to-1 margin.

In November 1940, when Wendell Willkie challenged FDR's precedent-breaking run for a third term, massive purchases of war matériel had made America's industrial heartland, including Milwaukee, prosperous once again. England, Germany and Russia were waging war on Election Day, and Paris had already become the second city of the Third Reich. If election results can be taken as a reliable indicator of social currents—and I believe they can—prosperity tended to emphasize rather than diminish the split between the core city and its small neighbor. In 1940, Willkie the Republican beat FDR by a 2-to-1 margin in Shorewood, while Roosevelt carried the City of Milwaukee by approximately the same margin.

The City of Milwaukee's politics was different from most of the rest of the United States's, as well as from the Village of Shorewood's. Three of the country's most vocal and visible opponents of both World War I and World War II called Milwaukee home. During World War I, Victor Berger, the Socialist mayor of Milwaukee, was sentenced to jail for breaching the Espionage Act with his antiwar speeches and writings. While his case was under appeal (he was eventually exonerated), he was elected to Congress, and a national furor followed when the House refused to seat him because he was a convicted felon. Senator Robert M. La Follette, also a Milwaukee resident, opposed U.S. entry into World War I, and his son, Senator Robert M. La Follette Jr., who succeeded him, opposed reinstitution of the draft in 1940 as well as lend-lease aid to Great Britain. While he voted for the United States declaration of war after the bombing of Pearl Harbor, his commitment to winning the war was only tepid. Chiefly because of his pacifism and his lukewarm support of World War II, Senator La Follette Jr. was defeated in 1946, after twenty years in the Senate, by an obscure Milwaukee judge who was also a war hero: Tail Gunner Joe McCarthy. The term "McCarthyism," meaning the unethical prosecution and interrogation of witnesses, came into the language because of Senator Joseph McCarthy's improper but highly visible conduct as a senator.

VII.

BETWEEN 1925 AND 1935 the Village of Shorewood built three handsome public school buildings on large, landscaped parcels of land. Ten percent of the village's land that was not dedicated to streets and parks was occupied by these public schools. The village's two elementary schools were built in the 1920s and were situated on eighteen acres of prime real estate with tree-shaded playgrounds. This contrasted with Milwaukee's custom at that time. Its public schools were built on small plots with cement schoolyards. Shorewood High School, with its twenty-five-acre tree-lined campus in the center of the village, had—and still has—the ambience of a small college campus rather than a midwestern public high school. Designed to serve less than one thousand students, it included five freestanding buildings: administration, classrooms, an auditorium, a gymnasium and a metal- and woodworking shop.

Neither the political acumen that resulted in Bill's receiving one of the most coveted appointments to which an American lawyer can aspire, nor the academic brilliance that made him a superstar at Stanford Law School, was apparent at Shorewood High School. He was a good student, but he was far from the top of his class. He was one of thirty-three members of the National Honor Society, but he was not a commencement speaker. Although he was a member of the student council and the features editor of a publication, his list of extracurricular activities was barely average.

Bill's abiding affection for both his hometown and Shorewood High School can be explained in one word: "community." After Bill moved from Shorewood, he was never again part of a community in the same all-inclusive way. At Stanford he was a bookish, serious student who had little time for social life or collegiate bonhomie. During the time that he worked on Senator Barry Goldwater's presidential campaign, he was the "house intellectual" rather than a coequal member of the campaign's inner circle. After he became a Supreme Court justice it was virtually impossible for him to establish casual relationships with his Northern Virginia neighbors similar to the ones that his parents had with their longtime neighbors and social peers in Shorewood.

Bill rarely, if ever, missed a Shorewood High School class reunion. When he attended one, he stayed with his parents or later with a classmate, Bob Brachman, a man of modest means who was president of a local salad-oil company. Brachman was the only non-Washingtonian to share in any of Bill's birthday parties at which I was present.

Bill's biographical entries in reunion booklets reflect the kind of candor people only show when they are among old friends. For the 1991 class booklet, he reported that his two older children were lawyers, while his youngest, Nancy, "belongs to that rather large class of people called, 'unpublished novelists.' "

VIII.

FOR MOST PEOPLE, the dozen years between first grade and high school graduation are the most intellectually formative. It is during this interval in the journey through life that ideas, biases, passions, relationships and traditions are embraced, rejected and revised—again and again. Bill's home, his school and his community were exemplars of tradition, stability and tranquillity when much of the United States was going through a period of depression, turmoil and travail. His ties to Shorewood ran deeper than nostalgia.

To try to directly relate Bill's youth in Shorewood to his political conservatism and to his judicial philosophy would be both futile and foolish. But it would also be both futile and foolish to deny that Shorewood left a lasting mark on his psyche.

THREE

GOLDWATER AND KITCHEL

I.

BILL REHNQUIST'S METEORIC rise to the pinnacle of judicial power has perplexed pundits and scholars ever since President Richard Nixon nominated him to the Supreme Court in 1971. No writer can fully explain how talent is fulfilled, why it grows and matures in some individuals and why it flames out in others. There will always be mystery about why a mediocre linebacker became a brilliant football coach, why an exciting child prodigy bored concert audiences as an adult, why the leader of a state assembly never won a congressional election and why a marginally successful business attorney in a backwater city became a brilliant chief justice. I can, however, cast some light on the trail of contacts, associations and friendships that put Bill in a position to accomplish great things.

Bill's appearance on the national scene can be traced directly to an obscure political machine in the Sun Belt city of Phoenix, Arizona. For one brief shining moment, Barry Goldwater made Phoenix an important gathering place for politically conservative intellectuals. Luck put Bill in the right place at the right time.

When Bill and Nan Rehnquist moved to Phoenix in 1954 as newlyweds, Bill knew that the small law firm he was joining was led by a financially successful, intellectually accomplished attorney who was active in Arizona's nascent Republican Party. But he had no way of knowing that within a few years, a presidential campaign would be managed from Phoenix and that the GOP's top brass would be made fully aware of his talents and competence.

Denison Kitchel, the Phoenix attorney who recruited Bill to become an associate in his law firm, was Barry Goldwater's closest confidant, lawyer and political mentor. In one short decade—almost single-handedly—Kitchel handcrafted Goldwater's public image. He changed a third-generation, second-tier department store scion into a conservative political icon and a United States senator. Kitchel's close ties to Arizona's conservative Republican senator gave Bill political access he had never dreamed of. Early in Bill's legal career, Kitchel introduced him to one of his prize clients, Goldwater Department Stores. Kitchel represented the Goldwater family's business interests as well as the senator personally. Bill would soon establish a relationship with Barry Goldwater that survived his subsequent estrangement from Kitchel.

II.

LIKE DOZENS OF other young couples, Bill and Nan had hoped to strike it rich in one of America's fastest-growing cities. There is no evidence to suggest that Bill harbored big-time political or judicial ambitions when he moved to the Southwest. If anything, his ambitions were just the opposite: he wanted to be a financially successful business lawyer in an environment without the social pressures that are usually part of a professional's life in big cities like New York and Los Angeles.

Arizona's economy was growing rapidly, but in the political firmament its star barely twinkled. It had only four electoral votes and no

Naomi topped it all off by being a country-club-champion tennis player.

During the years immediately preceding the Rehnquists' move to Phoenix, the Douglases were Arizona's glamour family as well as being rich and well-connected. They were regularly pictured in tabloids on both sides of the Atlantic. Naomi's cousin, Lewis W. Douglas, was President Truman's ambassador to Great Britain, where he and his wife were regular guests in the Royal Box at race courses and other British society events. Their daughter, Sharman Douglas, was a partying pal of Princess Margaret in both London and the Caribbean.

Denison and Naomi both chose to be listed in New York's Social Register more than fifty years after they moved to Phoenix. Until her death, Naomi maintained her membership in The Colony Club, an exclusive club for women on New York City's Park Avenue. Into the twenty-first century, The Colony Club continued to operate kennels (in its elegant Park Avenue building) for ladies who brought their poodles to town and wanted them out of the way at mealtime.

The Kitchels typified a popular post–World War II ditty about eastern slickers who went west to win fame and fortune:

> *We say we're real tough hombres,*
> *But we can't forget our Eastern ways.*
> *We always order barbecue,*
> *Then ask for sauce Béarnaise.*

V.

Bill was much too ambitious and independent to remain the protégé of a domineering intellectual for long. While it is likely that no other employer could have lured Bill to Arizona or opened as many doors for him as Kitchel did, personality conflicts started to show early in their relationship. A few years after establishing himself in Phoenix, Bill resigned from Kitchel's firm and went to work for a competitor.

As was probably inevitable, this led to a bitter—and lasting—estrangement. The break left a lasting mark on Bill, as I am sure it also did on Kitchel.

Their mutual interest in Barry Goldwater's presidential campaign, and the ascendancy of both the Republican Party and the conservative movement in Arizona, meant that communication lines between Bill and Kitchel were never totally closed. Still, during the nearly half century that ensued, they never met for a friendly meal or a casual chat about old times.

In 1960, six years after Bill had moved to Phoenix, he and a contemporary, James Powers, started their own law firm, Powers & Rehnquist. A native of Iowa, Powers moved to Phoenix in 1951 after graduating from Harvard Law School. Like Bill, he had been personally recruited by Kitchel. In 1952 he took a two-year leave of absence from Evans, Hull, Kitchel & Jenckes to accept an appointment as a "special attorney" in the office of the Internal Revenue Service's chief counsel. Through his many political contacts in the new Eisenhower administration, Kitchel had secured a plum job for one of his young associates, one that he hoped would generate big legal fees when Powers returned to Phoenix. An IRS "special attorney" represents the government in cases before the United States Tax Court. In the course of his Washington assignment, Powers got to know all of the top lawyers at the Internal Revenue Service, as well as many of the most respected private practitioners who regularly appeared before the Tax Court.

Powers and Bill originally met over lunch in the Supreme Court cafeteria when both young men were working in Washington. The luncheon was arranged by Ted Stevens, the future senator from Alaska, who had been a Harvard Law School classmate of Powers. He knew Bill as part of an informal group of young, conservative intellectuals who met regularly while working in the federal bureaucracy. In 1953, Stevens was a rising star in the Department of Interior's legal department. He had earned his job by writing an article for the *Har-*

vard Law Review on the conflict between property rights and public conservation programs.

The Powers and Rehnquist partnership grew and prospered, notwithstanding Powers's lifelong affiliation with the Democratic Party and Bill's active participation in Republican Party affairs. Bill believed that the partners' offsetting political affiliations helped attract business clients who feared being represented by a law firm that was too closely identified with one party.

VI.

In 1964, Kitchel and his team of amateurs wrested the GOP nomination for president from Nelson Rockefeller, the governor of New York, and his team of political professionals. Senator Goldwater's campaign strategy was atypical and unique. When it began to falter, the national media blamed Kitchel and his small coterie of Phoenix colleagues. They said that a complex nationwide presidential campaign was being mismanaged by a group of provincial hicks, the "Arizona Mafia."

Bill was part of the "Arizona Mafia." Even though in 1964 he was no longer friendly with Kitchel, he had personal relationships with most, if not all, of the campaign's top strategists. He had the unofficial title of "house intellectual." He wrote legal opinions for the Arizona Republican Party during the years immediately preceding Goldwater's presidential run. During the spring of 1964, he may have been the most visible Arizona Republican other than Senator Goldwater. While the senator was campaigning throughout the country, Bill was garnering headlines in his home state, where he represented the Republicans in the state's House of Representatives in a highly publicized impeachment trial before the Arizona Senate.

While he was still in his thirties, Bill was strategizing with the chairman of the Republican National Committee. In addition to giving general strategic advice to members of the campaign's leadership, Bill wrote position papers and speeches on complex and/or delicate subjects, including Senator Goldwater's ambiguous position on race relations. In the spring of 1964, Goldwater voted against the Civil Rights Act of 1964, probably the most important piece of civil liberties legislation enacted since Reconstruction. (The Civil Rights Act passed only because a majority of the Republican senators deserted their Deep South Democratic colleagues to support it.) Goldwater's vote against it eight weeks before the Republican National Convention may have seemed logical and rational to the senator, but it was a tough sell for the GOP's national campaign staff. One of Bill's major jobs was developing politically and socially acceptable talking points and speeches that campaign workers could use when explaining that the senator's vote against the Civil Rights Act did not mean he was a bigot.

William F. Buckley, in his Goldwater memoir *Flying High: Remembering Barry Goldwater*, said that Bill actually advised the senator on the underlying constitutional issues before he cast his vote. The quotation below is part of a colloquy between James Burnham, a *National Review* editor, and Brent Bozell, who ghostwrote *The Conscience of a Conservative*, Senator Goldwater's political manifesto:

> "We know that opposition to the act on constitutional grounds is a major contention of Goldwater's lawyer in Phoenix— William . . ."
>
> "Rehnquist." (Bozell supplied the name.)
>
> "Yes, Rehnquist. And we know that Barry is inclined to vote against it when it reaches the floor. . . ."

In the autumn of 1964, when it became apparent that Goldwater was going to lose by a large margin and funds were low, many of the foot soldiers in the army of political mercenaries (consultants, pollsters, speechwriters, public relations experts) began to desert the campaign. Their replacements were party loyalists and true believers;

either volunteers or semiprofessionals who received token stipends. Bill was one of them. In October, he took a four-week leave from his law firm to work full-time as Senator Goldwater's chief speechwriter.

During those weeks, Bill split his time between Phoenix and Washington. He was the chief author of Goldwater's concession speech. It was consistent with both Bill's and Barry's philosophies. It was defiant, notwithstanding the Republican candidate's overwhelming defeat. In the speech Goldwater restated his belief that the conservative principles on which he ran would eventually prevail and that the party's loss was due to internal differences. He specifically said that the moderates "have no difference at all with the Democratic concepts."

VII.

DICK KLEINDIENST, WHO served as attorney general of the United States from 1972 to 1973, was also discovered, sponsored and mentored by Denison Kitchel.

An Arizona native and Army Air Corps veteran with degrees from Harvard College (magna cum laude) and Harvard Law School, Kleindienst was recruited by Kitchel to work with the Arizona GOP leadership on a special assignment requiring sophistication and subtlety. He was to make sure that a majority of the state's delegation to the 1952 Republican National Convention in Chicago did not waver in its support for the conservative candidacy of Senator Robert Taft, who was being challenged by the internationalist, nonideological General Dwight D. Eisenhower.

This was a vastly more important assignment than is immediately apparent. Arizona's fourteen votes were split 10 to 4 in favor of Taft, and the vote on the convention floor was expected to be so close that every vote counted. On the original roll call Eisenhower received 585 votes and Taft 500, but a majority of 604 was needed to get the nomination. Eisenhower prevailed after Minnesota switched its vote from a noncontender, former governor Harold Stassen, to Eisenhower. (Incidentally, the chairman of the Minnesota delegation that swung the nomination to Eisenhower was Warren E. Burger, who preceded Bill as chief justice of the United States.)

Kleindienst's acceptance of Kitchel's offer led to a lifetime in Republican politics. Kitchel taught him to be a political organizer on both the local and national level. In a little more than a decade, he promoted him from a behind-the-scenes subaltern who handled intraparty squabbles to a widely known and respected national operative. He fit the mold of a Kitchel protégé perfectly. He was street-smart, tough, intellectually gifted and a dedicated right-wing conservative.

Dick and Marnie (Margaret) Kleindienst were the same age as Bill and Nan Rehnquist, and they became social friends as well as political confederates. Bill and Dick had both served in the Army Air Corps from 1943 to 1946 and were philosophically more conservative than the GOP's national leadership. They resented the eastern internationalists who had dominated the GOP since 1940, when both men were high school students. When Bill moved to Phoenix, Kleindienst was Kitchel's first lieutenant in charge of Goldwater's ideologically driven volunteer corps.

While Kitchel withdrew from politics after Goldwater's defeat in 1964, the political bond between his three protégés remained. Although Dick Kleindienst's and Bill Rehnquist's career paths diverged between 1964 and 1969, they remained intimate personal friends and continued to work closely on statewide Republican campaigns as well as GOP organizational issues. Dick devoted most of his time to Republican politics and Bill devoted most of his to building his law practice. Still, in 1967 and 1968, when Dick chaired the Arizona Republican Party, he arranged for Bill to be appointed general counsel to the Arizona GOP. In 1966 Bill was counsel to the Republican gubernatorial candidate and to his campaign organization.

In 1968, Dick Kleindienst became part of Richard Nixon's inner circle. They had worked together during Nixon's 1960 campaign against John F. Kennedy, and Nixon's staff was well aware of the fact that Goldwater's preConvention successes in 1964 were largely attributable to Kleindienst's organizational skills. When the new administration was being formed, Kleindienst was named deputy attorney general under John Mitchell, Nixon's campaign manager, law partner and personal confidant.

Almost immediately after Nixon's victory, while the transition team was still operating out of The Pierre Hotel in New York City, Dick and Bill began talking about a top-level job for Bill in the new administration. After Kleindienst was named to the number two post at the Justice Department, he arranged for Bill to interview with Mitchell for the job of assistant attorney general for the Office of Legal Counsel; the person who writes legal opinions for the president and advises him on the constitutionality of presidential executive orders. The Office of Legal Counsel also analyzes for the president the judicial opinions of potential Supreme Court nominees who have previously served as judges. It is considered the top "intellectual job" at the Department of Justice. A few weeks after his meeting with Mitchell, Bill was offered—and he accepted—the position. In January 1969, he resigned from Powers & Rehnquist and moved to suburban Washington, D.C. to be part of the Nixon administration.

VIII.

THE EXTERNAL FACTORS that led to Bill's nomination to be an associate justice of the Supreme Court two years after he became a top-level bureaucrat at the Department of Justice have been well-documented. Two successive nominees to fill Supreme Court openings were rejected by the Senate, notwithstanding the fact that both men had served with distinction as United States Circuit Court of Appeals judges for more than a decade. A hostile Senate Judiciary Committee made Nixon cautious. He wanted to nominate justices whose conservative credentials were impeccable but who had not created controversial paper trails as political officeholders or judges. With the deaths of Justices John Marshall Harlan II and Hugo Black in the autumn of 1971, Nixon had two new vacancies to fill. On October 22, 1972, he nominated Lewis Powell Jr., a former president of the American Bar Association and senior partner in Richmond, Virginia's, largest law firm, and Bill to fill the openings. While several hostile witnesses alleged illegal actions by Bill as a Republican Party worker at a polling place in Phoenix in 1964, he was confirmed by a wide margin, 68 to 26.

John W. Dean, the Watergate figure who was counsel to the president in 1971, and Dick Kleindienst have both written books that describe some of the behind-the-scenes maneuvering that preceded Bill's nomination. Each believes he played a crucial role in focusing President Nixon's attention on the obscure bureaucrat in the Department of Justice that he finally nominated.

Dean had been impressed with Bill when they worked together at the Department of Justice. As White House counsel he had direct, off-the-record access to the president. Kleindienst, on the other hand, had direct off-the-record access to both John Mitchell, Nixon's confidant—who as attorney general was charged with selecting and vetting Supreme Court nominees—and Barry Goldwater, who had been reelected to the Senate, and was one of the few members of Congress whom Nixon trusted and considered a personal friend.

I believe Dean's and Kleindienst's accounts are complementary rather than contradictory.

IX.

I CHATTED WITH Denison Kitchel in his hotel suite at Washington's Capital Hilton Hotel in 1998. Although Bill did not arrange the meeting, he indirectly initiated it. He and I discussed several times the fact that I had been invited to attend the meetings of The Mont Pelerin Society in the fall of 1998. I was proud of the invitation; he was curious about the meeting's intellectual content and quality.

Bill first became aware of the society when he lived in Arizona: Denison Kitchel was one of its earliest members who was not connected with a university or a think tank. (The Mont Pelerin Society is an international organization of intellectuals that first met in Mont Pelerin, Switzerland, in 1947 at the invitation of Friedrich Hayek. Members, then and now, share a belief in classical liberalism, a philosophy that says that personal liberty is undergirded by free markets, small governments and minimal regulation. Any erosion of these diminishes freedom proportionately.) Even though Kitchel was then ninety, Bill was sure he would attend if he was physically able. He rarely missed a meeting. Bill suggested I look him up. He was certain I would find Kitchel fascinating. I did not need any persuading. For many years I had been curious about the publicity-shy, intellectual "country lawyer" who had discovered and mentored Barry Goldwater, Bill Rehnquist and Dick Kleindienst.

When I contacted Kitchel and told him that I was a good friend of Bill's, he immediately invited me to his suite for a soft drink. While he was forthcoming about recently delivered papers and current politics, the meeting was frosty and awkward. He was not interested in personal chitchat. On behalf of my friend, I inquired about his health, his family and the legal community in Phoenix. To all of my personal inquiries, the answers were similar: gracious, precise—and cold. After about twenty minutes, Kitchel bombarded me with personal but superficial questions about Bill: Was he going to marry again? Was he still a chain-smoker? Did he belong to a country club? There were almost no follow-ups. It was apparent he did not really care about the responses. At the end of the meeting he wished me good luck and said he hoped to see me at the next day's session. He had no personal warm wishes for me to extend to Bill.

When I telephoned Bill to tell him about my meeting, his questions about Kitchel were also almost all personal—about his demeanor and attitude.

Although the details of my mission were never spelled out for me, I knew that I had flunked. I believed then—and now—that the underlying reason for Bill's suggestion that I meet with Denison Kitchel was a hope, deep in his psyche, that he would say something about his pride in Bill's achievements and successes.

X.

DENISON KITCHEL's STAR faded after Goldwater's defeat. After 1964 he never again took an active part in a political campaign. His work was done. He had played a major role in organizing and developing the intellectual underpinning for the conservative movement.

The single most important factor in Bill Rehnquist's journey from Supreme Court clerk to Supreme Court justice was Denison Kitchel, despite the fact that they were estranged during most of those years. It was Kitchel's charisma and intelligence that lured him to Arizona in the first place. Barry Goldwater's public career began when Kitchel persuaded his law client to run for Phoenix City Council in 1949. (The main inducement was Kitchel's agreement to serve as his campaign manager.)

Barry Goldwater and William Rehnquist changed the course of American history during the last half of the twentieth century. But without Denison Kitchel's insightful recognition of young talent, Goldwater would likely have ended his career as an inconsequential department store executive and Bill would have retired as a financially successful business lawyer. Kitchel never wanted to step forward and take credit. His interest was in accomplishment, rather than acclaim. It was why he was a mentor *par excellence*.

FOUR

HOME

I.

WHEN THE REHNQUISTS moved from Arizona in 1969, they settled in Northern Virginia, where they lived the rest of their lives. Except for contacts made through Bill's work, almost all of their social friends lived in the Old Dominion. The Rehnquist children graduated from Virginia public schools, and two of their grandchildren attended public schools in Arlington. For more than a decade, Bill and Nan belonged to a neighborhood swim club where they actively participated in party programs and watched their children star in athletic events.

Still, Bill never expressed warm feelings about Northern Virginia in the same way he did about Shorewood, Wisconsin. He always considered himself a midwesterner, not a southerner. And he wanted others to see him that way. By many measures, metropolitan Washington has the social ambience of a very large company town where the main employer is the federal government. In that environment, a Supreme Court justice is the equivalent of one of the company's big bosses, and that makes the establishment of casual friendships difficult—regardless of intent.

In the autumn, Bill always rooted for the Green Bay Packers and the University of Wisconsin Badgers, not the Washington Redskins or Stanford. In most circumstances this would be useless trivia, but in Bill's instance the Packers and the Badgers allowed him to make a statement.

While Bill faithfully read local newspapers, and was knowledgeable about state and regional politics, including the minor referendum issues that clutter Virginia election ballots, he was always an outsider looking in. He spoke often, both formally and informally, at local high schools, colleges, libraries and religious organizations. In his own way he tried to be a participant in local affairs—to be a good citizen.

II.

IN 1983, BILL and Nan were empty nesters. Their youngest child, Nancy, had graduated two years earlier from Amherst College in Massachusetts, and it was time to give up their large home in McLean, Virginia, for a townhouse in Arlington that was easier to maintain and closer to Bill's work.

An unexceptional three-bedroom, three-and-a-half-bath unit in The Birches, a twenty-four-unit townhouse development, fit the bill. Built on a five-acre plot, The Birches had a large common area whose shrub maintenance cost each resident $1,200 annually. Its history helped make it unique. From 1731 until the late 1950s, when it was sold to an investor, the land had been owned by the descendants of the family that had received it as part of a royal grant from King George II of England. Very few parcels of urban real estate anywhere in America were used as a homestead by one family for more than two centuries.

The Rehnquists paid $207,500 for the property in 1983, approximately 10 percent more than the assessed value. Two decades later, Bill's estate sold it for $747,000. In terms of both price and prestige, the Rehnquists' neighborhood was upper-middle-class. While The Birches was not a fashionable development, it was clearly on "the right side of the tracks." Bill's home was several notches below Arlington townhomes that face the Potomac River or those that are located near subway stops and include elevators and indoor parking for two cars. But it was near Country Club Hills, the municipality's most exclusive residential area, where the average home is assessed for substantially more than a million dollars. The Rehnquists' neighbors were teachers, shopkeepers, nurses, law firm associates and a few middle-level bureaucrats, some of whom had lower civil service ratings than Bill's secretaries.

Arlington has had highly restrictive residential zoning laws for more than a half century. Consistent with national trends in suburban development, most residential areas with expensive homes are clearly separated from commercial districts. Preliminary building plans that could result in business enterprises encroaching on residential areas draw large and boisterous crowds to public hearings, as well as lawsuits and editorials. Single-family residences that abut commercial areas are usually considered less desirable than those that are farther away.

But the small enclave where the Rehnquists lived was an exception. Bill's home was within three hundred yards of a liquor store, a diner, a drugstore and a gas station. The nearby shopping area was started as a few small shops almost one hundred years ago, long before Arlington's first zoning code was enacted. It was developed because it was near an important stop on one of Northern Virginia's early street railways.

III.

THE HOMES, APARTMENTS, parks, schools and shopping opportunities in Arlington appear to be little different from those in the near-in suburbs of other large American cities. But no suburb in the country has Arlington's unique characteristics.

Arlington was an integral part of the District of Columbia when it was established as the nation's capital during the administration of George Washington, and it remained so for almost six decades. How it became a part of Virginia a second time is a largely forgotten story. In the years that preceded the Civil War, those portions of the District of Columbia that were originally part of Virginia became a focus in the national debate about the expansion of slavery. The squalid, tiny municipalities (including what is now Arlington) along the southern shore of the Potomac River were important in the slave business. This situation embarrassed northern congressmen, abolitionists, writers and members of the diplomatic corps. The fact that the capital of the United States hosted one of the country's largest slave markets (with its pitiful and odiferous holding pens) and several slave shipping companies, which were among its larger businesses, created deep tensions within the District of Columbia government as well as in Congress. The problem was finally resolved in 1848 by Congress. It returned to Virginia the economically unimportant (except for slave commerce) hamlets it had originally given to the District of Columbia. Virginia accepted them with muted enthusiasm.

Although Arlington stopped being a constituent part of the District of Columbia 160 years ago, the communities are still inextricably linked. Many suburbs of great cities are self-sufficient economic entities that can prosper and grow without the core city. But that is not true of Arlington. Its affluence and its multibillion-dollar tax base are almost totally dependent on its proximity to Washington, D.C.

Notwithstanding their interdependence and contiguity, Arlington and the District of Columbia are vastly different municipalities. And Arlingtonians want to keep it that way. Their government and community organizations go to great lengths to keep Arlington separate and different.

Even though Arlington has world-class public schools and almost two-thirds of the population is college educated, neighboring Washington's public schools often place last in national testing and less

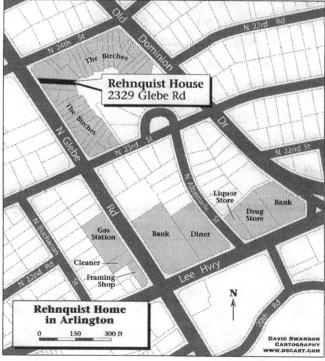

From 1982 until their deaths, the Rehnquists lived in a townhouse located in a business area of Arlington, Virginia.

than one-third of its population is college educated. The difference in the racial makeup of the two municipalities is even more dramatic: in the last census Arlington was nearly 70 percent white, while the District was 70 percent nonwhite.

The Virginia suburb's affluence allows it to support a local library with five hundred thousand books and a high-tech manuscript retrieval system, a sophisticated modern hospital, a resident theater with professional actors, a community-sponsored symphony orchestra, a planetarium and a municipal arts center. Still, visitors, foreign and domestic, view Arlington as an integral part of greater Washington. News with a Washington dateline often emanates from Arlington. Almost all news about war and defense starts in Arlington because the Pentagon is located there, as are scores of less-well-known federal commissions, bureaus and departments.

What would become Bill and Nan Rehnquist's final resting place, Arlington National Cemetery, was only a few miles from their home. The cemetery is Arlington's best-known and most popular tourist attraction, and Arlington County's official seal features a historic building that is part of the cemetery complex. For Bill, it was his village churchyard in more profound ways than geographic proximity. It is a burial place for those whose community is defined by patriotism— and he spent forty years in his country's service.

With a casual, offhand remark in the spring of 2003 Bill told me— unintentionally—that he considered Arlington his home and that he wanted to live there for the rest of his life. The previous autumn he had slipped on the stairs in his townhome. After a long and painful crawl, he phoned his daughter Jan, who took him to a hospital. While the ruptured ligaments in his leg were surgically repaired, the episode convinced him that his days of living alone were numbered. But he was unsure of when or where his next move should be. In the course of reviewing options, he visited an assisted-living facility in Arlington where his colleague, Justice Harry Blackmun, had spent his last years. When he described the visit to me, he praised the amenities and the various services provided to residents, even though he felt that he was not ready for "that." Still, he said he was finished looking. I asked him why he was quitting after visiting only one facility; he might find an environment more to his liking somewhere else in the Washington area. "Because Harry's apartment is in the middle of Arlington," he replied. "And that's where I belong."

IV.

When Bill and Nan moved to Arlington, they became part of an overwhelmingly Democratic municipality, a place that has supported every Democratic presidential candidate since 1960. James Moran, a doctrinaire, left-of-center Democrat, has been its congressman since 1991. For three decades, at least four out of the five members of Arlington's governing body, the County Board, have been Democrats. For more than half of that period, there has been no opposition party representation. Since Republican candidates for Virginia's Senate and General Assembly were unable to mount realistic challenges, Democratic incumbents usually ran unopposed.

Although the liberal-left Democrats who control Arlington politics object to the comparison, the situation reminds me of the Deep South during the years between Reconstruction and the Civil Rights Act of 1964: the only way to challenge incumbent power was in a Democratic primary. And challengers rarely prevailed.

V.

For more than thirty years, Bill was a man with *two* homes, not a Washingtonian with a vacation retreat. He had one residence in Virginia and one home in Vermont. While the environment and surroundings of each was totally different, the differences reflected the tastes of a man who was able to compartmentalize his life and fully enjoy each separate part.

Owning two homes was part of Bill and Nan Rehnquist's lifestyle. Shortly after they moved to Phoenix—while he was struggling to get established in a new professional environment—they bought their first vacation home in nearby Colorado. Bill described it as "a modest bungalow," but he felt he needed it to make his life complete. "In money terms, I couldn't afford to own my first vacation house," he once explained to me. "But in psychic terms, I couldn't afford not to."

Vacations were for resting the mind and body, preparing oneself for long periods of hard work. Bill did not find exotic travel, sightseeing and exploring particularly fascinating. He was a lifelong student of geography, and he enjoyed reciting obscure trivia about the earth's surface and how it was structured naturally and politically, but he spent little time visiting historic sites or scenic wonders. During the two decades when we were friends, Bill traveled to distant lands for a week or two each summer, but his trips were almost always add-ons after a law school teaching assignment or an official visit to speak at a foreign court system's or bar association's anniversary. Except for quasi-official visits to Australia and Egypt—and his Army service in North Africa—to my knowledge, he never visited Asia, or further into Africa or a Caribbean island.

In 1972, shortly after Bill started his life-tenured job in Washington, the Rehnquists began looking for a second home. Except for Bill's one year of graduate study at Harvard (and Army postings), neither Nan nor he had spent more than two weeks in New England. Still, they decided to look for a vacation home north of Boston. They wanted to locate in an authentic small, rural community. They searched for a village that was truly rural, neither a tourist attraction with curio shops and fast-food restaurants nor a rustic precinct for urban jet-setters with upscale restaurants, art galleries, cashmere sweater boutiques and gourmet cheese shops. Through a newspaper ad, they found Greensboro, Vermont, a unique community that fit their needs and personalities and which both enjoyed for the rest of their lives.

VI.

GREENSBORO, A COZY town of 770, tries to maintain the ambience of an early-twentieth-century village caught in a time warp. And it almost succeeds. Its two most noteworthy commercial enterprises, Willey's Store and Highland Lodge, are operated by fourth-generation descendants of the founders: affluent businesspeople who use computers skillfully while they artfully sell nostalgia. Northern New England's idiosyncratic lifestyle is disappearing rapidly; yet, some of its vestiges remain in isolated small towns like Greensboro, where change comes slowly.

Greensboro's seasonal visitors hail from every large city on the East Coast. It is a "destination resort" where visitors stay for weeks or months, rarely just weekends. The ski bunnies and snow jocks go elsewhere. The state's glitzy ski resorts—Stowe, Manchester, Killington, Woodstock and Stratton Mountain—are all at least fifty miles distant. At the same time it is not exactly an obscure, Joe-six-pack retreat. For three-quarters of a century, before the Rehnquists discovered it, Greensboro was one of the summer vacation areas most favored by the Princeton faculty. It has its own special form of glitz: its seasonal residents' academic credentials.

While Bill spent less than three months each year at his Greensboro, Vermont, hideaway, he probably had more good friends there than in Arlington. To a casual visitor, Greensboro is an isolated village where some remnants of the northern New England of Robert Frost and Norman Rockwell still survive. But it was not just another country town. Its summer community is self-contained, self-sufficient and homogeneous. Only its locale is small-townish. It welcomed into its midst accomplished, worldly people, many of whom could be properly classified as "intellectual elites." Almost none of its residents lived at the extreme ends of the economic class scale. The absence of great class differences, particularly within the summer resident group, created an environment where an unstructured, easy social life flourished.

In 1996, John C. Stone II, an enthusiastic Princeton alumnus and lifelong summer resident, wrote a privately published booklet entitled *The Princeton Connection: A Century of Princetonians in Greensboro, Vermont.* It lists more than one hundred Princeton faculty members, alumni and trustees who had summered in Greensboro during the twentieth century, most of whom had remained part of the Greensboro community for more than twenty years. As Bill saw it, the Princeton connection provided Greensboro with the critical mass necessary to attract intellectuals.

For many years, Princeton faculty members were a separate subset within Greensboro's social hierarchy. Princetonians represented one-fourth of the lifetime members of the Greensboro Historical Society in 1997, and "Princeton foursomes" regularly competed in Mountain View Country Club golf tournaments. The Greensboro Historical Society's archive includes a study of the Dartmouth-Greensboro connection, which was also quite extensive.

While Bill had a wide circle of friends in Greensboro, his closest friends—the ones whose homes he visited several times each summer—were not the typical residents of a northern New England mill town. They included Nate Smith, a mathematics teacher at the Phillips Academy at Andover; Lacey Smith, a retired professor of English history who spent his teaching career at Northwestern, MIT and Princeton; Bill Nicely, a business executive with degrees from Princeton and Harvard Law School; and Alan Lukens, a career foreign service officer who had several ambassadorial postings in Africa. His Greensboro friendships became particularly important to Bill after he became a widower.

VII.

FOR BILL, ESCAPING from Washington meant more than just trading the power and glory of the Supreme Court bench for a quaint, rustic village in northern Vermont. It also meant banishing much of modernity from his home. In 2000, when Betty Nan and I stayed with Bill for three days, there was no television set or VCR in his house. And he gave no indication that he missed them. A TV screen would have detracted from the relaxed ambience of his simple living room, with its large log-burning fireplace and its view of Lake Caspian. His flight from modernity extended into the kitchen, which did not include even the minimum equipment most people expect to find in a standard rental vacation home: coffeemaker, microwave oven, toaster.

The Rehnquists' home in Vermont was typically, quintessentially Bill. It was inelegantly furnished, but there were two extra-comfortable chairs placed so Bill and Nan could enjoy a pleasant view of the lake during the daylight hours. Reading was important to the Rehnquists when they bought the house in 1973—and that never changed.

Bill usually gave his guests detailed, written instructions on how to drive to his home from the Burlington, Vermont, airport. But they did not meet the minimum standards of clarity he set for his law clerks. The final half mile of the drive involved unmarked dirt roads that did not begin at a street but at the rear of the Highland Lodge's parking lot. The Rehnquist home and several others nearby were originally built in the 1920s by the owners of Highland Lodge, who had planned to develop a small satellite colony that never materialized.

Bill's house was painted white and timbered. It had the external look of a peasant family's home in the Swiss Alps or the English Midlands. The only outside accoutrements were an elaborate stone and brick grill, a hammock and a croquet court. The room arrangement was simple and practical: two bedrooms and one all-purpose room on the first floor and sleeping facilities for several couples and lots of children on the second floor.

Bill's overnight guests were expected to join the host in at least one round of croquet. His croquet lawn was laid out on a hill with holes burrowed out by rodents, rocks and weeds between the wickets: it was more like a recently abandoned battlefield or an obstacle course. This gave the host an unfair advantage. Every time we played, he won handily. When I called this to his attention, he responded, "At your age you should have learned that in every sport, the home team is supposed to have an advantage."

Bill's kitchen skills were limited, and he had no desire to improve them. This tended to limit the quality and complexity of home-cooked meals in both Arlington and Vermont. Since he did not do any complicated cooking, he did not pay any attention to how his kitchen was equipped. He gave me an unintended insight into this in Vermont. One evening he had planned to prepare hamburgers on his outdoor grill. However, shortly before dinnertime, a torrential storm blew in, and eating outside became impossible. After we abandoned the idea of grilling our hamburgers outdoors, Betty Nan offered to prepare them in a skillet, and Bill accepted. Following dinner we washed the dishes together until we got to the pots and the dirty skillet. Then Bill said, "Pots and pans are the host's job." It was his house, so we agreed: we left the skillet in the sink. In the middle of the night, when I went to the bathroom, I found Bill hunched over the kitchen sink, trying to scrape the skillet clean with a spatula. Our gracious host was embarrassed to admit that his "bachelor household's" kitchen did not include scouring pads.

The imperatives of his job and the country's business intruded in a small way on his vacations—by his choice. Like many of his predecessors, he could have been incommunicado while on holiday and the Supreme Court would have continued to function well. But he did not want to be out of touch. He called his chambers at a fixed time every day, and his secretary read from a prepared list of matters she considered important. He dealt with each quickly in the order it was presented, and rarely made notes on his end. He arranged his day so he could devote no more than an hour to his daily call to his chambers.

Bill was Greensboro's best-known and most visible resident. Everybody knew who he was. He enjoyed exchanging greetings with passersby as he walked his daily route from his home to Willey's Store and then to the post office. At Willey's he picked up his *Burlington Free Press* and one day's supply of groceries. (A full larder would have deprived him of the pleasure of making small talk with Greensboro housewives about fresh produce and food prices.) His circumstances also forced him to make conversation each day at the post office. While the Greensboro post office had approximately three hundred individual boxes for prices that in 2008 ranged from $38 a year to $98 a year, Bill preferred to pick up his mail each day at the general-delivery window, where there was no charge. This required him to identify himself each day at a counter and, if asked, to present a photo ID.

VIII.

Mountain View Country Club, where Bill played tennis and bridge, is one of the nation's few—maybe its only—century-old country clubs that does not have a restaurant, a bar or a swimming pool. It reflects Greensboro's unique character. Mountain View's golf course is over one hundred years old, one of America's oldest. In 1898, when the general public still considered golf a quaint sport for high society, like polo, Mountain View built its first three-hole course. The nine-hole layout was completed five years later, less than a decade after the founding of the United States Golf Association. There are no membership restrictions. Any summer resident of Greensboro or its environs, or any visitor passing through the area, is welcome to play the course for a modest fee, but only members can participate in its handicap golf competitions and round-robin tennis events.

Greensboro's main tourist facility is Highland Lodge, a two-story wooden hotel that was built at the end of the nineteenth century. It offers eleven guest rooms and the town's only restaurant. Its promotional literature boasts about its old-fashioned atmosphere, including a front porch with a line of wicker rocking chairs that overlooks the region's largest lake.

Since the day they answered the newspaper ad about the availability of a home in Greensboro, the Rehnquists have had a connection with Highland Lodge. The land on which their house is situated was originally part of the property that surrounded the farmhouse that later became Highland Lodge. During the thirteen years he summered in Greensboro as a widower, Bill often ate his evening meal at Highland Lodge.

IX.

IN THE MID-1980s Bill was invited to join the ROMEOS (Retired Old Men Eating Out in Style), a group of seven older men who summered in the Greensboro area. Each Wednesday at noon they met for lunch at the Highland Lodge following a late-morning cocktail or two at a member's home. A diverse group of intellectually accomplished men, the ROMEOS expanded an informal luncheon group into dinner visits to one another's home, occasional card games and an annual outing to nearby Lake Memphremagog, which is half in Vermont and half in French-speaking Quebec. The outing included a ferry trip to Canada, where members had a chance to show off their linguistic skills.

They also had several Washington "outings" when they had preferred seating for the oral arguments in a marquee case before the Supreme Court followed by a ROMEO lunch at a round table at one of Bill's favorite Capitol Hill restaurants. Lunch was usually followed by a visit to the latest "big show" at the Smithsonian or the National Gallery, where VIP treatment was arranged by Bill, whose job description included "chancellor of the Smithsonian Institution."

Although Bill boasted about the fact that he was the only member who had a full-time job, all of the others had had successful careers in business or academia. The ROMEOS were the summer colony's equivalent of the Social Register. When Bill joined the group, five of the six other members were the children or grandchildren of couples who had started summering in Greensboro before World War II.

X.

TWELVE YEARS AFTER the Rehnquists bought a simple, unostentatious home behind a country hotel, the underlying paperwork became a national cause célèbre. In August 1986, during the Senate Judiciary Committee's confirmation hearings on Bill's nomination to be chief justice, it was disclosed that there was a clause in the Rehnquists' Vermont deed that barred the sale or lease of the house to "anyone of the Hebrew race." The restrictive clause originated in 1928, when four land developers assembled several farms in the Greensboro area as part of a residential real estate promotion scheme that the Great Depression kept from coming to fruition. Since exclusionary covenants have been unenforceable since the mid-1950s, subsequent owners never bothered to have the restrictive language expunged from their deeds. Neither did the Vermont title attorney who represented Bill at the closing.

When confronted with the fact that the deed to his summer home, which he loved, included a clause that prohibited sale or rental to Jews, Bill said he never read the details of the deed but had depended on his title attorney in Vermont to do so. However, he believed his Vermont title attorney was not obligated to advise him to have it expunged since it was unenforceable boilerplate, and making the change would have increased his closing costs.

Still, the Democrats on the Judiciary Committee, particularly Senators Edward Kennedy and Howard Metzenbaum, tried to make the point that while the exclusionary clause was legally meaningless, failure to have it removed from the deed reflected ethnic and racial insensitivity on Bill's part. Even though the deed had been tucked away in a safe-deposit box for fourteen years before its existence was discovered, it offended several senators who said it tended to remind Jews that, until very recently, they were considered socially inferior and undesirable neighbors. It was being gratuitously hurtful, they argued. An editorial writer likened it to telling anti-Semitic jokes in the presence of Jews.

A reader may fairly ask how I, a devout Jew, feel about the Kennedy-Metzenbaum position. The answer is: ambivalent. I still cringe when I am reminded that it is only a few years since my neighbors thought that my being Jewish made me defective or inferior. I recall that one of the reasons I applied for admission to Dartmouth in 1941 was because it was one of the few colleges in the East where Jews were welcome to join any fraternity. At most of the others, only Jewish fraternities welcomed them. Before World War II almost every Ivy League college had a Jewish quota, and their leaderships were quite open about them. Large law firms and medical staffs at hospital centers also had Jewish quotas. I do not think the language in Bill's deed was significant, but I feel happy to know how far America has traveled away from its bigoted past during my lifetime.

Near the end of the Judiciary Committee hearing, Senator Patrick Leahy, a liberal Democratic senator from Vermont, closed off discussion of the "Hebrew race" exclusionary language in the Rehnquists' deed: "The question of restrictive deeds has been somehow blown out of proportion and is a 'red herring,' " Leahy stated. "Under Vermont law, it is indeed null and void," he continued, "and I can state that with a great deal of certitude it would certainly be null and void under any federal law . . . This was a covenant added to your [Bill's] deed. It was brought forward from an earlier deed. The fact that that covenant is in there, I find regrettable . . . But its inclusion in no way suggests to me any kind of an anti-Semitic background. . . ." This statement is particularly significant since Senator Leahy voted against Bill's confirmation when the final tally was taken. For the two days before Senator Leahy's remarks, tiny Greensboro's attitude toward minorities—past and present—led the evening TV news reports.

XI.

I BELIEVE BILL'S problems with his Vermont deed are attributable to his near-obsessive frugality, nothing more. Saving money was a fundamental part of his character and it manifested itself in almost all of his activities. (I discuss this detail in "Personality Quirks.")

The Vermont attorney who handled the legal details of his house purchase advised him that the restrictive clause in his deed could be ignored because it was unenforceable. To have it expunged would have involved a costly legal procedure whose sole purpose would have been "cosmetic"—and the cleaned-up deed would likely have rested unread for decades in a safe-deposit box.

Bill's decision not to have the restrictive covenants expunged from his Vermont deed was likely a deliberate decision, but that decision had nothing whatsoever to do with racial or religious bias. It was just another expression of a personality quirk that made him choose to pick up his mail at the post office's general-delivery window instead of paying a nominal rental fee for a private, locked post office box.

PART TWO

FIVE

IMPEACHMENT

I.

THE ATTEMPT TO remove President Bill Clinton from office by impeachment in 1999 was viewed by much of the public as little more than political theater. But Bill Rehnquist, who played a highly visible role in the proceeding, understood its true significance. He probably knew more about impeachment trials at both the state and federal level than any impeachment trial presiding officer in United States history.

While most news reports focused on statements and votes by individual senators, Bill's function was virtually ignored by the media. In many broadcast venues, the chief justice's part was dismissed as largely symbolic. But, in reality, it was *central*.

Even though presidential impeachments are once-in-a-century occurrences, Bill had been thinking about the role of the impeachment process in democracies for more than three decades. He was convinced that when a constitution granted a legislature the power to remove a duly elected executive or an appropriately appointed member of the judiciary on unspecified grounds, it had created a ticking time bomb which would someday explode with catastrophic consequences.

In *Grand Inquests*—a book about two famous nineteenth-century impeachment trials that Bill wrote eight years before he presided at the Clinton trial—he explains that the impeachment process as outlined in the United States Constitution could provide ambitious and clever politicians with a lawful way to destabilize a government. Specifically, he feared that large congressional majorities, of either party, could use impeachment—as well as its threat—to intimidate both the judiciary and the executive branches.

While Bill had undoubtedly written more and read more about impeachment trials and their history than any other participant in the Clinton impeachment proceedings, he was also the only person in attendance who had actually *taken part* in an impeachment trial. He alone understood from experience, as well as research, an impeachment trial's unique dynamics.

II.

FOR THREE MONTHS in the spring of 1964, Bill was likely the most visible figure in a politically inspired—and politically decided—impeachment trial before the Arizona Senate. After the overwhelmingly Republican House of Representatives impeached (indicted) two Democratic corporation commissioners on multiple charges of fraud, bribery and financial malfeasance, the House managers hired Bill, who was part of the GOP's inner circle, to organize and lead the prosecution.

While Barry Goldwater's come-from-behind Republican primary campaign was big news nationally, the top news story in Goldwater's home state was a politically freighted impeachment trial before the Arizona Senate. Bill's name appeared on the front page of Phoenix's *Republic* and Tucson's *Arizona Daily Star* an average of twice a week between March and June of 1964. Ironically, in 1999, none of the national media connected Bill's personal experience as "chief prosecutor" at an impeachment trial thirty-five years earlier with his role in the Bill Clinton trial.

As usual, Bill did his homework fastidiously. By the time he appeared before the Arizona Senate, he had read widely about impeachment trials and their history. He knew why trials before legislatures are vastly different from trials before courts of law, civil or criminal. He was prepared to answer challenges by the chief justice, as well as by opposing counsel.

The Arizona Senate was presided over by Chief Justice Jesse A. Udall, a member of a political family whose prominence continues. (In November 2008, two of Chief Justice Udall's grandnephews were elected to the United States Senate, and a grandson—Gordon Smith of Oregon, an incumbent senator—was defeated.)

At one point early in the trial, Bill called one of the defendants to the witness stand, and the defense counsel objected. Chief Justice Udall ruled that a defendant in an impeachment trial cannot be forced to take the stand. Bill still objected. "This is more like a civil case than a criminal proceeding," he told Arizona's chief justice. "In a criminal case, the defendant is never required to testify. But he can take the stand in a civil case, like this is." But Arizona's chief justice was unmoved. And the witness did not testify.

At another point in the proceedings, when Bill felt that a ruling by Chief Justice Udall was more appropriate for a criminal trial than an impeachment, he explained to the Arizona senators that the only penalty they could impose on the defendants was the loss of their jobs. The Senate—and the chief justice—should be aware of their very limited powers.

Bill's experience as an impeachment trial "prosecutor" in the rough-and-tumble environment of Arizona's state capital in 1964, undoubtedly left an indelible mark. It is difficult to imagine someone as decorous as Bill forgetting the following statement about him that appeared in a front page story of the *Arizona Daily Star*:

The questions from Mr. Rehnquist are exactly similar to sticking a hot branding iron on a bull's rear, pulling it off, and telling the bull it never was there. Well, the bull knows it was there.

The defense attorney who made this statement before the Arizona Senate was accusing Bill of breaching a procedural rule about the sequence in which witnesses were to be questioned, and then trying to cover up the alleged breach.

III.

THE 1964 IMPEACHMENT trial gave Bill a chance to show off his legal skills in a well-publicized political dispute. The appointment was a political plum, and Bill knew it. While he and his Republican clients realized they had little chance of prevailing in the Arizona Senate, where the Democrats controlled with a 6-to-1 margin (24 Democratic senators to 4 Republican senators), the Republicans foresaw that an impeachment trial provided a great opportunity to expose the majority party's chicanery to public scrutiny, and part of Bill's job was to help them do it.

When the Arizona Senate voted overwhelmingly to acquit the two corporation commissioners, Bill was not surprised. From the beginning he understood that, even if he proved his case completely and conclusively, the fraud and bribery charges were window dressing. He was an actor in a show trial. That was part of the deal. But the experience allowed him to further solidify his position as "house intellectual" within the top echelons of Arizona's GOP.

A member of the Arizona Senate issued a press release at the impeachment trial's midpoint that said the trial was contrived by the House managers and their counsel (Bill) at the behest of the Republican Party's political boss, Eugene Pulliam, the owner of Phoenix's daily newspapers. Part of the press release said:

> The main purpose of this impeachment trial is to flagrantly drag through the pages of the press the dirty linen, if any, of the Democratic Party . . . by the Pulliam press-motivated leadership of the Arizona House.

Although Bill had no personal relationship with Eugene Pulliam, Pulliam's role in Arizona politics became a minor conversation factor in his life for several years after Pulliam's grandson, Dan Quayle, was elected vice president. Bill and Vice President Quayle saw each other at official functions with some regularity, and they usually talked about the only thing they had in common: nostalgic remembrances of Eugene Pulliam's role in the development of the Republican Party in Arizona.

In 1964, Chief Justice Jesse Udall, like Bill Rehnquist thirty-five years later, was the only participant in the proceedings who had actually taken part in an impeachment trial—and this led to his firm-handed management of the proceedings.

In 1933, while in his second term in the Arizona House of Representatives, Udall made the motion for impeachment and was one of the House managers at the only other impeachment trial in Arizona's history. One of the defendants at the trial outwitted Udall, and Udall wanted to make sure nothing similar happened when he was presiding.

A few days before the 1933 impeachment trial was to begin, one of the defendants resigned from his office. As a result, evidence concerning the briberies and extortions with which he was charged could not be introduced into the public record under oath. The impeached official who resigned claimed that impeachment was a political smear tactic, nothing more. In the next general election he ran for the job from which Udall had resigned—and he won by a large margin.

IV.

GRAND INQUESTS TELLS the stories behind the impeachment trials—and acquittals—of Supreme Court Justice Samuel Chase in 1805 and President Andrew Johnson in 1868. Bill considered them classic examples of how the impeachment process could be used for partisan political gain. As he viewed it, the impeachment procedure gave Congress the power to tyrannize both the judiciary and the executive branches.

Even well-informed people know very little about impeachment. This greatly concerned Bill. He thought the subject should be discussed more often in high school civics courses as well as in college-level political science classes. If either of the nineteenth-century trials had succeeded, they would have set dangerous precedents—and, he believed, American democracy would be less sturdy than it is today.

In his methodical, lawyerly way, Bill explained that one of the reasons he saw impeachment trials as so threatening was because defendants at impeachment trials usually do not have the same protections as criminal defendants, specifically the right to call witnesses and the right to refuse to testify. While a criminal defendant can lose his liberty and, maybe, his life if found guilty, the most a defendant at an impeachment trial can lose is his job. However, as *Grand Inquests* states, the consequences of a president or a Supreme Court justice losing his or her job through an impeachment proceeding would be long-lasting, with far-reaching effects. At an impeachment trial, the political system is often more on trial than the individual defendant.

V.

In *GRAND INQUESTS* Bill easily established both the legal and the political cases for impeaching President Andrew Johnson. He made both seem persuasive, appropriate and worthy. He concluded that while President Johnson probably breached his oath "to faithfully execute the Office of President of the United States"—which is generally interpreted to mean enforcing the laws passed by Congress—the case against him did not rise to the level of an "impeachable offense." He believed Congress's case was more political than legal. The Senate was correct to have acquitted him (by a single vote).

The facts leading to President Johnson's impeachment can be stated succinctly. The majority in Congress in 1866 and 1867 passed laws whose main objective was to hamper and harass a president with whose policies they disagreed. One such law required the president to secure the Senate's "advice and consent" before dismissing a cabinet officer, just as he is constitutionally required to do when he names a new cabinet officer. President Johnson promptly vetoed the law, and a hostile Congress, with equal promptness, overrode his veto. Within days President Johnson defied the express will of Congress. He fired the secretary of war, with whom he disagreed politically. Three days later the House of Representatives impeached the president.

The events that led up to Justice Samuel Chase's impeachment were more complicated. A signer of the Declaration of Independence, Chase was appointed to the Supreme Court by President George Washington. A political conservative who abhorred Thomas Jefferson's populism, he repeatedly made public statements about his low opinion of and dislike—almost hatred—of President Jefferson.

Jefferson, who had been inaugurated as president in March 1801, was frustrated when the Supreme Court repeatedly found large portions of his legislative program unconstitutional. Since all members of the Supreme Court were appointed by his predecessors who did not share Jefferson's political philosophy, he decided to partially cure his Supreme Court problem through the impeachment process. Chase became Jefferson's designated candidate for impeachment.

Several years before Justice Chase's impeachment, two events occurred in his courtroom (when he was sitting as a trial judge) that formed the basis of the charges. (During much of the nineteenth century, the only federal court was the Supreme Court. As a result, Supreme Court justices spent part of each year sitting as trial judges in specified geographic areas.) In the first, Justice Chase made offensive, hostile remarks about President Jefferson and his political party during a trial, probably while drunk. In the second, at another trial, Justice Chase refused to allow the attorney for the leader of a small antitax revolt who was being tried for treason to offer an argument on the definition of "treason." In a bizarre sequence of events, the defendant's lawyer quit in protest and Justice Chase took over the role of "defense counsel" from the bench. Still, at the end of the trial he sentenced his own client to death by hanging. Although the tax revolt leader was later pardoned, the second charge against Justice Chase was based on his bizarre conduct in the tax revolt–treason case.

The Jeffersonian majority in the House of Representatives impeached Chase on appropriate grounds in Bill's view. But the Senate, when sitting as an impeachment court, also acted correctly when it voted to acquit him.

Bill made it clear in *Grand Inquests* that he believed both Justice Chase and President Johnson would have been guilty as charged, if they had been tried as part of a routine civil action. But they were not. They were tried before the United States Senate sitting as an impeachment court. The question before the Senate was: Were the charges important enough to justify impeachment (removing from public office persons who were properly elected or appointed), or were the trials carefully staged judicial events whose sole objective was partisan political gain? In both instances Bill thought the Senate's acquittal votes were prudent and responsible.

VI.

SINCE I WAS only vaguely aware of the underlying circumstances that led to the impeachment of Justice Chase and President Johnson, I asked Bill to recommend a book to fill in some of the large voids in my knowledge. As much as anything I have previously written, the text he suggested tells about the wide lens through which he viewed the world. Instead of recommending one of the several dozen American history books he had read while doing research for *Grand Inquests,* he urged me to read Thomas Babington Macaulay's *Warren Hastings.*

One of Britain's most eminent historians and a master of English prose, Macaulay wrote a short book describing the eight-year impeachment trial (1787 to 1795) of Warren Hastings, the first governor-general of British India. The "high crimes and misdemeanors" with which Hastings was charged were heinous: extortion at gunpoint, murder, aiding in the mass killings of natives and tolerating a policy of rapine that resulted in a devastating famine. Although the evidence offered at the trial was copious and often unchallenged, Hastings was eventually acquitted on all charges. Many of the offenses with which he was charged were capital crimes. If he had been tried by a jury of his peers, he likely would have been hanged.

The Warren Hastings story gave me a broad understanding of impeachment trials and why they are different than all other trials, both civil and criminal. Like Samuel Chase and Andrew Johnson, Warren Hastings was probably guilty as charged. And like his American counterparts, his guilt was likely proven at the trial. Nonetheless, all three were acquitted.

When required to perform a judicial function, both the House of Lords, which tried Hastings, and the United States Senate, which tried Chase and Johnson, acted differently from the lower houses of their legislatures that had indicted (impeached) the three. In Hastings's case, the House of Lords acknowledged the fact that he, more than any other person, created the united and financially productive India that became the British Empire's crown jewel for a century and a half. This fact was weighed in the balance against each specific charge. In the end, the Lords believed they were expected to render judgment on Hastings's loyalty and service to the Crown—and on the basis of his loyalty and service, they acquitted him.

For someone like me, who was thinking about the impeachment process for the first time, Warren Hastings was a helpful read. Macaulay made it clear that impeachment trials are, by definition, both political and judicial—and it was ever thus. He pointed out that both Cicero and Tacitus were, at different times, active participants in politically inspired impeachment trials before the Senate of Rome.

106TH CONGRESS—FIRST SESSION

United States Senate

Impeachment Trial of the
PRESIDENT OF THE UNITED STATES

DATE JAN 14 1999

ADMIT BEARER TO THE SENATE GALLERY

Sergeant-at Arms United States Senate

Only those with special tickets were admitted to the Senate Gallery during the impeachment trial of President Bill Clinton in 1999.

VII.

BILL NEVER DISCUSSED with me the details of the Clinton impeachment trial. But a careful reading of *Grand Inquests* leads me to believe that, had he been a senator instead of an impartial presiding officer, he would have voted for acquittal. While Bill Clinton probably committed perjury and obstruction of justice in the course of trying to hide his extramarital sexual encounters—the crimes for which he lost his license to practice law in Arkansas and paid a large settlement to Paula Jones—the Senate decided that his crimes did not cross the "impeachable offense" threshold. He extoled the Senates of 1805 and of 1868 for rising above partisanship, for seeing themselves as participants in a special kind of court, for being more than mere triers of fact.

In early 1999, when the Senate met as an impeachment court with Bill presiding, the trial entered the verdict stage. Like a jury in a trial court, the senators debated President Clinton's guilt or innocence in secret.

Everybody who attended the closed sessions of the Clinton impeachment trial—sergeants-at-arms, parliamentarians, lawyers, law clerks, doorkeepers, stenographers—except the chief justice and the senators, whose attendance was constitutionally mandated, signed confidentiality pledges. And to my knowledge none has ever been breached.

While the substance of the deliberations was never disclosed publicly, several senators commented publicly on the fair and evenhanded manner in which Bill conducted the proceedings. He won special kudos from the senators because, among other things, he and his law clerks had done extensive preparatory research on the rules and procedures for conducting impeachment trials. During the months preceding the trial, they created their own parliamentarian's guide for the task. Bill's law clerks were his parliamentarians. While I am unaware of any serious conflicts between Bill's young law clerks and the Senate's respected and scholarly parliamentarian staff, all participants were impressed with the serious and efficient way in which he approached his new short-term job: the United States Senate's presiding officer.

While Bill fastidiously avoided discussing the details of the Senate's secret sessions, he did tell me how much he enjoyed working with the senators over a period of several weeks on a familiar basis, much of it behind closed doors. They came to respect one another. In a special way, they bonded.

At the conclusion of the trial, the Senate presented Bill with a "golden gavel," a token of its appreciation for the fair manner in which he conducted the trial. A particularly delicious moment for him came at the very end when two Democratic senators told him that they were sorry that they had voted against his confirmation in 1986. This was something he was totally unprepared for, and he was deeply touched. He never revealed to me the names of those senators.

Grand Inquests' conclusion reaffirms Bill's concern with the impeachment process's potential for abuse. It concludes:

> The importance of these two acquittals in our constitutional history can hardly be overstated . . . [D]ecided not by the courts, but by the United States Senate . . . [they] surely contributed as much to the maintenance of our tripartite federal system of government as any case decided by any court.

SIX

DISPUTED ELECTION

I.

LESS THAN TWO years after the Senate rendered its verdict in the Clinton impeachment trial, Bill was garnering even larger headlines around the world. The Supreme Court's decision to bring the disputed presidential election of 2000 to closure was a cataclysmic event. The aftershocks will be felt for generations. It was also likely the most newsworthy and historic event in Bill's public life.

I feel quite certain that until December 2000, Bill believed that history would recall him as the author of erudite and artfully crafted opinions, and a chief justice who led the Supreme Court in the direction of less regulation, more federalism and stricter law enforcement. But minutes after the court decided *Bush v. Gore*, his place in history had changed. The court that he led had effectively chosen the forty-third president of the United States, and no Supreme Court had ever done anything remotely similar.

The *Bush v. Gore* decision and Bill's passing were separated by slightly less than five years, and time tends to dull memories, both individual and collective. Still, a large percentage—probably most—of the articles published immediately following his death included in the lead paragraph a reference to his role in naming the winner in the 2000 presidential election. Current indications are that history will connect his name with *Bush v. Gore*, just as Chief Justice Earl Warren's name is identified with *Brown v. Board of Education*.

Books about the Supreme Court during Bill's tenure fill two shelves in my library. Half of them concern *Bush v. Gore*. Most are serious, thoughtful books about an important event. The final denouement in that presidential election will continue to fascinate serious people as long as the republic survives. The election saga's intricate plot could not have been contrived by a fiction writer.

While I feel compelled to review in detail Bill's and my relationship during those tempestuous weeks in late 2000, it should be noted that nothing hereafter should be interpreted as my personal commentary on the merits of the Supreme Court's involvement in *Bush v. Gore*. A surfeit of that has already been produced by lawyers, scholars, pundits, politicians and historians, including Bill himself.

II.

MY INVOLVEMENT WITH Bill and the presidential election of 2000 began late in the afternoon of November 6, 2000, the Monday before Election Day. Betty Nan and I had just faxed our election picks to Bill's secretary, Janet Tramonte, and she had faxed his back to us.

The fact that a one-dollar election bet among three old friends was never paid off might seem unworthy of special treatment. But it merits it here. It is revealing in profound ways.

Betty Nan, Bill and I began betting on elections shortly after Nan Rehnquist's death in 1991. In the beginning, it was simple. We each bet one dollar on one or two close races, shook hands and paid off the next time we had dinner together. But in a few years, without deliberate planning, the scope of our betting expanded. The money involved remained insignificant. The wagering terms, however, became complicated. On some Election Days we each wagered a dollar on two dozen or more individual races. To add complexity and variety to our game, we changed the terms regularly. Sometimes we simply chose a winner. More often we wagered on spread, voter percentage or by what percentage each party would win in a legislature.

After our election cards grew lengthy and complicated, it became necessary to record our bets in writing. Conversation on movie dates during October often focused on how we would organize our betting cards for an upcoming election. The arrangement by which we exchanged our picks was efficient and easy. Betty Nan and I faxed our selections to Bill's secretary and, after receiving our choices, she faxed Bill's to us. This allowed the bettors to keep their choices secret.

I had some reticence about using the chambers of the chief justice of the United States as a betting parlor. But when I questioned Bill about it, he brushed me aside. "Janet loves being part of all this," he explained.

Our betting cards in November 2000 were comprehensive and complex. We bet one dollar on each of twenty-two different contests:

- which presidential candidate would prevail in ten closely contested states

- which party's candidate would win in nine tight Senate races

- the Electoral College vote for president

- the spread between Republicans and Democrats in each house in the next Congress.

The day before the election, Bill bet George W. Bush would trounce Al Gore by 320 to 218 electoral votes. While Betty Nan and I also picked George W. Bush, we thought he would win by substantially smaller margins: I bet 292 to 246; Betty Nan bet 280 to 258.

Bill's final Electoral College numbers do not tell the full story. A re-

Supreme Court of the United States

1 First Street, NE, Washington, D.C. 20543

FAX COVER SHEET

To: __M. & Mrs. Obermayer__   From: __Janet__

Company Name: _____   Description: __Here's the Chief's__

FAX Number: _____   __count!!__

Number of Pages (including cover page): _____

Date Sent: __11 / 6 / 00__   Time Sent: _____ a.m. _____ p.m.

If there are any problems receiving this transmission please call. _____

(Cover Page)

The Obermeyers and the chief justice exchanged betting cards by fax on the Mondays before elections. The chief justice's secretary was the exchange agent.

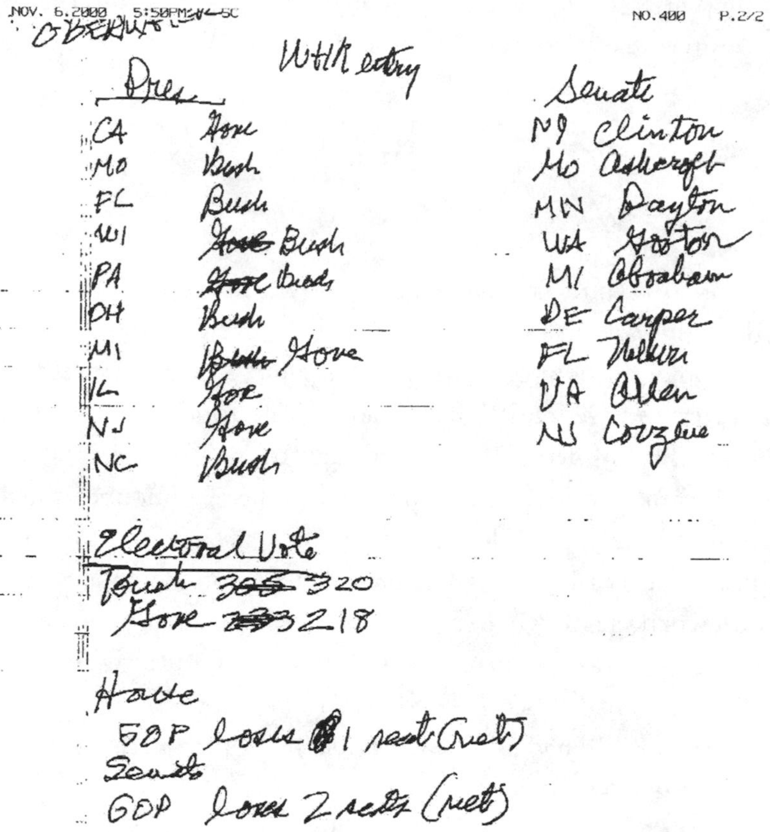

NOV. 6.2000 5:50PM... NO. 400 P.2/2

[handwritten worksheet]

OBERLIN

With entry

Pres.

CA	Gore
MO	Bush
FL	Bush
WI	~~Gore~~ Bush
PA	~~Gore~~ Bush
OH	Bush
MI	~~Bush~~ Gore
IL	Gore
NJ	Gore
NC	Bush

Senate

NY	Clinton
MO	Ashcroft
MN	Dayton
WA	Gorton
MI	Abraham
DE	Carper
FL	Nelson
VA	Allen
NJ	Corzine

Electoral Vote
Bush ~~305~~ 320
Gore ~~233~~ 218

House
GOP loses 1 seat (net)
Senate
GOP loses 2 seats (net)

view of his longhand worksheet shows that between the time he originally prepared his betting entry (Sunday evening) and the time it was
faxed to our home (Monday afternoon) he changed his mind about
the races in Wisconsin, Pennsylvania and Michigan. His last-minute
changes resulted in his adding fifteen electoral votes to Bush's total. Bill
rarely, if ever, switched his faxed bets impetuously or on the basis of his
personal preference: his betting card confirms that as the moment of
truth grew closer, his belief in a Republican sweep grew stronger.

While he was dead wrong in switching his bets on Pennsylvania
and Michigan from Gore to Bush, the tally in Wisconsin was almost as
close as the one in Florida. Gore carried Wisconsin by 5,708 votes out

of a total of 2,480,266 votes cast, a margin of 0.2 percent. The final Wisconsin vote was not certified until the Thursday after the election.

III.

BY NOON ON Thursday, November 9—two days after the general election—it had become clear that Florida's vote would likely decide the outcome. Without counting Florida's vote, Al Gore had 267 electoral votes and George W. Bush had 246 electoral votes. With 270 needed to prevail, whoever won Florida's twenty-five electoral votes would become president. According to the official—but uncertified— Election Day tally, Bush led in Florida by 1,784 votes out of nearly 6 million votes cast. Florida law provided for an automatic machine recount when the margin in an election was less than 0.5 percent, and Bush's margin was less than 0.03 percent. The statutorily mandated machine recount was completed on Friday, November 10. It confirmed that Bush had won in Florida by a margin of 327 votes (2,910,198 to 2,909,871).

Al Gore's team challenged the recount in more than a dozen different forums. Media attention, particularly TV coverage, focused on how military ballots were distributed and mailed, how election machines were calibrated, how voters were registered, how polling place workers conducted themselves and how well Palm Beach County's punch card machines worked. At the same time, out of the public's view, the final outcome was being plotted. Two former secretaries of state—James A. Baker III, George H. W. Bush's secretary of state, and Warren Christopher, Bill Clinton's secretary of state—were organizing the equivalent of two multiservice national law firms whose sole reason for existence was to litigate various aspects of Florida's election process.

During the week following the election, Bill and I chatted on the phone about the turmoil and the ineptitude with which Florida officials appeared to be handling their mushrooming problem. We particularly talked about the TV coverage, which we saw as too sensational, full of sound and fury but signifying nothing. We feared how America's inability to name a president a week after Election Day would affect the United States's image in the rest of the world and how it would sooner or later roil financial markets. The notion that Bill could be involved in resolving the contested election never crossed my mind. If it had crossed his, he certainly did not let on.

Meanwhile, our betting cards were still open. In addition to the presidential race, several congressional and gubernatorial races were still being recounted.

On Saturday, November 11—four days after the election—I faxed Bill a preliminary score sheet indicating that, after almost a week, six out of the twenty-two races on which we had bet were still undecided. The even political split in the country went far beyond the Bush-Gore contest. My cover note said:

> Dear Bill:
>
> Half time report—Like everything else this year, it's too close to call.
>
> Obe's post election prediction: If there is no concession statement before Friday night, Dow Jones will be 1,000 points below Election Day's close.

Actually, the financial markets remained calm throughout the chaos. Between November 7 (Election Day) and December 12 (the day the Supreme Court declared a winner) the Dow lost 1.7 percent. It declined from 10,952 to 10,768: 184 points. The Standard & Poor 500 Index's loss was greater, but it was far from catastrophic. The S&P declined from 1,432 to 1,371, 4.3 percent.

IV.

WHILE TV ANCHORS reported nightly on the sideshows—hanging chads, protest rallies and street demonstrations, faulty voting machines and late delivery of military ballots—Katherine Harris, Florida's secretary of state, the state's top election official, was supervising vote tallies out of public view. According to Florida's election law, she had the statutory authority, unilaterally, to declare a winner. It was her responsibility—alone.

On Tuesday, November 14, the legally mandated deadline, Harris certified Bush as the winner in Florida by less than one thousand votes. Gore's legal team immediately appealed to Florida's supreme court. They sought an order that would nullify Harris's certification because several large counties were still conducting recounts on November 14, the day Harris made Bush the official winner. The following Tuesday, November 21, Florida's supreme court ruled in Gore's favor, invalidating Harris's certification.

V.

ON THE SAME day, Bill faxed the following letter to Betty Nan and me:

> *Dear Obie and Betty Nan:*
>
> *It now appears remotely possible that the Florida election case might come to our Court. I therefore feel obliged to cancel all my election bets in any way dependent on the Florida vote. I hope you will agree to let me do this.*
>
> *Sincerely,*
> *Bill Rehnquist*

Supreme Court of the United States
Washington, D. C. 20543

CHAMBERS OF
THE CHIEF JUSTICE

November 21, 2000

Dear Obie and Betty Nan,

It now appears remotely possible that the Florida election
case might come to our Court. I therefore feel obliged to
cancel all my election bets in any way dependent on the Florida
vote. I hope you will agree to let me do this.

Sincerely,

Bill Rehnquist

11/21/00 — 11:20

*Of course!! lets cancel
the entire 2000 election bet.
We're off tomorrow PM to
celebrate Thanksgiving in
Boston with my brother. I'll
telephone tonight to set up
movie date in Dec.*

Obie

Two weeks after Election Day in 2000, when it became apparent that
the Florida dispute might be appealed to the Supreme Court of the
United States, Chief Justice Rehnquist asked to be excused from a one-
dollar election bet.

Although Bush's legal team did not appeal the Florida decision to the Supreme Court of the United States until the next day (November 22), it was a foregone conclusion that within a few hours of the Florida Supreme Court announcing its decision—regardless of which candidate prevailed—the loser in Tallahassee would appeal to the Supreme Court of the United States.

It is also likely that before Bill faxed his letter to us, he knew that his court would become part of the Florida vote dispute, even if its role was limited to a vote not to accept jurisdiction in the Florida appeal. Bush's lawyers probably gave the Supreme Court staff an advance heads-up on the details of how, when and where they were going to file their appeal. An intricate and complex government, like that of the United States, functions as smoothly as it does because bureaucrats—of both parties—understand that efficient operations depend on keeping surprises to a minimum.

To the surprise of many scholars and pundits, the Supreme Court agreed to rule on *Bush v. Palm Beach County Canvassing Board*. It heard oral arguments beginning on Friday, December 1. On Monday, December 4, three days after the oral arguments, the justices rejected the Florida Supreme Court's decision by a 9-to-0 vote.

In their unanimous decision, the justices observed, "As a general rule, this Court defers to a state court's interpretation of a state statute. But in the case of a law enacted by a state legislature applicable . . . to the selection of Presidential electors, the legislature is not acting solely under the authority given it by the people of the State, but by virtue of a direct grant of authority made under Article II." (The U.S. Constitution's Article II says that presidential electors are to be appointed by each state "in such manner as the legislature directed.") This set in motion the chain of events that led to the *Bush v. Gore* decision on December 12.

After Bill notified me that he might be involved in the Florida election controversy, we never discussed the election until mid-December, after the Supreme Court had issued its final ruling. We both understood the rules of the game. We talked about cases before the Supreme

Court only when Bill initiated the discussion. Although we spoke on the phone several more times between receipt of his letter about our bet and the day the election dispute was brought to closure, we limited our conversations to small talk: football, the *Washington Post Book World,* family Thanksgiving celebrations and arrangements for a movie date in early December.

VI.

Notwithstanding the justices' unanimous decision, the question of extending the deadline for counting Florida's votes in the previous month's presidential election was back before the U.S. Supreme Court five days later, on December 9. In its second incarnation, the case had a new caption: *Bush v. Gore.*

Exactly three weeks after Bill's letter saying that it was "remotely possible that the Florida election case might come to our Court," he and his fellow justices in Washington heard oral arguments for the second time on Bush's appeal of the decision by the Florida Supreme Court.

A careful reading of Bill's book *Centennial Crisis* makes it clear that he believed the Supreme Court of the United States acted properly when it decided to get involved in the Florida dispute. He saw a constitutional crisis developing; if it was allowed to continue unchecked, it could quickly destabilize the entire country.

It is instructive to read Bill's explanation in *Centennial Crisis* about the disputed election of 1876, and why a deadlocked Congress considered various ways by which the Supreme Court could resolve the election contest:

> It was quite natural for Congress to turn to the justices of
> the Supreme Court. . . . Unless it was to go totally outside of
> the government it had little choice. . . . The third branch—the

judiciary—was chosen by default. This was a dispute; disputes are traditionally resolved by courts.

Florida's General Assembly (state legislature) had been advised that it had the "constitutional duty" to name Florida's twenty-five electors by December 12, in accordance with Secretary of State Harris's certification. Since Harris certified George W. Bush as the winner, the Florida General Assembly had formally announced that it was going to certify Bush in direct defiance of an order from the Florida Supreme Court. If, as seemed likely, Al Gore was later declared the winner as a result of recounts by various legally constituted county election boards that were authorized to act by Florida's supreme court, the Sunshine State would end up with two sets of certified electors, each with instructions to vote for a different candidate. Each group of electors would believe that they had been elected lawfully. Until a higher legal authority made a selection, their conclusion would be correct.

There was no precedent for the constitutional crisis that appeared to be almost inevitable. Although Bill used that term several times in his book, he never defined or fully explained it. (Since I have been unable to uncover a concise definition of "constitutional crisis," the following will have to suffice: a constitutional crisis occurs when a conflict between the different branches of the government—executive, legislative and judiciary—or within the federal system—state and federal governments—cannot be resolved in a timely and orderly manner.)

On December 9, when the justices agreed to hear *Bush v. Gore*, it was clear to many thoughtful observers that a potentially cataclysmic event loomed on the horizon. But the justices did not all agree that it was their job to resolve it. The justices also understood that if the disputed election was resolved by non-Floridian judges, a victory—by either candidate—would be tainted and unpopular. Their action would be unprecedented. It would likely do long-term harm to the credibility of the institution they respected and that they served with pride. But it would also—in Bill's opinion—be courageous and appropriate.

VII.

Everyone in the Supreme Court's courtroom on December 11, 2000, knew they were sharing in an extraordinary, transforming situation. The entire world was watching and waiting with bated breath.

Since there are less than 350 seats in the Supreme Court Building's courtroom, preference was given to members of Congress, cabinet officers, prominent public figures, political party leaders, Florida election officials and members of the diplomatic corps. Approximately forty seats were reserved for the general public on a first-come, first-served basis (many stood in line throughout the night). But in every theater, there are "house seats" that are specially put aside for friends of the leading actor or the playwright, and the Supreme Court of the United States is no different. Notwithstanding our friendship, I was reluctant to bother Bill on that Sunday afternoon about priority seating for Betty Nan and me the next day. I began by apologizing for interrupting what I was sure was an all-work, high-pressure Sunday reading briefs, having texts of relevant cases sent to his home, meeting with his law clerks and responding to demands by the world's press for additional access. Before I could finish, he graciously interrupted. "I'm on my second football game," he said. "The only thing you're interrupting is Dick Enberg's trivia." He then said he would tell Janet to put both of us on the special-seating list and also to arrange for our parking in the Supreme Court Building.

Legal scholars and historians have written articles and books on the lawyers' arguments as well as the questions posed by the justices between 11:00 a.m. and 12:30 p.m. on that Monday in December 2000. But very little has been written about the mood and ambience in the courtroom. Except for the forty "general-public seats," all seats were assigned to well-connected people who had arranged to be on the marshal's "guest list." Personnel from the marshal's office began admitting those on the list shortly before 9:30 a.m. Guests were seated in

the order they were cleared, regardless of how important they were—
or thought they were. Everybody on the guest list had gone to great
lengths to have their names entered there. It was compiled and vetted
by various government security agencies between 3:00 p.m. on Saturday, when the Supreme Court agreed to hear the case, and early Sunday evening, when the guest list was closed and finalized.

During that short interval, all government offices, including the Supreme Court, were officially closed for business. Still, in less than
thirty hours, proposed attendee lists were submitted from Congress;
protocol offices at the State Department and the White House; both
political parties; Florida's secretary of state, attorney general and supreme court; bar associations and law schools; as well as individual
justices who wanted their own friends and family added to the list.
Since a list of slightly over three hundred names is only a few pages
long, Bill personally checked the guest list on Monday morning. (The
names of the occupants of the forty seats assigned to the general public
were not on the list.) At dinner on the following Saturday, he told
how he was "amused" to find that some of his colleagues had requested seats for celebrities, and several of the congressional seats
were assigned to familiar names from Hollywood and big business.

Bill enjoyed reviewing lists (invited attendees at important oral arguments in his court, invitees to diplomatic receptions, members of
business boards and patron lists at charity balls and political fund-
raisers); they gave him insights into subtle and often important relationships, the kind that often eluded media gossip columnists. Before
attending a reception at an embassy or some branch of the federal government, he often had a member of his staff request a list of attendees.
I saved for him the programs from political events that listed "spon-
sors," "patrons" and "supporters" and identified each group with a
particular level of giving: $2,000, $1,000, $500, etc. We often talked
about why the details of these lists so rarely appeared in the media.
They almost always told more about the local political scene than a
report on the candidate's partisan-babble to the faithful.

VIII.

ALTHOUGH EVERY SEAT in the Supreme Court courtroom—in front of the public seats—was occupied by an important politician or a prominent member of the Washington establishment (most of whom knew each other) forty-five minutes before oral arguments were scheduled to begin, there was no chitchat. Political types, who almost reflexively make conversation with friends or colleagues they recognize in a crowd, were silent in their assigned seats, some for as long as ninety minutes.

One prominent senator who was in the row in front of me rose to change his seat when he saw a colleague nearby. A deputy marshal stopped him in his tracks. Seated near me, in addition to legislators, were Warren Christopher, former secretary of state; William Daley, secretary of commerce; George Will, a syndicated columnist; Mort Zuckerman, editor and publisher of U.S. News & World Report; Jesse Jackson, the civil rights activist; Geraldo Rivera, a Fox News commentator; Stephen Hess, the Brookings Institution historian; and Ben Ginsberg, counsel to the Republican National Committee. Even the candidates' families wanted to be in the Supreme Court on that historic date. Mary Cheney and Elizabeth Cheney Perry, the daughters of Bush's vice presidential running mate, Dick Cheney, were in attendance, as were three of Al Gore's four children: Karenna, Kristin and Albert III.

Part of the thrill of attending oral arguments at the Supreme Court is the place's solemnity. All of those gathered in the courtroom conduct themselves with dignity, decorum and respectfulness, from justices, to lawyers, to media, to invited guests, to the ordinary citizens who are assigned seats in the back rows. There is almost never even a hint of group laughter or applause. But an exception happened during Bush v. Gore.

In addition to the Republican and Democratic candidates, Katherine Harris, Florida's secretary of state, was technically a party in the suit. She was represented by a prominent Florida attorney with little or no Supreme Court experience. He was allotted ten minutes to present his arguments. After Harris's lawyer had spoken for a few minutes, Justice Stephen Breyer asked him a question. He replied, "Well, Justice Brennan [*sic*], the difficulty is . . ." Whoops. Justice William Brennan had retired a decade earlier and died in 1997. Justice Breyer, in a low-key way, corrected the confused lawyer. But then, less than a minute later, when Justice David Souter asked the Florida lawyer a question, he replied, "No, Justice Breyer, what I'm saying is that . . ." But he was quickly interrupted. "I'm Justice Souter," he said. "You've got to cut that out." On a tense historic day, the entire courtroom burst into raucous laughter. Standards of decorum were forgotten for a minute or two.

The next day the Supreme Court of the United States, by a 5-to-4 vote—with Bill in the majority—overturned the Florida Supreme Court's decision that ordered the manual recounts to continue. This action effectively reinstated the Florida secretary of state's certification of George W. Bush as the winner in Florida. With Florida in his column, the Republican candidate won the election of 2000. And a potential constitutional crisis was averted.

Later that week I was unwinding with some friends at the Washington Golf and Country Club's tennis facility when Justice Antonin Scalia walked by. A member of my group stopped him and said, "Thanks for what you did last Saturday afternoon." (At approximately 3:00 p.m. on Saturday, December 9, immediately after the Supreme Court agreed to hear the *Bush vs. Gore* appeal, Justice Scalia had issued an order terminating the manual recounting of disputed ballots in Florida.)

"Just a lawyer doing his work," the justice replied.

IX.

On Saturday, December 16, four days after the *Bush v. Gore* decision, our movie threesome saw *Bounce,* a character drama with a romantic twist. It was not the genre we most preferred, but it was playing at an Arlington cineplex where we could park in a multilevel garage and enter the movie theater without walking on the street. It was the first and only time during our friendship that Bill was concerned about being harassed in public. After the movie, over dinner in the Obermayer's kitchen, Bill explained that he was concerned about subjecting us to loud, hateful speech and obscenities. He said he feared that we might get hurt if someone decided to hurl a rock at him.

After having authored dozens of opinions on controversial issues like abortion, school busing and racial preferences in college admissions, Bill thought he was prepared for hate mail and mean-spirited placards. But the public's response to *Bush v. Gore* was very different. Although they were always orderly, the number of protestors demonstrating in front of the Supreme Court reached mob proportions. On Inauguration Day six weeks later, there were more than one hundred protestors with hostile placards in front of the Supreme Court Building alone. The justices' guests needed police escorts to guide them past the crowded, boisterous sidewalks as they walked from the Supreme Court's preinauguration breakfast to the viewing stands. The court's decision in *Bush v. Gore* did not affect just one specific segment of the body politic; it affected everybody.

Attending a movie in Arlington's Ballston Common Mall with the Obermayers was Bill's first exposure to a potentially hostile public following *Bush v. Gore.* Our almost furtive entrance and exit from a movie theater felt out of character. On other Saturday nights, Bill was totally open about who he was, where he was going and who he was with. But from another—and more important—perspective, it was in character. Many other people in his position would have demanded—and received—protection from the United States Marshals Service or some other government agency. As a matter of fact, if he had wanted protection 24/7, he would not have had to request it from another branch of the federal government. The Supreme Court has its own police force and its chief reports to the chief justice. He is its boss.

The official duties of the Marshals Service includes giving protection to federal judges when they receive threats during criminal trials. (Former attorney general of the United States Michael B. Mukasey, as a Federal District Court judge, received Marshals Service protection 24/7 beginning in 1993 when he presided at the trial of the al-Qaeda operatives who attempted to bomb the World Trade Center. How long Judge Mukasey was protected is secret.)

X.

THE 2004 PUBLICATION of *Centennial Crisis*, a scholarly book that analyzes and explains the disputed election of 1876, allowed Bill to explain to the public—and to history—some of his feelings about the Supreme Court's actions in December 2000.

Ironically, he began *Centennial Crisis*, approximately a year before he became involved in bringing the election of 2000 to closure. When he contracted to write the book, he believed there was high political drama in the story of a presidential election in which the time-tested political machinery did not work and the popular-vote loser became the winner by the vote of one Supreme Court justice. He and his publisher were enthusiastic about the book's commercial prospects.

But *Bush v. Gore* and its aftermath necessitated a partial change in the book's focus. Bill, as well as his publisher, Alfred A. Knopf, understood that if the author did not acknowledge the many similarities between the disputed elections of 1876 and 2000, reviewers and critics would do it anyway.

Prudence dictated that Bill preempt the line of commentary which would focus on his "political insensitivity" because he failed to relate the two events. He accomplished this by forthrightly acknowledging that the readers would likely see a connection between the two events, as well as between Bill, the historian, writing about 1876 and Bill, the chief justice, who played a central role in the 2000 drama. In *Centennial Crisis*'s prologue, Bill clearly established a direct relationship between his writing a book about the first presidential election that was decided by a Supreme Court justice, and his own participation in the second.

There are many parallels between the 1876 and 2000 presidential elections, from the type of candidates to the denouement. In 2000, as in 1876, neither candidate was tainted with scandal. The Democrat won the popular vote by a substantial margin. While in 1876 the results in four states were challenged, the most contentiously disputed vote was in Florida. In both years, battalions of lawyers failed to get vote tally differences satisfactorily resolved in state courthouses.

In 1876, after it became clear to the leaders of both parties that they had reached a stalemate, Congress stepped in. It empowered a fifteen-man commission to name the winner. The commission was to be made up of five Republican and five Democratic members of Congress and five Supreme Court justices. Congress was to select two justices appointed by Republican presidents and two justices appointed by Democratic presidents for the commission. Then the four congressionally selected justices were to name a fifth impartial justice.

As anticipated, the electoral commission split evenly along party lines: seven for the Republican and seven for the Democrat. This made the vote of Justice Joseph R. Bradley the deciding one. Bradley had been named to the Court by a Republican president, but he was the only justice serving in 1876 who had not been active in politics before his appointment to the Supreme Court. Bradley voted for Rutherford B. Hayes, the Republican governor of Ohio. On the basis of a single vote by a Supreme Court justice appointed by a Republican president, the Republican candidate became the sixteenth president of the United States.

In *Centennial Crisis*'s prologue, Bill unequivocally ties together the presidential elections of 1876 and the presidential election of 2000:

> There were undoubted similarities between the two events (1876 and 2000). . . . [I]n the disputed election of 2000 (as in 1876) the Supreme Court of the United States and the supreme court of Florida were the principal post-election actors. There was profound dissatisfaction with the process on the part of the losing parties in both 2000 and 1876. Perhaps when such a dispute erupts, there is no means of resolving it that will satisfy both sides. *But for all of those whose interest in the process of electing a President was quickened by the disputed election of 2000, a review of what happened in 1876 should be interesting and perhaps instructive. To that review, this book is dedicated.* [Emphasis mine.]

Laurence H. Tribe, a Harvard Law professor who presented the losing side's argument to the Supreme Court in *Bush v. Palm Beach County Canvassing Board,* wrote an analysis of the 2000 election cases for the *Harvard Law Review* the next year. In it he discusses the low esteem in which much of the country held the Court's majority after its final decision. He, almost alone among active participants on the losing side, has written respectfully and generously about the justices in the majority. He said he understood how difficult it was to identify and define partisanship on the part of honorable judges:

> It makes little sense to talk . . . about whether partisan considerations really provided the final motivation for the majority's action in *Bush v. Gore.* . . . [In] something as complex and elusive as partisan bias, the danger is great that the bias will be as much in the eye of the accuser as in the heart of the accused.

Centennial Crisis's epilogue is a twenty-eight-page discussion of extrajudicial patriotic service by Supreme Court justices from 1794, when President George Washington asked Chief Justice John Jay to negotiate a treaty with Great Britain, to 1964, when President Lyndon Johnson asked Chief Justice Earl Warren to chair the commission that investigated the assassination of President John F. Kennedy.

Even though the Supreme Court's involvement in *Bush v. Gore* was not an extrajudicial proceeding (it traveled from the Florida Supreme Court to the Supreme Court of the United States through appropriate judicial channels), it is apparent to me that Bill believed the case had characteristics that made it different from a routine appeal from a decision by a state supreme court to the Supreme Court of the United States. The justices could easily have refused to accept the case. They could have let the decision of Florida's supreme court govern in what many saw as an intrastate dispute. There was ample precedent for such a decision. When the Rehnquist Court's long-standing deference to the independence of states is viewed in conjunction with *Centennial Crisis,* it is clear that Bill considered the Florida election appeals in 2000 as special, outside the usual rules. This is at least partially confirmed by the speedy manner in which the Supreme Court processed two different and separate appeals from the Florida Supreme Court (*Bush v. Palm Beach County Canvassing Board* and *Bush v. Gore*); in twelve days two sets of briefs were written, printed, delivered and studied two different oral arguments were presented, with the Democrats fielding two different teams and the justices rendering vastly different opinions in each case.

Throughout *Centennial Crisis's* epilogue, Bill examined how extrajudicial service by justices—their participation in treaty negotiations, criminal investigations, international tribunals, military inquiries and arbitration commissions—impacted the Supreme Court and the nation. He concluded it was rarely, if ever, worthwhile, either in terms of the results achieved or its effect on the Supreme Court.

Bill had unequivocal praise for only one instance of extrajudicial service by Supreme Court justices. He thought that those who agreed to serve on the 1876 Electoral Commission rendered an invaluable service to the republic—and were also individually brave. He pointed out that if they had not accepted an onerous, unpopular assignment, the consequences for the country might have been disastrous. "Even before the first meeting of the Commission," Bill explained, "each one of them could surely see that its work would be the subject of violent and prolonged criticism from the party against whom it ruled. They would be deciding who would be the next President of the United States. Members of the Court . . . would participate in a decision that had enormous political consequences." He could have been writing about his own colleagues in 2000.

Centennial Crisis states unambiguously that Supreme Court justices have an obligation to act when the country faces a constitutional crisis:

> Critics, including Earl Warren, have expressed the view that the justices serving on the Electoral Commission (1876) demeaned the Court. But here one must be reminded of Lincoln's comment when he was accused of acting contrary to the Constitution: "Shall I save the Constitution, but lose the nation?" Four of the five justices, according to Garfield, would rather this cup passed from them, but the consequences of their refusal would have been grave, if not entirely foreseeable. *They may have tarnished the reputation of the Court, but they may also have saved the nation from, if not widespread violence, a situation fraught with combustible uncertainty. In the view of this author, in accepting membership on the Commission, they did the right thing.* [Emphasis mine.]

In the final sentence, Bill makes it clear (to me) that he believed that he and his fellow justices in the majority acted valorously in December 2000. They knew that by bringing the disputed election to closure they invited derision, disdain, scorn and potential personal danger. They understood that their votes might impugn the credibility of the court they served and loved. But when duty beckoned, they answered its call.

SEVEN

RELIGION

I.

BILL, A DEVOUT Lutheran, visited Washington's Roman Catholic cathedral often—to pray. He considered the cathedral's dean, Theodore Cardinal McCarrick, a friend. And I feel certain the feeling was mutual. When Cardinal McCarrick greeted the congregation at the beginning of Bill's funeral service in 2005, he said how pleased he was to be able to loan Washington's grand cathedral to the Rehnquist family for the last rites of a man he knew well and admired.

Bill rarely missed the Red Mass, celebrated each year in the Cathedral of Saint Matthew on the Sunday before the Supreme Court convened in October. The Mass, which is always led by a cardinal or a bishop, is attended by several hundred top-level government officials as well as lawyers and law professors and sometimes the president. They join in special prayers asking that the judiciary be divinely guided in its deliberations.

The term "Red Mass" refers to the scarlet vestments worn by the cardinals or bishops who conduct the service. Its origins hark back to the thirteenth century, when worshippers were praying that God's steady hand would guide the ecclesiastical judges who were part of the

Roman Catholic Church's hierarchy. Throughout much of Western Europe from the Middle Ages until the late nineteenth century, the Roman Catholic Church operated its own judicial system. More than a dozen countries hosted ecclesiastical courts that had equal status with the nation's civil and criminal courts. Matters involving marriage, annulment, bastardy and inheritance were usually tried in church courts, where canon law prevailed. All other matters, civil and criminal, were tried in secular courts.

Bill found the Red Mass uplifting. He considered it important and relevant. He also had a better attendance record than any of his colleagues, including those who were devout Catholics. The John Carroll Society, a Catholic lay group charged with administering the Red Mass, emphasizes that attendance is voluntary. Any hint that attendance is required—or even strongly urged—would likely breach the church-state separation line.

The John Carroll Society started keeping Red Mass attendance records in 1991. During the fourteen years between 1991 and Bill's illness, he only missed three Masses. His faithfulness was particularly noteworthy in light of the fact that, during his last years, he participated in few public events when his attendance was not required.

In light of his aversion to participating in public events, I once asked why he felt that it was important to attend the Red Mass every year. The answer was direct and short: "Because I enjoy it." Anything more would have confused the truth.

II.

FOR THE FIRST several years of our friendship, Bill and I rarely, if ever, discussed our religious faiths. Lutheranism and Judaism share little, except a belief in one God and respect for a moral code whose origins are in the Old Testament.

Then we discovered that the lay and clerical leaders who are represented in the media as speaking for Evangelical Lutherans and Reform Jews often did not speak for us on public policy issues. We shared something important: a feeling of frustration and resentment. Once we began talking about how our religious beliefs were often at odds with the public personas of our religions, it became a favored topic.

Both the Jewish and Lutheran religions have several different branches. Bill's Lutheran Church of the Redeemer in McLean, Virginia, is a constituent member of the Evangelical Lutheran Church in America, and Temple Rodef Shalom in Falls Church, Virginia, to which I belong, is a member of the Union for Reform Judaism. The constituent assemblies of their umbrella organizations (they are not "governing bodies") are made up of lay and clerical leaders, selected by local congregations, ministerial associations and professionals who occupy positions within clerical and philanthropic bureaucracies. These central organizations issue position papers (usually presented as constituent resolutions) on a wide variety of public policy questions, most of which have little or nothing to do with theology, rites of worship, religious education or the passing on of traditions. In the past few years the Union for Reform Judaism (URJ) has passed resolutions on diverse subjects ranging from gun control to abortion, from gay marriage to Supreme Court nominations and from campaign finance reform to capital punishment, none of which are areas in which I feel that my religion should publicly endorse positions, pro or con. Furthermore, I do not enjoy explaining to non-Jews that the URJ's position on these issues has nothing to do with me.

While the autonomy of individual parishioners in matters of politics is acknowledged and reaffirmed in the officially sanctioned literature of both religions, membership resolutions and convention votes are usually treated in the mainstream media as if they had the canonical authority of medieval papal bulls. The Evangelical Lutherans and the Reform Jews are the largest denominations within each religion. This makes policy statements by their leadership assemblages particularly newsworthy. They are also the most liberal subsets within the denominations, both in terms of their interpretation of religious dogma and ritual and their orientation within America's political and cultural infrastructure.

Bill's support for capital punishment has been well documented. Several scholarly tomes have been written about it. It is a subject on which we agreed with each other, but not with those who spoke for our religions. The Evangelical Lutheran Synod and the Union for Reform Judaism are in agreement in their categorical opposition to capital punishment. On the other hand, the Missouri Synod, the second largest Lutheran group in the United States, supports the death penalty unequivocally, as do almost all organizations of Orthodox Jews.

III.

OUR SHARED INTEREST in church-state questions led Bill to invite Betty Nan and me in 1994 and again in 1997 to sit in the box reserved for justices' guests during oral arguments in two cases that he believed would be landmarks in the ever-evolving legal status of organized religion in the United States.

Since Bill knew that we did not have access to the briefs or other explanatory documents before we heard the arguments, he explained the underlying issues to us in advance at dinner after a Saturday movie. Bill was helping us get the most out of our Supreme Court visits, but he was also doing something he thoroughly enjoyed. He was analyzing complex legal issues in colloquial, easy-to-understand English while telling friends about *his* court and *his* job in a way that did not impinge upon the Supreme Court's institutional code of secrecy.

The 1994 case *Board of Education of Kiryas Joel Village School District v. Grumet* arose after an ultra-Orthodox Jewish sect settled in upstate New York, where they sought, and received, a state charter to incorporate as an independent municipality. The new town, Kiryas Joel Village, all of whose residents were Orthodox Jews, later decided to establish a local public school for handicapped children. The question before the Supreme Court was: Since all attendees at the small school were Orthodox Jews, was the government subsidizing a religious school, even though the curriculum was secular and nontheological? Or was the Kiryas Joel School for Handicapped Children a legitimate public school where all the pupils just happened by quirk to be Orthodox Jews? The Supreme Court in a 6-to-3 vote (Bill voted with the dissenters) decided that the Kiryas Joel School District was not eligible for taxpayer support. The majority said that creation of the special school district where all the residents were members of a Jewish sect amounted to support of a religious school, even though the faculty fastidiously avoided teaching religion.

In 1997 we attended the oral arguments in *City of Boerne v. Flores*, another landmark religious freedom case. Catholic archbishop Patrick F. Flores of San Antonio, Texas, filed a request for a building permit to enlarge a famous old church in suburban Boerne. The church at the center of the controversy was built in 1923, in a location that later became a historic district. When it could no longer accommodate a burgeoning congregation, it filed plans to expand into its own parking lot. But Father Flores was denied a building permit for his church because a change in the church's façade would breach the historic district's restrictions. He then sued the City of Boerne, claiming that a federal statute (the Religious Freedom Restoration Act) required the City of Boerne to exempt the church from its historic preservation laws. In a 6-to-3 decision (with Bill joining the majority), the Supreme Court struck down the Religious Freedom Restoration Act. It said that the City of Boerne's zoning laws trumped an individual church's need to expand its facilities when the two interests collided.

Almost immediately following the *City of Boerne v. Flores* decision, a coalition of religious advocacy groups decried it and plotted strategies to frustrate the decision's impact. The coalition included both the Lutheran Office of Public Policy and the Religious Action Center of Reform Judaism.

The denunciation of the decision by Rabbi David Saperstein, the Religious Action Center's director, was so strong that I gave Bill a copy.

It said, in part, "Today's decision in *Flores* . . . will go down in history with *Dred Scott* . . . allowing a preoccupation with extraneous issues to blind it to the real issue in the case—are Americans going to remain free to practice their religion?"

IV.

HOW OUR ADULT children approached each of our religions was a topic that we returned to repeatedly. Most of our children married spouses who were brought up in different faiths than ours.

Jim Rehnquist's decision in the mid-1990s to settle in Sharon, Massachusetts, was a deliberate, carefully considered action that made him part of a community where the majority's religious beliefs were vastly different than his own. It was a decision about which his father spoke of often—and always with pride.

Sharon is an unusual community of 17,500 that is part of Boston's exurbia. Several local websites say that it has a larger percentage of Jews in its population than any similarly sized community outside Israel. Since the census does not collect religious affiliation statistics, there is no official data as to the number of Jews in any particular political subdivision. Still, Sharon's largest Catholic church, Our Lady of Sorrows, when describing its environment says "the town is roughly 75 percent Jewish with seven synagogues." A 2008 report on Harvard's Pluralism Project's Boston area programs says that unofficial estimates place Sharon's Jewish percentage at sixty-five.

When Jim, a former sports star at Amherst and a rising young litigator in one of Boston's oldest and most established law firms (a name partner served as attorney-general in President U. S. Grant's cabinet), decided to move to Sharon, in preference to an elite suburb with a country club, an old private school and charity boards where ambitious lawyers can troll for clients, he was making a statement. No thoughtful person could miss it.

Bill says that Jim and Anna Rehnquist's chief motivation for deciding to bring up their young family in Sharon was a belief that its demographics almost guaranteed a well-funded, academically superior public school system. A 2006 *BusinessWeek* article that listed Sharon among the "25 Best Affordable Suburbs in the U.S." concluded the section on Sharon by quoting a local real estate agent as saying that 96% of the town's high school seniors go on to college: "Our school system is no secret . . . In fact, that is what drives a large number of families."

V.

BOTH BETTY NAN'S and my ancestors were Jewish as far back as anyone can trace. However, Bill and Nan's affiliation with Lutheranism was an adult decision. He was brought up in a Congregationalist church, where his entire family was active. In addition to his parents, two members of his father's family served on various boards and committees at the Plymouth United Church of Christ in Milwaukee. Bill was baptized and confirmed there, and his name is on the honor roll of congregants who served in the armed forces in World War II. Both of his parents were given final rites according to Church of Christ ritual.

Bill informally reaffiliated himself with the Congregational Church (United Church of Christ) during his summers in Greensboro, where there was no Lutheran church. The nearest Lutheran church with a full-time pastor was more than fifty miles distant.

After Bill's death the *United Church of Christ News* distributed on its national newswire a report on his long connection with the church. It included this statement: "Older members at Milwaukee's Plymouth UCC still remember that, at approximately age 12, Rehnquist won a pair of roller skates for knowing the most scripture that year at a church school."

It is not surprising that T. S. Eliot's "Ash Wednesday" was one of

Bill's favorite poems. It was also one of my favorites. Bill was fascinated by Eliot as a person as well as a poet. He was an erudite, learned intellectual who valued tradition, but was able to convey his thoughts in a contemporary idiom. Several times we talked about the meaning of:

> Because I do not hope to turn again
> Because I do not hope
> Because I do not hope to turn

Many critics believe that "Ash Wednesday" was Eliot's way of explaining his own rejection of the Congregationalism of his New England forefathers and his conversion to Anglican Catholicism (Episcopalianism), which he perceived as a Roman Catholic ritual adapted to England's language and culture. Bill viewed his own voyage from the Church of Christ to Evangelical Lutheranism somewhat similarly. He described Lutheran rites as the traditional Roman Catholic order of service adapted for German and Scandinavian worshippers.

VI.

IN 1996, BILL got to know my extended family on an intimate basis when he attended our family Passover Seder. He was the only nonfamily member to do so since World War II. Bill's desire to participate in a religious event with my family meant a great deal to me. Apparently it meant the same to him, or he would not have attended multiple times.

Seder is a ceremonial meal served at Passover, a Jewish holiday that commemorates the Israelites' flight from Egyptian slavery four thousand years ago. Because it memorializes what is generally believed to be the first recorded successful revolt of an enslaved minority (the

Jews) against established royal authority (Egypt's Pharaoh), Passover is widely accepted as a secular as well as a religious holiday. Seder is not a synagogue celebration but a familial one in which ritual prayers are combined with an evening meal. It is observed on a date in the spring close to Easter (Christ's Last Supper with his disciples was actually a Seder).

Bill's involvement with my extended family was unplanned. At dinner one evening in late February, Betty Nan out of the blue casually said, "We talk about religion often. Would you like to join us at our Passover Seder next month?" I was aghast when Bill immediately replied, "I'd love to."

By the next day, I was apprehensive. This was something new and different. An important public figure who was also a devout Christian would be joining our family group. And for us it is as much a family get-together as a religious event. Obermayer Seders are not always decorous. Infant and toddler grandchildren are welcomed at our service, and they rarely show regard for religious ritual or prayer. They make noises, play under tables and between adults' legs and demand almost constant attention from their parents. Still, I have always considered a little baby noise in the background appropriate at a religious service dedicated to the passing on of traditions from generation to generation.

One member of my extended family particularly fascinated Bill: my cousin Erna. Erna was a short, wizened, shy old lady who spoke heavily accented English falteringly. While he was intrigued with her, she was absolutely unimpressed with him. She described him as the "tall, goyische [Christian] politician Obe brought to Seder." Cousin Erna was a Holocaust survivor, a symbol of Jewish survival, the real thing. She was reticent, and did not want to talk about her past.

In order to sustain an awkward conversation, Bill asked Aunt Erna a simple, innocent question: "Where do you live?" She responded, "In a Jewish old folks' home where the food is okay." She actually lived in a sleek, modern assisted-living facility with many programs, a diverse menu and costly amenities. The word "Jewish" was not part of its name, and the director would have blanched to hear his institution described as an "old folks' home" where the food was mediocre.

Seder is a participant ceremony where every adult is assigned a portion of the service to read. Bill was always assigned a part. And he participated with gusto and enthusiasm.

While details of the Seder ritual have varied according to historic and geographic imperatives, the Madrigal of Numbers has been an important part of the service since the Middle Ages. Its purpose is to test a family's understanding of Judaic history and tradition and to confirm its competence to pass them on to succeeding generations. The head of the family asks questions numbered one through thirteen. Then the assembled family members are expected to answer in unison as quickly as they can. Each response repeats the preceding numbers and responses until number thirteen is asked and answered. The routine goes like this:

The head of the household asks: "Who knows one?"

The family responds: "I know one. One is the God of the world."

The head of the household next asks: "Who knows two?"

Then the family responds: "I know two. Two are the tablets of the commandments. One is the God of the world."

After three and four, the leader asks: "Who knows five?"

The family responds: "I know five. Five are the books of the Torah. Four is the number of the matriarchs. Three is the number of the patriarchs. Two are the tablets of the commandments. One is the God of the world."

Finally the head of the household asks: "Who knows thirteen?"

By the time the leader gets to thirteen, the last question, a broad range of biblical events and ritual customs have been covered. Long before you get to question thirteen, the Madrigal of Numbers has become a tricky tongue twister. Most members of the family cannot complete it without slurring their words, mumbling and giggling a little.

Ever since I first began attending Seders as a boy, I considered the Madrigal of Numbers fun. My siblings and I viewed it as a high-spirited family game. Now, as when my father conducted the Seder, various family subsets are pitted against each other to see who can answer a particular sequence of questions most rapidly without slurring, mumbling or cheating by skipping a word or number. For example, my four daughters might be pitted against each other for "Who knows seven?" Then all persons under thirty, all women at the table, all sons-in-law and, finally, my brother Arthur and I. There is much merriment. I, as the head of the household, am the arbitrator in all contests except those involving me. Sometimes we take a vote to determine if a particular family member has cheated.

In 1997, the second year Bill attended, I announced that we had "a real live judge" in our family group. He would judge the Madrigal of Numbers. At first several Madrigal contestants were awed by the "real live judge" and conducted themselves with unaccustomed decorum. But long before Bill reached question thirteen, family members, particularly my brother Arthur, tested the judge's mettle. They did not

Chief Justice Rehnquist often took part in the Obermayer family's Passover Seder. Doug Atnipp, an Obermayer son-in-law, is between Betty Nan Obermayer and the chief justice.

always follow his instructions and made their cheating obvious. And Bill joined in the fun wholeheartedly. When he found somebody mumbling or slurring their words, he disqualified them. When a contest was too close to call, he ordered a rerun.

VII.

ANTI-SEMITISM BECAME A factor in my relationship with Bill posthumously. On September 4, 2005, the day after Bill's death, Alan M. Dershowitz, a prominent Harvard Law School professor, author and TV personality, wrote an article for the online news site The Huffington Post alleging that Bill was an anti-Semite.

Over the years, our friendship allowed us to examine each other's thought processes. We understood each other. Group prejudice of any kind was contrary to Bill's intellectual approach to life. By its nature, group prejudice is arbitrary and irrational. I never heard him use a racial or religious adjective, let alone an epithet. I believe with all my being that bigotry was as abhorrent to him as it is to me.

Dershowitz's piece was entitled "Telling the Truth about Chief Justice Rehnquist." It included the following, *without attribution:*

> When he [Rehnquist] was nominated to be an associate justice in 1971, I learned from several sources who had known him as a student that he had outraged Jewish classmates by goose-stepping and heil-Hitlering with brown-shirted friends in front of a dormitory that housed the school's few Jewish students. He also was infamous for telling racist and anti-Semitic jokes.

This is a cheap smear: if you could libel a dead man, I believe it would do so. Dershowitz should have known better than to repeat hearsay as fact. His reference to "heil-Hitlering" and "goose-stepping" makes the story sound particularly suspicious to me. Between 1946 and 1948, when Bill and I attended college on the GI Bill, a large portion of the student body (often a majority of the men) were veterans, many of whom had fought the Nazis, some of whom may have been maimed by them. While there likely were anti-Semitic groups at Stanford at that time—as there were at all colleges—I believe the wounds of war were still far too fresh for any group to have openly conducted a "goose-stepping, heil-Hitlering" march on a college campus.

The Harvard professor's diatribe was apparently written hastily, in a moment of ire. "Within moments of Rehnquist's death, Fox News called and asked for my comments," Dershowitz explained in The Huffington Post. "Presumably they were aware that I was a longtime critic of the late Chief Justice. After making several of these points to Alan Colmes (who was supposed to be interviewing me), Sean Hannity intruded, and when he didn't like my answers, he cut me off and terminated the interview."

Following the aborted, anti-Bill interview on *Hannity & Colmes*, Dershowitz says he received dozens of hateful and obscene e-mails that convinced him he should memorialize his view that Bill was an anti-Semite in The Huffington Post. The piece ends, "All this, for refusing to put a deceptive gloss on a man who made his career undermining the rights and liberties of American citizens. My mother would want me to remain silent, but I think my father would have wanted me to tell the truth. My father was right."

In 2001, Dershowitz wrote *Supreme Injustice*, a lawyerly polemic (that is not an oxymoron in this context) about the presidential election of 2000. He, like millions of other Americans, vigorously disputed the legal reasoning and intellectual undergirding of the Supreme Court's actions. That is fair and proper.

But the chief justice's feelings about race and religion had nothing whatsoever to do with the majority opinion in *Bush v. Gore*. Yet, in over three pages in the notes section at the back of his book, the Harvard law professor presented a list of hazy (and disputed) recollections and vague innuendos concerning Bill's alleged bigotry. They have no relevance to the book's thesis that I can discern. The only reason for their inclusion in the book is that, if true, they would tend to prove that Bill was a man whose character was so flawed by irrational prejudices that he would betray his judicial oath to accomplish a partisan political objective.

I conclude that Dershowitz placed the information outside the book's main text (but listed in the index) because he understood that it was gratuitous. The notes entry includes the following sentence from a *New York Times* editorial opposing Bill's confirmation in 1986: "A Chief Justice can be less than inspiring or less than an ardent civil libertarian, but he cannot be less than a champion of truth." Dershowitz's comment on the editorial was:

> What the polite editors of the *Times* were saying, in their understated language, was what several senators had already concluded, namely, that Rehnquist had lied under oath at his confirmation hearings, in an effort to deny his *bigoted* background. [Emphasis mine.]

In the course of Bill's fourteen years as an associate justice, the *New York Times,* in closely reasoned editorials, had criticized his socially and politically conservative judicial opinions. It also opposed his confirmation as chief justice in 1986. But in the *New York Times* editorial on which Dershowitz commented, the strongest word used to describe Bill's attitude toward race was "insensitive." Even if that word is accurate (which I vehemently dispute), it is a vastly different word than "bigoted."

One anti-Semitic charge against Bill is memorialized in the public record. It is in the transcript of the 1986 Senate Judiciary Committee hearings before his confirmation as chief justice. Even though the committee's record refutes the charge of anti-Semitism unambiguously, the charge itself remains in the transcript. The Senate Judiciary Committee concluded that a "Hebrew race" restriction in a deed that all parties knew was unenforceable is not evidence of anti-Semitism.

The Harvard law professor's 2005 article in The Huffington Post includes this sentence:

> Rehnquist later bought a home in Vermont with a restrictive covenant that barred sale of the property to "any member of the Hebrew race."

The only possible rationale for Dershowitz's decision to include that sentence in the article was character assassination, a desire to smear the reputation of a dead man.

I am a proud and devout Jew. I have been exposed to anti-Semitism many times in the course of my life. I can almost always recognize an anti-Semite when I see one or when I hear one. I certainly could not have shared a close, honest and candid friendship for almost two decades with a man who was an anti-Semite. I am also quite certain an anti-Semite would not have found pleasure in a long-term relationship with me. This is particularly true of a relationship in which neither party had anything to gain from the other except the joy of warmth, comradeship and shared values.

In summary: Alan Dershowitz and the others who have repeated similar canards did not know the subject of their unfounded accusations.

I did.

EIGHT

MEDIA

I.

LIKE MOST RESIDENTS of Arlington, Bill began his day by reading the *Washington Post*. He enjoyed the newspaper, but he did not read it in the same sequence as the pages are numbered—and only on rare occasions did he deviate from his routine.

After glancing at the day's headlines, he skipped the entire front news section (that included most Supreme Court reportage as well as all editorials and opinion pieces). The first part of the newspaper that he read carefully was Metro (local news and courts). This was followed by Sports, Style (book and movie reviews, chiefly) and the puzzles, in that order. While he loved crossword puzzles, he never took to Sudoku.

While Bill had an encyclopedic memory, there were certain areas of knowledge that he considered "special." In those areas—by his personal crossword puzzle rules—it was acceptable to seek outside help. One such area was Yiddish or Hebrew words and Jewish ritual. Several times a year he phoned asking for help with a crossword lead that involved these subjects. Another gap in his knowledge was Greek mythology, and he had another "live source" that he used for mythology-based clues that stumped him.

Bill's enjoyment of newspaper puzzles received considerable publicity in 1999 when he correctly solved a riddle posed by Dr. Gridlock, the author of a column on traffic congestion that appears regularly in the *Washington Post*'s Metro section.

> What automobile is referred to in a license plate that reads 1
> DIV 0?

On Supreme Court stationery, Bill wrote the *Post*'s columnist the correct answer:

> *Dear Dr. Gridlock:*
> *I believe it refers to an Infiniti, since when you divide 0 into 1*
> *the result is infinity.*
>
> William H. Rehnquist

Bill showed his interest in local news when I visited him in Vermont. Each morning, like a good host, he bought two newspapers at the nearby general store, the *New York Times* for his guest, and the *Burlington (VT) Free Press* for himself. Later, when I offered to swap, he responded that he had finished reading newspapers for the day. He was already working on his current book.

II.

ONE OF THE reasons our friendship matured and flourished was that in the course of pursuing our respective careers we never ran into each other—unless we tried to. Although we shared certain core values, viewed expanded government power as threatening and had similar tastes in poetry and literature, we had somewhat different approaches to media restrictions and the First Amendment.

Our different professional backgrounds and career paths made this almost inevitable. One subject that we disagreed on was cameras in courtrooms. While zealots on both sides saw the issue in black-and-white terms, both Bill and I viewed it as nuanced and complex.

In three important First Amendment cases, Bill invited me to attend oral arguments before his court. All involved subtle understandings of when, or if, small liberties with the truth constituted libel. None involved clear-cut, right-or-wrong questions. While Bill and I agreed on all three, my professional peers saw the underlying issues somewhat differently.

Most of Bill's firsthand knowledge of courtrooms was learned as a judge, and all of that in the rarefied atmosphere of the Supreme Court of the United States. During his fourteen years as a practicing attorney in Arizona, his professional practice consisted chiefly of advising corporate clients, crafting complex business documents and drafting wills. While he made court appearances now and then, litigation was not his specialty.

On the other hand, I had observed the judicial system in low-level trial courts. When I was a card-carrying member of the American Newspaper Guild, the journalists' trade union, I spent nearly two years reporting the seamy side of life in New York City magistrates' courts, specifically in Flushing and Far Rockaway, offbeat precincts, even in the 1950s. While the Constitution's Sixth Amendment requires that all trials be subject to public scrutiny, and the First Amendment guarantees the press's right to publish reports of actions taken within courtrooms, both public scrutiny and press coverage are still more matters of theory than of practice in the real world of magistrates' courts in many jurisdictions.

III.

Today, just as when I was a working journalist, many local governments do not maintain either stenographic records or videotapes of what happens in the lowest-level trial courts. Most days there are no observers in these courtrooms, except insiders. Notwithstanding the Bill of Rights and the protections it guarantees, a large percentage—probably most—of the criminal proceedings at the magistrate's court level are conducted in an environment where journalists are considered intruders, and careful public scrutiny is seen as a form of voyeurism.

When justice is administered outside the public's view, venality and corruption flourish. It is inevitable: the temptations are too great. It is unrealistic to expect that all of the humble—and relatively poor—civil servants who are charged with operating magistrates' courts will turn their backs to the blandishments of money. This is particularly true when they feel they are operating outside the view of the public—or of the law.

The fact that all but marquee criminal trials are conducted in what is tantamount to secrecy is partly attributable to the economics of a free press. The cost of staffing all the courts where petty criminals are tried would bankrupt most media companies. Additionally, most of the reportage would be tedious. Only creative storytellers and skilled writers can produce fascinating stories about small-time lawbreakers.

When I began to cover magistrates' courts, my bosses made it clear that they did not want highbrow stories on how justice was meted out in Gotham's sordid byways. I was to listen to each day's cases until I found one or two sensational, sexy stories. In the summer, this usually meant writing a leering, innuendo-laden article about the arraignment of an exhibitionist or sexual predator who had been arrested on one of Far Rockaway's beaches after a complaint had been filed by a good-looking girl whose photo would add sex appeal to my yarn. In winter, it usually meant describing the trivial but lurid details of a domestic dispute, a pool hall mêlée or a barroom brawl. During my years at magistrates' courts, I observed lowborn and poor people lose their liberty and/or their property in New York City courthouses where there was virtually no public scrutiny and no transcript.

IV.

VIDEOTAPING IS A relatively inexpensive process. When done properly, it is also unobtrusive and automatic. If courtroom activity from gavel to gavel was recorded on tape, the media cost factor would be negligible. A major impediment to broad coverage of criminal courts would be virtually eliminated.

I believe strongly that videotaping courtroom proceedings at all levels would serve the cause of justice. But it is most important at the lowest rung of the judicial ladder. Tape recording magistrate's court trials would help protect the accused from exploitation by all those who are tempted to take advantage of the weak and the defenseless. Bill had considerable sympathy with this. He understood that the administration of justice in low-level trial courts is often rough and sometimes unfair.

Still, he had many problems with how such a record would be used. There is no practical way to create a video archive for the exclusive use of lawyers, defendants and judges. The tapes would have to be made available to the media—and thereby to the general public the media is dedicated to serving. Newsroom personnel would have to edit long, tedious videos down to snippets to make them marginally interesting. The power to reduce and rearrange videos of lengthy courtroom proceedings puts considerable power in the hands of journalists. Many in the legal profession—both lawyers and judges—fear that power; sooner or later it will be abused.

Misgivings that broadcasting video snippets may distort the facts in a particular case is not particular to camera coverage. Distortion is part of the subjective selection process—in journalism, as well as in the writing of history and judicial opinions. It is an essential component of reporting. To some degree, it makes all reportage biased—and it also separates the outstanding from the mediocre and the bad. The pencil-and-pad reporters who cover the Supreme Court give their editors three- or four-paragraph summaries of the day's proceedings, the equivalent of a forty-second snippet.

The change from print to video, however, is more than just a change in medium. It is substantive. TV has a dynamism of its own. I agree that this is justification for judges to consider TV reportage as different from print.

Bill and I agreed that cameras in courtrooms could pose serious problems outside the world occupied by journalists and judges. In highly charged criminal trials—particularly those involving the Mafia and terrorist organizations—videotaping jurors and witnesses could put them at risk of bodily harm. To my knowledge there has never been any serious study of this risk. How realistic is it? How prevalent?

Bill and I both understood that once videotaping was an established practice in courtrooms, posturing and preening on the part of judges, lawyers, witnesses and jurors was inevitable. However, we evaluated the importance of posturing and preening quite differently: I dismissively, he seriously.

Notwithstanding our differences—or maybe because of them—in the spring and summer of 1995, Bill and I talked at least weekly about the bizarre twists in the O. J. Simpson murder trial. We agreed that gavel-to-gavel coverage had turned that particular trial into cheap, sensationalist theater. I believed it was the exception that proved the rule. He, on the other hand, saw it as confirmation of how cameras can pervert and distort the administration of justice as well as the public's perception of the judicial system.

V.

ONLY ONE OF Bill's colleagues, Justice David Souter, was able to talk from experience about cameras in courtrooms. Over more than two decades, he had served as assistant attorney general, attorney general and Supreme Court justice in New Hampshire, where all judicial proceedings are videotaped. At all levels his experience with cameras was bad. He was quite certain that the net effect of cameras in courtrooms had been deleterious. His statements in opposition have been categorical and passionate. They also have been made public.

While he was serving as New Hampshire's attorney general, a reporter for the state's second largest newspaper, the *Concord Monitor*, sought his comment on an aspect of the state's "right-to-know" statute, that mandates camera coverage in all state courts. He responded that the law was a piece of "vague and lousy legislative drafting. [It] stinks!" In 1996, while testifying on the Supreme Court of the United States's budget, he told a congressional panel, "The day you see a camera come into our courtroom, it's going to roll over my dead body."

After Bill's death, the *Washington Post*'s Supreme Court reporter, Charles Lane, disclosed to the public how Bill voted on the issue of cameras in the Supreme Court. In an article about the Rehnquist funeral, Lane wrote, "Rehnquist was opposed to allowing televised proceedings of the high court, and the same rule prevailed at his send-off." When Lane wrote his piece about Bill's funeral, he did not know that the public relations department of the Archdiocese of Washington had arranged to have the entire funeral unobtrusively videotaped, from the opening prayers to the closing hymn. One copy was deposited in the Archdiocese's archives, one copy was donated to the Supreme Court archives and one copy was given to the Rehnquist family.

Two of the most important justifications for video coverage of lower courts do not apply to the Supreme Court. First, stenographic transcripts of all oral arguments are made available to the press and public on a timely basis. Second, covering the Supreme Court is a plum assignment. As a result, most reporters assigned there are talented, experienced professionals who study briefs and the underlying issues before they report on oral arguments or decisions.

VI.

SHORTLY AFTER BILL became chief justice in 1986, he announced that he would give no press interviews while he held the office. Still, while he never allowed a journalist to conduct a freewheeling one on one, he publicly answered questions—none of which he had seen in advance—on at least two dozen occasions during his tenure.

The nonjournalist questioners fit into two categories:

First: broadcast book reviews. He was interviewed on TV at least once about each of the four American history books he wrote. It was stipulated before each meeting that no contemporary Supreme Court questions would be asked. If an interviewer tried to slip one past Bill, he was cut off politely and promptly.

Second: Q and A sessions following formal speeches. Most of Bill's talks were made to university audiences or organized groups of lawyers and judges. With both of these groups he was able to keep the questions focused. There was little risk that he would inadvertently answer a question that would embarrass him or his court. The chair almost always explained in advance that questions would be limited to the topic of Bill's talk or the agenda of a panel of which he was a part. If a member of either group made an off-topic query, he gently reminded the questioner of the rules of engagement.

Advocates of cameras in courtrooms and free-press activists have attempted to say that Bill had a double standard when it came to interviews: one standard for questioners whose efforts would help promote books he authored, as well as those who represented constituencies with whom he identified (lawyer organizations, judicial conferences and law schools); a second standard for professional journalists whose job it was to communicate the actions of a democratic government, including the judiciary, to the citizenry.

I disagree with my activist peers. I do not believe Bill operated on a double standard. The difference between a literary discussion and a hard-hitting, no-holds-barred journalist interview is substantive and fundamental. It is a difference in kind.

An interview with a chief justice who allows questions about the development of opinions, the conduct of justices, the Supreme Court process and a justice's approach to abstract questions cannot be compared with a book reviewer's queries. Whether or not the Supreme Court's institutional regime of secrecy is appropriate in a democracy is a different, albeit important, question. However, it did not begin in 1986 when Bill became chief justice, and it did not end with his death.

VII.

At dinner on the Saturday following *Bush v. Gore,* Bill and I discussed the pros and cons for filming the oral arguments in his court five days earlier. Almost every major media organization in the world was signatory to a petition to allow TV coverage. While the justices turned down the request for live TV coverage, they did allow an audio feed and a typed transcript of *Bush v. Gore* to be released a few minutes after the arguments ended.

That evening Bill told me that he had begun wondering whether the intensity of the passions aroused by the Court's involvement in the presidential election justified approaching live TV coverage with even more skepticism. He had a new concern, he said. It was one I had never thought about. I do not know whether the notion had been buried in his psyche for a long time, or if he had learned about it from one of his colleagues when they discussed the hateful and vicious way they were being described in the press.

Bill's new reason for opposing videotaping the Supreme Court can be explained simply: After several years of taping oral arguments before the Supreme Court, hundreds of tapes would be in the public domain. They could easily be aggregated and manipulated to demean and denigrate particular justices or to diminish the stature and legitimacy of the Supreme Court itself. A TV producer could easily cobble together a program in which a group of justices were shown repeatedly picking their noses, cleaning their teeth, dozing off, scratching their behinds, popping pills, doodling erotic obscenities, winking at old friends or asking foolish questions during an oral argument. In the course of a decade or two on the Supreme Court bench, it was inevitable that a sizable number of unflattering, silly and demeaning poses would have been recorded for each justice. Images gathered to advance the people's right to know could easily be used as raw material for editorializing, propagandizing and creating polemical attacks on the Court as an institution. A talented video editor could likely enlarge a justice's doodling and discern, as well as memorialize, never-articulated thoughts about lawyers, colleagues, cases, maybe even domestic or medical problems. Unedited videotapes in the public domain have a potential for mischief that has rarely been discussed. I had never thought about it before our dinner.

Bill saw this post–*Bush v. Gore* scenario as a threat to the Supreme Court's stature and status. I acknowledged his main point that the existence of a film library of court proceedings would allow clever editors to manipulate tapes to make points that had nothing to do with news gathering. Like all aggregations of knowledge, a video library can be used for good or ill. But I still believed the advantage of making videos outweighed the disadvantages.

VIII.

ON SEVERAL OCCASIONS, when a contemporary political leader was in the news extolling the wonders of full disclosure and transparency, Bill would rhetorically query me as to whether I thought the extoller had read about the totally secret convention in Philadelphia in 1787. After four months of secret debates and negotiation, approximately forty men who had volunteered their time and their talents produced the Constitution of the United States, one of the most remarkable political documents ever written. At one of the Constitutional Convention's opening sessions in May 1787, the delegates voted to station guards at all doors to keep out journalists and curious citizens and to secure from each delegate a lifetime pledge not to write about or discuss the proceedings.

Bill was convinced that secrecy was an essential element in the Constitutional Convention's success. The details of the Constitutional Convention's deliberations were virtually unknown for several decades. James Madison, the Convention's unofficial secretary and note taker, lived more than fifty years after ratification. As a result, the Constitutional Convention's minutes remained secret until 1840, fifty-three years after the Convention adjourned.

One of the few times in the twentieth century that the full United States Senate has met in secret session, when the matter before it did not involve intelligence gathering or national security, was when Bill was the presiding officer during Bill Clinton's impeachment trial in 1999. Before the trial opened, the Senate voted to invoke a century-old rule that provided that the deliberative portion of an impeachment trial be secret. Any senator who breached the rule would be expelled. While the press and some senators decried the secrecy rule, others credit it with keeping the emotionally charged, bitter proceedings orderly. The senators and the chief justice honored their pledges in 1999, just as the delegates to the Constitutional Convention had done two centuries earlier.

IX.

I INTRODUCED BILL to the subject of media/communications theory casually, almost by accident. It was during a talk about sports. From the first time we chatted after a tennis game until our final sad evening together, sports was part of our conversation. Although Bill rarely attended events in stadiums, and turned down all potentially compromising invitations to visit VIP skyboxes, TV sports consumed many hours of his time.

Marshall McLuhan, the Canadian media theorist, wrote extensively about sports. Since he was an important and original thinker in my field, I had read several of his books; Bill, on the other hand, had not. Still, he knew that McLuhan was the author of the phrase "The medium is the message." In various contexts we had discussed the notion that an individual's response to a message delivered by a particular medium, like TV or a local newspaper, is affected by the medium. Despite the fact that Bill's understanding of McLuhan's most famous phrase was pertinent to our discussions of cameras in courtrooms, and the nature of satire, we only applied it to sports broadcasting—and in that area we made reference to it often.

McLuhan wrote that the future popularity of various kinds of contests would not be determined in stadiums or on schoolboy playing fields but on how well they adapted to TV. One of his favorite topics was how football would replace baseball as America's favorite sport. McLuhan argued that football's dynamism and split-second timing, and the ability of players to switch positions in the midst of play, made it a TV natural, while slow-moving, fixed-position baseball was not.

In 1964, three years before the first Super Bowl, McLuhan wrote at length on the relationship between instant replay and sports viewership, particularly in professional football. He said that without instant replay, football would not be an engaging TV sport. With it, football would quickly become America's most popular sport. Professional football would be tedious without instant replay's clear explanation of complex plays and off-screen infractions. Once millions of TV viewers had football's complicated strategy and tactics explained to them, they would become hooked. Eventually stadium owners as well as homebodies learned McLuhan's lesson. Today, every arena in which an NFL team plays is equipped with a billboard-size TV screen on which stadium fans can also enjoy instant replay. Often when Bill and I watched

TV together, and instant replay explained a strategy we would not have understood without it, one of us would comment, "McLuhan Factor."

X.

Once during a half-time break in a football game, we fantasized about how TV coverage of the Supreme Court with instant replay would affect the proceedings. We visualized the Supreme Court's "John Madden" as a former governor or senator with proven TV skills whose career had included a brief judicial appointment. Instant replay would make Supreme Court viewing hugely popular, and several justices would become folk heroes and superstars. The justices would recognize that the medium is an integral part of the message. They would change the oral argument format so that at the end of each half hour of oral argument, there would be a fifteen-minute break so the Court's John Madden would have time for a chalkboard analysis of the attorneys' arguments and the justices' queries. Our McLuhan fantasy's denouement came when the justices unanimously decided that scheduling oral arguments in prime time was in the people's interest—and the court began convening at 8:00 p.m. instead of 10:00 a.m.

XI.

Early in each court term, Bill would tell me if there were interesting First Amendment cases on the calendar. At his invitation I heard oral arguments in three important First Amendment cases, all of which had a common theme: How far can journalists stray from the straight reportage of facts without hurting innocent persons or destroying their own credibility?

The first case I heard was *Hustler Magazine, Inc. v. Falwell* in 1988. The question at issue can be stated simply: What are the appropriate legal limitations, if any, on sexually crude speech and satiric exaggeration in a civilized society? Can speech be restricted because it causes pain and emotional distress, or because it breaches the bounds of good taste and conventional manners?

The facts in the case were clear-cut: *Hustler,* a financially successful magazine with a large national circulation, was generally considered pornographic, even though it published a few serious articles in every issue. It was best known for its gynecologically explicit pictures of women, its reader letters seeking kinky sex advice and its offbeat humor, scatological as well as sexual. Jerry Falwell was a TV personality and a prominent fundamentalist Protestant minister who headed the "Moral Majority," a lobbying group interested in the promotion of conservative social values. The Supreme Court was asked to rule on whether *Hustler* crossed the line when it published a parody advertisement that said that the Reverend Falwell had drunken sexual liaisons with his mother in an outhouse.

The Supreme Court's unanimous opinion, which Bill authored, concluded that the parody advertisement was so outlandish that it had to be judged as satire, not a misstatement of fact. Bill's opinion discussed the role of political satire in American history. He considered the *Hustler* ad in the same genre as Thomas Nast's hard-hitting cartoons a century earlier. Nast's cartoons were credited with bringing the public's attention to the personal thievery of William Tweed, the political boss whose organization controlled New York City. Press freedom mavens hailed Bill's opinion, which greatly expanded the limits of permitted commentary.

However, in the *Masson v. New Yorker Magazine, Inc.* case in 1991, Bill concurred in a majority opinion that was condemned by most of the leading journalist and press associations. Once again the question before the Court can be stated simply: Do quotation marks mean that a speaker actually said the words attributed to him? Can a journalist alter what was actually said and still attribute it to a speaker with quotation marks?

Jeffrey Masson, a famous Freud scholar and the author of books on psychoanalytic theory, was the subject of a *New Yorker* article based on forty hours of interviews. The reporter admitted that the quotes in the article were inaccurate but claimed they captured the essence of multiple interviews with Masson; quotation marks around appropriate paraphrasing did not constitute substantive misstatements of fact. The Court found that the psychiatrist had been libeled. Quotation marks are supposed to tell readers that the speaker actually said the words between the punctuation marks.

I, as opposed to most of my professional peers, believe the Masson decision helped the media. While it may have made it easier to file lawsuits against journalists who use quotation marks haphazardly, overall it contributed to the credibility of reportage. It said that long-established rules of punctuation and syntax are firm. They cannot be adjusted or adapted to accommodate journalistic contingencies.

I also observed the 1990 proceedings in *Milkovich v. Lorain Journal Co.* Bill again wrote the majority opinion. This time the issue was: if a pundit misstates a known fact, one that can easily be verified, is such an error covered by the *Hustler* decision and other precedents that say that writers of commentary can exaggerate and misstate incidental facts without breaching the libel laws?

Bill and a majority of his colleagues decided that when a sports columnist at a small newspaper in Mentor, Ohio, said that Mike Milkovich, a high school wrestling coach, had lied in court about a riot after a wrestling match, when he had actually told the truth, the sports columnist should have checked his facts before he wrote his column. The facts were easy to locate. Even though press groups were disappointed with the *Milkovich* decision, which to some extent restricted the free expression of opinion, they were not outraged. It is difficult to defend a sports columnist who knowingly prints an untruth under the rubric "Opinion." I thought that it, like the *Masson* decision, tended to increase the credibility of the press. And nothing is more important than credibility, if the press is to function optimally as the people's watchdog.

XII.

ALTHOUGH BILL AND I followed different career paths, those paths crisscrossed often. The editor-publisher and the judge were able to find many areas of common interest—because they tried to.

PART THREE

NINE

PERSONALITY QUIRKS

I.

BILL WAS A frugal man. It was one of his most basic character traits. And it was one that was constantly manifesting itself—in his chambers, in restaurants, in shopping malls, at the public library, at his home in Vermont, on the tennis court. His colleagues, clerks, friends and family all joked about it. They usually substituted the words "tight," "cheap" or "parsimonious" for "frugal." Occasionally he kidded himself about it.

Bill viewed spending money carefully as a high virtue. Resisting the temptation to be wasteful or self-indulgent was a moral act. Extravagance offended him. Frugality was part of a value system that respected discipline and self-control. Spending money frivolously was like wasting time: he did not like to do either.

II.

My first experience with Bill's feelings about waste came on the tennis court a few weeks after we met in 1986. Before beginning our third or fourth singles match, I followed a custom that I had long understood to be country club etiquette: I opened a new can of tennis balls.

Bill then casually asked me how often I played. After he had determined that I rarely played more than once a week, he explained that he did not like people who confused extravagance with courtesy. If the balls we had played with the previous week were not worn out, we should continue using them. After a month or two of weekly play, we should examine the balls we had used. If they showed signs of wear, then one of us should buy a new can of balls—but only if they showed obvious signs of wear. Obvious "signs of wear" to him meant there was almost no discernible fuzz on the balls. At the time I viewed this as quirky: for the cost of a can of tennis balls, why make a fuss? Only later did I realize this was a typical manifestation of his basic character trait.

III.

After a year or so of weekly tennis, we had lunch together for the first time. When it came time to tip the waitress, Bill inquired how I calculated the amount of the gratuity: Did I figure it before, or after, the District of Columbia's 10 percent restaurant tax? Tax collection and invoicing for goods and services were two different functions, he explained. They should be considered separately. No business should get extra compensation for helping the government collect taxes. Restaurant tips should be calculated on the basis of the "invoice for services"—before taxes. At the time I thought he was making a political statement about Washington's sock-it-to-the-commuter restaurant tax. Only later did I learn that politics was the lesser part of the statement.

We never patronized well-known or pricey, gourmet restaurants. We enjoyed neighborhood eateries with simple menus, paper napkins, no flowers on the tables, butter in foil wrappers and cream for coffee in small plastic cups. When Bill, Betty Nan and I went out for dinner on a Saturday night, as we did several times a month for more than a dozen years, Arlington and the nearby suburbs of Falls Church and McLean had more than enough small restaurants to provide a little variety. Although my home is less than one mile from the District of Columbia and Bill's was only a little farther, we almost never shared a Saturday night dinner at a Washington restaurant. Our avoidance of tony, well-reviewed D.C. restaurants was consistent with our desire to enjoy Saturday evenings together, uninterrupted and unobserved. But it was also consistent with Bill's near-obsessive sense of frugality. (Among other things, the tax on restaurant meals in Washington was two and a half times the tax in Arlington.)

If the server at an Arlington restaurant finished reciting the evening's "specials" but failed to tell the price of each item, Bill would invariably inquire about the prices, although he rarely ordered one of the specials. No matter how often we visited a restaurant, the routine never changed. In his own subtle way he was making a statement. He considered price an essential part of a merchandise offering, even the verbal presentation of a chef's specials. His preferred before-dinner drink was light beer. Since most restaurants charge a premium for imported beers, when he inquired about what brands the restaurant served, he would almost always begin, "What are your *domestic* light beers?"

A Supreme Court justice's job is highly visible, but its sartorial demands are minimal. On the bench justices wear robes that completely cover whatever they are wearing underneath. When not hearing oral arguments, most of their time is spent reading and writing in their chambers, where casual clothes are often appropriate. Since justices park in the basement of the Supreme Court Building, during many working days they have no need to be in "proper business attire."

One afternoon while visiting Bill at his vacation home in Vermont, we stopped by Willey's Store in Greensboro for ice cream. I selected three Häagen-Dazs bars from the freezer. He immediately quizzed me: "Could you explain to me what's better about premium-priced ice cream?" "It tastes better," I answered. I had bested him. That was a value judgment he could not challenge. Still, I doubt he found it convincing.

At the end of a movie date we always settled accounts down to the last nickel. It did not occur to him that sometimes it might be easier to round accounts to the nearest half dollar. Since I was always the "treasurer," he would inquire about whether I had included parking fees, coat check tips and even the one-dollar premium that is charged by most cinemas if movie tickets are reserved in advance by phone.

IV.

BILL'S SENSE OF frugality and self-discipline extended beyond his own pocketbook. He showed similar concern for that portion of the public treasury of which he was the steward. His predecessor, chief justice Warren Burger, had always employed four law clerks and three secretaries. Fourteen years as an associate justice convinced Bill that three law clerks and two secretaries could take care of all of his needs, despite the fact that, at the time of his elevation to chief justice, he was in the midst of writing his first history book.

When his longtime colleague and friend Justice Harry Blackmun, after several years of retirement, requested extra secretarial help to assist him in organizing his papers for presentation to the Library of Congress, Bill turned him down. He knew he would incur his old friend's wrath, but since all retired justices have the services of one secretary, he considered it wasteful for Justice Blackmun to have more, even though a single secretarial salary would have been lost in the Supreme Court's budget.

V.

BILL USED ARLINGTON'S public library extensively. He personally picked up and returned books. Not surprisingly, he was always prompt. At the dedication of its new Central Library facility in 1992, he was the main speaker, a grateful and satisfied user of its services.

After he became a senior citizen, the library notified him that his fines for "late" books would be reduced in the future. He thought this reduction reflected distorted priorities and said he was going to write the head librarian about it (I do not know if he actually did). Seniors generally had more time to read than working people, he reasoned. Therefore, they should pay the same fine, or a greater one, than working people, who were more legitimately pressed for time—and therefore, usually, had more legitimate reasons to return their books late. (The Arlington Public Library gave up this niggling bit of reverse age discrimination more than ten years ago.)

He asked me if I agreed. I responded that I really did not care. The amount of the levy was insignificant. At our age, and in our circumstances, we should not be concerned with late fees if our schedules made it difficult to return library books on time, I further explained. But late fees always concerned Bill. If we rented an occasional movie, we shared the cost . . . but he would almost reflexively ask when I picked the film up at the video store. He wanted to be sure I had not incurred any late charges before we actually viewed it.

VI.

AT THE RECEPTION following Bill's funeral, I was expressing my sympathies to his son-in-law Tim Spears when Tim interrupted, "You'd be interested to know that the family talked about you as we were driving to the cathedral this afternoon," he said.

I was surprised—and curious.

"With last-minute hairdo tinkering and eulogy editing," he continued, "we did not have time to sit down for lunch. En route, we snacked on 'Obe-bars' that we found in the refrigerator."

One of the favors at my eightieth birthday party, a year before Bill's death, were specially wrapped chocolate bars with my picture and the words "Obe's 80th": Obe-bars. Although Bill was still in Vermont on the day of my party, I was aware of his fondness for sweets, so I delivered half a dozen "Obe-bars" to his house after his return. Like everything else in his life, he carefully rationed his candy stock. When illness struck six weeks later, he had eaten just two of his chocolate bars. The uneaten bars were still in the refrigerator on the morning of his funeral.

Betty Nan often baked homemade cakes and cookies for Bill. It was one of the few gifts he genuinely appreciated. Four weeks after she delivered them, it was not unusual for him to tell her how much he had enjoyed one of her cookies the previous evening.

VII.

I ENJOY AND treasure my library. When I work, read or snooze surrounded by familiar books, I feel I am in the presence of old friends who have guided me through good times and bad. Betty Nan calls it my "security blanket"—and there is more than an element of truth in that.

Bill, on the other hand, had virtually no library. While he read voraciously, he never saved books. He believed personal libraries were wasteful indulgences. Once he had read a volume, he was done with it. He commented often about my deep affection for my library, usually derisively. In one of his books he inscribed: "For Obe, who not only collects books, but reads them, too."

In addition to the Arlington Public Library, which was near his home, most of Bill's reading requirements were fulfilled by the Supreme Court's own vast library. Its professional staff's main function is to service the intellectual and professional needs of the nine justices. New-release purchases and interlibrary loans are quickly arranged for them. The Supreme Court library also arranges for tutorials, films and demonstrations about a case before the Court if one or several justices believe they are inadequately informed. He had a special fondness for the library staff—and they for him.

My small collection of rare books and first editions never piqued Bill's interest, with one exception. Over the years we both found enjoyment in my copy of Samuel Johnson's *Dictionary of the English Language* (not a first edition). Originally published in 1755, it was written and compiled by a remarkable genius whose only help was approximately six (the number varied) amanuenses, or clerks. Dr. Johnson defined forty-two thousand words by examples of how they had been used by great writers from antiquity to his contemporaries. His dictionary can be viewed as a compendium of systematically organized quotations. It includes more than one hundred thousand examples of English usage. He used different quotations to demonstrate special nuances or subtleties of meaning. It took nine quotations from Shakespeare, Bacon, Dryden and Spenser to fully define a commonly used word like "brave," and it took twenty citations to define "passion," many from obscure Greek and Latin classics. Dr. Johnson's extraordinary, almost limitless memory was the source of most of the quotations. The main job of the amanuenses was to confirm the accuracy of his recollections.

For two men who enjoyed using quotations in routine conversations to illustrate ideas and make points in arguments, Dr. Johnson's intellectual achievement was fascinating, even awe-inspiring. While having a drink in my library before dinner, we would often look up familiar words to see what quotations Dr. Johnson had used to define them. While Dr. Johnson's quotations were almost never familiar to us, it was always an enjoyable exercise. The pleasures a man gets from a library in his home are almost always lonely, almost impossible to share. But my copy of Dr. Johnson's dictionary was an exception. Over the years Bill and I found several hours of happiness checking out the work product of the quotation game's greatest master.

VIII.

I HAVE NEVER viewed any car I owned as anything more than transportation, and I have never longed to own anything expensive or fancy. It was another subject on which Bill and I agreed. While he was driven to and from work by a Supreme Court police officer in a government-issue Lincoln Town Car, the automobile he used on weekends and at his vacation home in Vermont was a bottom-of-the-line Subaru.

But in 2003 I succumbed, buying my first high-end foreign car. I justified the purchase of a BMW 325xi to myself—and my friend Bill—by explaining that it contained more safety features than any other compact car. At my age, I explained, eight air bags, four-wheel drive, a unique braking system and other high-tech safety gimmicks made my purchase an investment in accident prevention, not ostentation. When I showed my new toy to Bill a few weeks later, his only comment was: "Still looks like a Chevy to me."

IX.

Bill was probably addicted to cigarettes. They were very important to him. During the two decades of our friendship, I do not recall any time when he was trying to break, or even curtail, his tobacco dependence. While he was not furtive or secretive about his habit, he was not in-your-face about it, either. When the three of us had dinner together at our home or at a restaurant, he always had a cigarette after the meal. After we attended a movie, he occasionally had a smoke with his light beer before dinner.

But if Bill was at a dinner party with several couples around the table, he did not light up until someone else did. If no one else had an after-dinner cigarette, he did not have one, either. However, if he did not have a smoke at the table, or soon afterward, he usually left for home shortly after the meal. He profusely apologized to his hostess. He explained that he was "very tired" and had a lot of reading to do for the next day's conference or oral arguments, or whatever. "Very tired" was code. He never hinted that he would have enjoyed continuing the after-dinner conversation, if he could have smoked a cigarette without appearing to be impolite or breaching an evolving community standard. This carried over to restaurants. In the smoking section, we relaxed. If we were seated in a nonsmoking area, the end of the evening was rushed.

I often speculated as to why a man who was smart, disciplined, intellectually focused and strong-willed could not break the tobacco habit. Whenever I brought up the subject, he explained that he knew he could quit. As a matter of fact, he said he had gone cold turkey for extended periods several times in his life. But he greatly enjoyed cigarettes. And he knowingly accepted the trade-offs. Several times he explained his addiction in an idiom he particularly liked: "Let's just say I am an informed bettor."

X.

BILL LOVED TRIVIA. His ability to quote an obscure—and relevant—fact in almost any social situation carried over to cigarette smoking. On several occasions, Bill pointed out to me that Frank Sinatra smoked two packs of cigarettes a day during most of his adult life. He achieved superstardom during World War II when we were soldiers—and, notwithstanding his tobacco habit, he was still performing in sold-out concert halls when we were senior citizens. Sinatra's voice had changed with age, but it still had timbre and vitality when he was in his mid-seventies.

Once, while telling me about an opera he had attended, Bill shared with me another bit of cigarette trivia: Enrico Caruso was a chain-smoker. The first male vocalist to earn one million dollars from his recordings, and the Metropolitan Opera's star tenor in the first two decades of the twentieth century, was so addicted to cigarettes that he sometimes smoked onstage during performances—with the Met's tacit approval.

After all, smoking was the "in" thing for Bill's generation. In the 1930s and 1940s, world leaders, war heroes and movie stars openly enjoyed their tobacco habit. All World War II soldiers (like Bill) received a weekly cigarette ration of more than a carton (two hundred cigarettes). Among his contemporaries, there were lots of quiet "closet smokers"—and he knew it.

XI.

FOR EIGHT SEMESTERS in the early 1990s, I was an adjunct professor at the University of Maryland's College of Journalism. At the end of each semester, I asked my students to write an essay on the conflict between the First Amendment's guarantee of free speech and the federal government's banning of tobacco advertising from radio and TV. Each semester, after I had marked the papers, I would discuss them with Bill. He looked forward to these semiannual discussions: all of the issues involved were close to his heart.

The specific question on which my students were asked to write was: Is it threatening to liberty, and particularly free speech, when a government prohibits advertising (commercial speech) for a product that is lawfully manufactured, lawfully marketed and lawfully distributed in all fifty states, like cigarettes? I usually explained beforehand that, if the health hazard was clear and unambiguous, then Congress had a duty to make the manufacture and sale of cigarettes unlawful. But it never had.

After I had finished grading their essays, I told my students my position. I feared that other lawful activities—even certain political ones—could be restricted by an aggressive government under the broad rubric of health and welfare. I believed the precedent created a serious threat to all civil liberties.

The exams were scored on the basis of good writing, orderly reasoning and the student's understanding of the underlying issues. Students did not have to agree with me; only half did. Year after year, University of Maryland journalism majors split almost evenly on the question of whether public health concerns, like restricting the promotion of tobacco products, trumped the constitutional guarantee of free speech.

The fact that aspiring journalists consistently split evenly on freedom of speech guarantees versus community health protections perplexed both Bill and me. Analyses by sex, race and overall grade scores did not reveal any group patterns. My intuition is that the split was between students who aspired to become professional journalists and those who had little interest in pursuing media careers.

To my knowledge, none of Bill's friends, colleagues or close family tried hard to help him break his smoking habit. They, like me, were probably convinced that if he really wanted to free himself from his addiction, he would have done so long ago. The one exception was his youngest child, Nancy Spears. He said she was outspoken in her disapproval of his smoking. She thought he set a bad example for her children. Consequently, he rarely smoked in her home. Since she also did not think she could teach an old dog new tricks, she requested that in mild weather he smoke on the stoop, away from her daughters.

XII.

THYROID CANCER KILLED Bill a few weeks before his eighty-first birthday. I, like his other friends, colleagues, family and the general public, wondered to what extent his cancer, which started in a gland located in the throat, could be attributed to his cigarette habit. There is, of course, no clear answer.

The almost unanimous view of the distinguished physicians who gave opinions in the press—but never examined Bill or had access to his medical charts—was that smoking was not the most important factor in the development of his condition.

The *New York Times* and the *Washington Post*, as well as respected medical Internet sites, conjectured on the real nature of Bill's illness. And they all came to the same unhappy conclusion: he had anaplastic cancer of the thyroid gland.

The anaplastic type is the most virulent and deadly form of thyroid cancer. It affects between 250 and 350 people in the United States each year. (Of fourteen thousand diagnosed cases of thyroid cancer in 2004, slightly more than 2 percent were anaplastic.) It often develops in people who have been exposed to radiation in early childhood. The cure rate is "very low." And "very low" is a medical euphemism for "virtually nil."

While there was no concrete evidence about Bill's exposure to radiation in his youth, he harbored suspicions that he had been exposed. If so, it could have played a more important role than cigarettes in the development of his disease. Radiation treatment for many childhood medical problems—many located in or near the throat, including enlarged tonsils, adenoids and thymus—was a well-respected, popular medical procedure in the 1920s. There is extensive literature from that period covering the disagreement between distinguished physicians on the question of surgery versus radiation for enlarged tonsils and adenoids. Between 1939 and 1967, more than four thousand patients, mostly children, received X-ray treatment for nonmalignant enlargement of the tonsils and adenoids in Michael Reese Hospital, one of the Chicago-Milwaukee area's largest and most respected medical institutions.

XIII.

Frugality and punctuality are related traits, but only friends and family were exposed to Bill's penny-pinching. His near obsession about punctuality affected most of his relationships—with colleagues, subordinates, friends. It was hard to ignore, and it was often annoying. Bill was always on time. And he expected everybody with whom he had any kind of dealings to do likewise. No exceptions. If I agreed to pick him up at 4:10 p.m. to go to a movie, and I arrived at 4:12 p.m., he would be pacing up and down the sidewalk or sitting on the stoop and scowling. On all but the coldest days of winter, if I was a few minutes late, he gave me his unspoken punctuality message. If I arrived at 4:05 p.m., I parked in front of his townhouse. Then at 4:10 p.m. (exactly!) he would come bounding down the steps. If we planned to watch a football game (usually at my house because I had a larger TV screen) at 1:00 p.m., he always rang the doorbell between 12:58 p.m. and 1:00 p.m. If he arrived in my neighborhood a few minutes early, he parked unobtrusively on a nearby street. Then he rang the doorbell at what he perceived as the proper time.

When Bill and I went out to lunch together, I always arrived at his chambers a few minutes early. At the appointed hour (exactly!) he arrived at the chief justice's waiting room, already dressed in his overcoat, scarf and cap if it was winter. He was ready to leave. Sometimes his schedule allowed us to spend an hour at lunch, and sometimes an hour and a half. He always told me in advance the amount of time he could spare. Our lunches together were relaxed and fun, but there was always a clock ticking in the background.

The chief justice has only one important job outside the federal judiciary: by statute, he serves as a member of the Smithsonian Institution's board of regents and, by long-established custom, the regents always choose the chief justice as chancellor. It was an assignment Bill enjoyed. He rarely missed a board of regents meeting and fastidiously read the regents information packets. Board of regents meetings were conducted by the clock, just like meetings of the Judicial Conference of the United States, over which he also presided.

Everybody who worked in Bill's marble palace understood that punctuality was a nonnegotiable concept. It extended beyond punching in each morning at the appointed hour. It included many winter days when the region's schools were closed and most other federal bureaucracies were operating on a "liberal leave" policy. A few inches of slush or snow rarely excused Supreme Court employees from arriving at work on time.

Although Bill delegated authority easily and well, he personally decided when the Supreme Court would close down because of extreme weather conditions. On mornings following weather forecasts of snow the preceding day, his administrative assistant telephoned him promptly at 6:00 a.m. to report what she had learned about weather conditions from the Internet and local TV stations. On the basis of his assistant's reportage, he alone determined if the Supreme Court would be open for business. What policy other branches of the vast federal bureaucracy were following on that day did not influence his decision. Lawyers who were scheduled to argue cases before the Supreme Court usually arrived in Washington two days or more in advance. They knew that a continuance plea based on airport delays in Chicago or Atlanta would be looked on with disfavor.

All eight associate justices drove their own cars to work each day. They understood that they were expected to be in their places when oral arguments began. Bill was firm in his belief that "minor climatic events" like snowstorms should not—*would* not—interfere with the timely operations of the Supreme Court of the United States. Occasionally, on snow days, associate justices and certain essential functionaries were driven to the Court in police cars.

XIV.

Historians are in almost universal agreement that one of the best sources—often *the* best source—of information about historic events or personalities are private letters, hastily scribbled memos and longhand marginal notes. All were written with the "presumption of transience," a phrase that is part of the lexicon of historians and archivists. It describes writings that were created with the assumption that they would be destroyed shortly after they were read.

Postcard writers make this assumption almost reflexively. Bill and I exchanged postcards whenever either of us was away from Arlington for more than a week. Bill's postcards reveal a great deal about him and our relationship. What he wrote on postcards, as well as the fact that he felt compelled to write them, tells much about his capacity for friendship and what he thought was important.

Even though postcards are "unsealed" and the message is subject to scrutiny by postal employees, in a strange way they are more personal than most other types of mail. I have few friends and family members who regularly send me postcards when they are away from home. I have none who send them faithfully whenever they go on a trip of a week or more. Postcards are special. They reflect caring. They indicate a desire to share. They are also old-fashioned, like most postcard writers. They are usually written in haste. Small errors in syntax and spelling are expected and forgiven.

The younger generation perceives postcard exchanges between good friends as a quaint anachronism. They are not totally wrong. As a matter of fact, their judgment is similar to that of the commercial enterprises that operate kiosks in hotel lobbies. Two decades ago, the postcard racks in hotel gift shops were loaded with several dozen choice views. Today many hotel gift shops do not sell postcards. Those that do offer a limited choice of views.

For Bill, the exchanging of postcards was part of friendship. It was neat, uniquely personal and uncomplicated. Cards from faraway places often contained tidbits of knowledge he could store away for future use. The picture on a postcard was important to him. When I returned from a trip, he would invariably ask questions about the cathedral, museum or historical site on my card's front side. He expected me to have similar questions about the pictures on his postcards. While his Tucson cards were usually freebies from the Arizona Inn where he stayed, he never sent "hotel cards" from Europe, only those he had carefully selected.

Bill's postcards almost always had two messages: a comment on the historic or scenic locale he was visiting and a report on whether he was having a good time, particularly if his back was bothering him. He did not think postcard writers had to express themselves in complete sentences.

Bill's last postcard to me was written in July 2004 from Cambridge, England. It said:

> This is a traditional view of Cambridge—the Cam River with someone punting on it—I have had a very good time here.

The nonsentence in Bill's final postcard tells a lot about the bond between us. He knew that I knew that punts are identified with Cambridge, just like gondolas are identified with Venice.

XV.

WHEN ONE OF my daughters read an early draft of this book, she urged me to retitle this chapter "Character Traits." While the chapter gives unique—and important—insights into the protagonist's personality,

Whenever the Obermayers or the chief justice was away from Arlington for more than a week, the homebody received a postcard.

habits and psyche, she viewed the word "quirks" as diminishing and demeaning. But, after reflection, I decided to stick with the original title.

"Frugal," "addicted" and "punctual" are not among the traits authors typically consider when trying to help readers understand a contemporary leader, particularly one the writer holds in high esteem. But Bill Rehnquist was not typical. He was unusual, different. He is best understood by examining some of the less-traveled byways of human experience. "Quirks" by definition are atypical. And so was Bill.

TEN

BETTING

I.

Bill Rehnquist loved to bet. He would bet on almost anything: how much snow would fall in the Supreme Court's courtyard on a particular morning, which football team would next sack the quarterback, the point spread between the top contestants in a California primary election. Friends, law clerks, colleagues—almost anyone he saw regularly—had wagered with him on something. It was a personality quirk that was also known to many people who knew him only fleetingly, from elevator operators in the Supreme Court Building to Charlie Rose after a PBS interview about one of his books.

Still, he did not consider himself a gambler: he was a bettor, nothing more. He said this to me categorically, repeatedly. The distinction between the two was clear in his view: gamblers put meaningful amounts of money at risk; bettors, on the other hand, found pleasure in wagering small, insignificant amounts. He never bet more than three dollars with me on anything, and I am not aware of his betting more than five dollars with anybody else. For Bill the joy, of course, was in winning. He hated to lose at anything: tennis or cards or one-dollar bets.

Betty Nan's and my election bet with Bill played a disproportion-ately important part in our relationship during the autumn of 2000. More typically, we prepared betting cards in October and conducted brief postmortems in November. Additionally, we regularly bet on county and state races as well as referendum issues. (In Arlington, Vir-ginia, our home, the citizens vote on referendums often, occasionally several times in a year.)

Bill had both the intuition and inclination to be a big-time gambler. But he also had the willpower and self-discipline to limit his obsession into a benign game. He was a compulsive bettor. Hardly a week passed when he did not bet with somebody about something. Still, it never got out of control, which tells a great deal about his character and per-sonality. He was probably the most disciplined person I have ever known. For example, he enjoyed a beer with meals and while watch-ing sports on TV. While I do not recall his ever ordering a restaurant meal without a beer, I also do not recall him ever ordering more than one. Even during the course of three or four hours of Sunday after-noon football; he limited himself to a single bottle.

While Bill regularly bet with Betty Nan and me on local, state and national elections, he and I also bet on sporting events like baseball and football games, particularly while watching them on TV. Before a game's start, we always bet on the final outcome. But that was rarely enough betting excitement for Bill. Sometimes in the second quarter of a football game, he would say, "The game's getting dull. You want to bet a dollar on which team will score next or which team will be penalized next?" Shortly after that bet was completed, he would be eager for more. With baseball, he might suggest betting one dollar on the next team to get an extra-base hit, or whether the batting star would get a hit the next time he was at the plate. By the end of a game, we had usually made at least three or four one-dollar side bets.

II.

WAGERING MERITED MENTION by two of the eulogists at Bill's funeral. His Stanford Law School classmate, lifelong friend and Supreme Court colleague Justice Sandra Day O'Connor concluded her poignant remembrance with a reference to his passion for betting: "The Chief was a betting man," Justice O'Connor said. "If you valued your money, you would be careful about betting with the Chief. He usually won. I think the Chief bet he could live out another term despite his illness. He lost that bet, as did all of us."

In her funeral talk, Bill's daughter Nancy Spears combined an anecdote about her father's ability to recall historic trivia with his love of betting. When Spears was in high school, she recalled, one evening he called from his bedroom to hers and offered to bet her five dollars she could not name the date of Queen Elizabeth I's death. When she correctly replied that the queen had died in 1603, she heard "muffled curses" coming from his bedroom. After her victory, she explained, she had to face a summerlong effort by her father to win back his money. She did not disclose whether he prevailed.

It is significant that, in their brief funeral eulogies, Bill's daughter and his closest friend-colleague—independent of each other—saw fit to mention his love of betting. It was a personality quirk that they wanted to memorialize.

III.

THE ENTIRE NOVEMBER 2005 issue of the *Harvard Law Review* was dedicated to Bill's memory. While the publication's tone was somber and erudite, most of the authors knew Bill personally and included in their articles a bit of nostalgia or personal reminiscence. The lead piece was written by his successor, Chief Justice John G. Roberts Jr. (Bill's law clerk in 1980–81). Roberts, like those who delivered funeral eulogies, found it appropriate—maybe necessary—to also include a reference to Bill's fondness of betting. "He enjoyed small wagers on anything," his successor wrote, "athletic contests, presidential elections, and the day of the first snowfall."

The *Legal Times,* a weekly periodical devoted to news about the legal profession, published remembrances by nine former law clerks shortly after Bill's death. Two of them thought his love of betting worthy of commentary: R. Ted Cruz, solicitor general of Texas (Bill's law clerk in 1996–97), said, "He [Rehnquist] would wager on anything— football, baseball, election results—almost always for a single dollar."

David Leitch, vice president and general counsel of the Ford Motor Company (Bill's law clerk in 1986–87), said, "A particular love of the Chief's was wagering—not for high stakes, by any means, but just for the sport of it. A memorable wager during my clerkship took place in January 1987, as weather forecasters called for a massive snowstorm to hit Washington, D.C. These predictions permitted the Chief to combine his love of wagers with his keen interest in weather [he'd served as a meteorologist in World War II]. He organized two betting pools—one in his Chambers and one among the members of the Court—on the amount of snow that would fall on the Supreme Court plaza by 10 a.m. the next day. The next day, we [his clerks] trudged out to the plaza, with rulers in hand to measure the snow. . . . My co-clerk, Bill Lindsay, won the Chambers pool, and Justice Powell won the Conference pool." (The words "Chambers" and "Conference" are Supreme Court code words. Bill's law clerks and members of his personal staff participated in the "Chambers" betting pool. Only the nine justices participated in the "Conference" betting pool.)

Richard W. Garnett, an associate professor of law at the University of Notre Dame Law School (Bill's law clerk in 1996–97), told Slate, the online current events magazine, the following anecdote about the importance Bill attached to his small-stakes betting. A few days after the 1996 election, while the Court was in the midst of hearing oral arguments, Bill sent a note from the bench to his clerks. A bailiff handed the note to Garnett, who assumed that his boss was requesting a law book or some other document pertinent to the case that was being argued. But when he opened the note, he learned differently. Bill requested that a clerk return to the chief justice's chambers and check by telephone who had won a House race on which he had an outstanding bet.

IV.

IN THE AUTUMN of 2004, a year before Bill's death, his fascination with betting was discussed in a two-thousand-word article in *PS: Political Science & Politics,* a publication of the American Political Science Association, the largest professional organization in the field. The article, written by three political science professors at The George Washington University in Washington, D.C., viewed his "habit" from an entirely different perspective than mine. The professors found significance in the details of a game in which almost all adult Americans have participated: a small-stakes office betting pool.

The article is based on a longhand betting pool chart prepared by Bill for six of his fellow justices who bet one dollar per state on the presidential election of 1992. It was discovered in the personal papers of Justice Harry A. Blackmun that were donated to the Library of Congress following his death in 1999.

The article, which was "peer reviewed" and approved by an editorial board of prominent political scientists, states in its first paragraph:

> Until now no hard evidence has existed of just how fixated the Court is on presidential elections . . . Fortunately, now we have proof positive.

The notion that Supreme Court justices could be compromised or influenced in any way whatsoever by a one-dollar bet in an office pool is so preposterous that I am reticent to give it permanent status in this book. Still, it was published in *PS: Political Science & Politics,* which the American Political Science Association describes as "the journal of record for the profession." I have given some thought to the notion that the entire piece, including its twenty-five source notes, is a spoof, but an inquiry to the editor's office came back with an unequivocal statement that *PS: Political Science & Politics* never publishes satire.

V.

I NEVER DOUBTED Bill's categorical statements that he was not a gambler. Self-control, discipline and restraint were fundamental traits and essential parts of his character.

Still, I was happy when I discovered a document that proved Bill did not enjoy putting meaningful amounts of money at risk, even in benign ways that are not generally considered gambling. The inventory of his estate, as filed by his executors with the Clerk of the Circuit Court of Arlington County, Virginia, indicates that in addition to his modest homes in Virginia and Vermont, household goods and a stamp collection, his entire estate consisted of $708,689 in "plain vanilla" savings accounts at banks with branches a few hundred yards from his home.

Many—probably most—Americans with six-figure salaries, guaranteed six-figure lifetime pensions, paid-off house mortgages and adult children who are gainfully employed tend to invest in stocks, bonds or mutual funds. In varying ways and in varying amounts, people in Bill's circumstances usually "gamble" on Wall Street.

People who can afford to invest in marketable securities and do not are usually reticent because they do not understand the nomenclature of business, cannot read financial statements or believe stock and bond exchanges operate like casinos. But none of these reasons explains Bill. He had studied graduate-level economics at both Stanford and Harvard. As a practicing attorney, he had represented both large and small businesses, and as a Supreme Court justice he had opined on hundreds of cases involving complex questions of commerce, finance and contract.

I feel certain that Bill's decision to keep all his money in deposit accounts at local banks was based on a desire not to do anything that might harm the institution he served and loved. He relished being the center of controversy, so long as critics could not question his motives or his personal integrity. Bill's last will and testament also confirms the fact that, while he was a "betting man" (Justice O'Connor's term), he definitely was not a gambler.

VI.

BETTY NAN, BILL and I bet on at least twenty elections between Nan Rehnquist's death in 1991 and Bill's in 2005. The only precondition for our betting on an election was full coverage in the *Washington Post*. While we had access to several other newspapers and periodicals, and had friends who were supposed to be especially knowledgeable, our one common information source was the local daily newspaper. While the *Washington Post*'s coverage was the standard by which we determined if there was enough campaign news available so the bettors could make informed wagers, Bill and I both had access to privately circulated political analysis.

VII.

MOST REGULAR BETTORS on horses or stocks or elections rely on some special intelligence or insider tip sheets to give them an edge. Bill and I were not exceptions. Each of us had his own unique source of worldly-wise political intelligence.

I relied heavily on Rudy Boschwitz's street-smart weekly handicap report. A Republican senator from Minnesota from 1979 to 1991, Rudy was a top GOP national fund-raiser, both before and after his Senate tenure, a position that afforded him access to several proprietary polls, forecasts by party strategists, "opposition research," political consultant newsletters and a fat Rolodex. Distribution of his "poop sheet" was an integral part of Rudy's solicitation technique.

Bill had his own special sub-rosa political intelligence organization: his former law clerks. They constituted an informal network of wily, savvy political observers. He could, and did, call on them for off-the-record advice on local political trends and likely election outcomes. Bill felt that his former law clerks, as a group, understood the political scene in their home states as well as or better than most pundits and pollsters.

Typical was Tom McGough (Bill's law clerk in 1979–80), a senior partner in ReedSmith, a large international law firm headquartered in Pittsburgh. Although McGough usually attended clerk reunions and he and Bill had met informally several times over the years, they did not keep in touch with any regularity. Then, without advance notice, in the first week of November 1992 McGough received a phone call from the chambers of the chief justice. Bill had called his former clerk to ask how he, as a local political activist, thought Pennsylvania would go in the following week's presidential election. He needed to know, Bill explained, because he was working on an election bet.

VIII.

IN 2000, THE Republican presidential primary election season lasted only five weeks. (The first primary, in New Hampshire, was held on February 2. California's primary, which solidified George W. Bush's victory, was held on March 7.) Still, in that short period we were able to schedule three primary election bets.

Supreme Court of the United States

Memorandum

N.H. PRIMARY BET

CHAMBERS OF
THE CHIEF JUSTICE

DEM: GORE 54%
BRADLEY 45%

REP: MCCAIN 40%
BUSH 36%

The chief justice's bet on the New Hampshire primary was far off the mark, by more than twenty percent.

In New Hampshire's Republican primary, Senator John McCain, a decorated Vietnam War hero, faced Texas governor George W. Bush, an Andover-Yale-Harvard scion who before he entered politics headed the Texas Rangers, one of the state's two Major League Baseball clubs. In the Democratic primary, Al Gore, the incumbent vice president, faced Senator Bill Bradley, a former Rhodes scholar at Oxford and a basketball star with the New York Knicks. Bush and Gore represented the incumbent leadership of their respective parties.

When the results were in from the New Hampshire primary, our betting threesome did not look like prescient political observers or even smart bettors. We selected the incumbent vice president, Al Gore, who won the Democratic primary easily. But in the hotly contested GOP race between Bush and McCain, we were not even close. All three of us totally underestimated McCain's strength. Betty Nan gave McCain 42 percent of the GOP vote, while Bill and I gave him 40 and 38 percent, respectively. He actually received 49 percent.

IX.

TEN DAYS LATER, we determined how we would bet on Virginia's primary, which was scheduled to take place at the end of February. Since it was already clear that Al Gore had locked up his party's nomination, we decided not to bet on Virginia's Democratic primary. While the network polls all showed Bush beating McCain by a substantial margin, loyal supporters of both candidates were expected to vote. It was believed that the spread would influence primaries in other states, particularly California, where the race was still too close to call.

In our home state's Republican primary, all of our picks were close to the actual vote. Our betting in Virginia's Republican primary on February 28, 2000 was:

Candidate	Betty Nan	Bill	Obe	*Actual Final Tally*
BUSH	**53%**	52%	51%	**53%**
McCAIN	40%	43%	**44%**	**44%**

If there had been a payoff, Bill would have continued his losing record, and Betty Nan and I would have shared his money. But our wagers were never settled. The press of official business forced Bill to cancel our Virginia primary bets. He telephoned Betty Nan to apologize, and explained the circumstances that led to our first election bet without a payoff. Bill forgot to give his selections to his secretary, Janet Tramonte, before he left for a meeting. When he returned late Monday afternoon, his office staff, had gone home. Since he had no reason to learn how to use office machines, he did not know how to send his picks by fax. Therefore, he felt compelled to cancel.

The next day he wrote us a formal letter of explanation that included the following:

. . . as I explained to Betty Nan on the telephone, these guesses were put on paper shortly after 5 p.m. on Monday, and were that Bush would receive 52% of the vote and McCain 43%. The actual vote was Bush 53% and McCain 44%. This means that Obe hit McCain's percentage right on the nose, and Betty Nan hit Bush's percentage right on the nose.

I, therefore, owe each of you one dollar. I may be pardoned for expressing the view that although I lost out to you on the percentages, I got the percentage separating the two candidates exactly right, whereas neither of you did. Unfortunately, we didn't bet on that percentage.

X.

POLLING DATA INDICATED the GOP primary in California would be close, and the winner would likely be his party's nominee. We made three bets of one dollar each on the California GOP vote: on the percentage of the total vote George W. Bush and John McCain would each receive, and on the spread between them.

Our choices in the California Republican primary on March 7, 2000 were:

Candidate	Betty Nan	Bill	Obe	Actual Final Tally
BUSH	52%	57%	55%	61%
McCAIN	48%	38%	40%	35%
SPREAD	4%	19%	15%	26%

Bill won in all categories. We attributed this to the fact that he alone could claim California expertise. He had spent six formative years in Palo Alto as a student at Stanford and Stanford Law School, and the Rehnquist

Supreme Court of the United States
Washington, D. C. 20543

CHAMBERS OF
THE CHIEF JUSTICE

March 1, 2000

Herman J. Obermayer
Betty Nan L. Obermayer
4114 North Ridgeview Road
Arlington, VA 22207

Dear Obe and Betty Nan:

I have not yet forwarded to you my guesses in the Virginia Primary yesterday; as I explained to Betty Nan on the telephone, these guesses were put on paper shortly after 5 p.m. on Monday, and were that Bush would receive 52% of the vote and McCain 43%. The actual was Bush 53% and McCain 44%. This means that Obe hit McCain's percentage right on the nose, and Betty Nan hit Bush's percentage right on the nose.

I therefore owe each one of you one dollar. I may be pardoned for expressing the view that although I lost out to you on the percentages, I got the percentage separating the two candidates exactly right, whereas neither of you did. Unfortunately, we didn't bet on that percentage.

Sincerely,

Bill

3/5/00

Bill –
One time is luck. Two a tree in a dow may justify a claim to talent or prescience.
Let's add a new betting category, "spread," to both CA (beauty contest) and NY next Tuesday.

Obe

The above letter tells how serious the chief justice was about his election wagering.

family kept in close touch with several of Nan's siblings who continued to live in the San Diego area, where they had been brought up.

XI.

OUR BETS IN the presidential election of 2000, and the fact that they were never paid off, has been fully covered in Chapter Six. Two years later Bill suggested that we develop a "betting card" for the upcoming 2002 congressional elections. I asked if he was sure that he wanted to bet on elections again in light of his experience in 2000. He was adamant. He had no doubts. He wanted to bet. The 2000 election was an anomaly, he explained. It would probably never repeat itself. Life is too short, we agreed, to abandon a fun custom because of a once-in-a-lifetime event.

Still, it was hard to develop a good betting card for the 2002 gubernatorial and congressional elections. To us, most of the races looked dull. After the election of 2000, all election contests were, to some degree, anticlimactic. Still, we bet on more than a dozen individual races. And Betty Nan was as usual the big winner. She won nine dollars: four-fifty from each of the male bettors.

The last time we went to the movies together, October 16, 2004— three days before Bill entered Bethesda Naval Hospital for his thyroid surgery—we devoted a considerable amount of time to compiling a betting card for the 2004 presidential race as well as the make-up of Congress and several senatorial contests we believed would be close. Until the weekend before the election, I thought he would complete his betting card in the hospital. A few days after he entered the hospital, Janet Tramonte had telephoned requesting a duplicate of our betting card. He had misplaced his. She knew it was an activity he had enjoyed. She thought working on his picks might "pep him up." But in the end, it involved more mental work than he was up to.

XII.

IN THE SUMMER of 2005, a few weeks before Bill's death, we discussed how we would format our betting in Virginia's gubernatorial election that autumn. We decided to focus our betting on Tim Kaine, the lieutenant governor. We would bet several different ways on how he fared in Richmond, where he had served two terms as mayor, and in Arlington, where we lived. We acknowledged a nostalgic interest in Kaine, the eventual winner in November. He is the son-in-law of former Republican governor Linwood Holton, a member of the "dream" tennis game whose dysfunctionality brought Bill and me together. Reminiscing about the "dream team's" antics provided us with a few hearty laughs at a time when subjects we could laugh about were few and far between.

ELEVEN

MOVIES

I.

A FEW MONTHS after Nan Rehnquist's death in 1991, Bill, Betty Nan and I began going together to dinner and a movie several Saturday nights each month. Our routine was simple: we would attend a late matinee at an Arlington cineplex followed by dinner and drinks in a neighborhood eatery. Dinner was relaxed, without time pressures. There was always time for Bill to enjoy his after-dinner cigarette.

We were avid moviegoers before we became a regular threesome. But we were not film "buffs": we were not conversant about the particular styles of directors and screenwriters. Celebrity gossip bored us. For us, movies were an enjoyable, relaxing, uncomplicated escape, nothing more. A production won "four stars" from us if it helped us forget the day's angst.

Bill's loneliness after Nan's death was apparent to anybody who saw him regularly. He did not try to hide it.

At our Sunday morning tennis games, I could tell that Saturday nights were the loneliest of the week for him. After routine greetings, he would almost always ask what Betty Nan and I had done the previous evening. I would describe a typical suburban couple's Saturday night

(dinner with friends, neighborhood party, movies, a charity event, etc.).
Bill would then sometimes tell me about a quasi-official party that
sounded glamorous but that he found tedious. More often he would
describe a dinner of hot dogs, canned vegetables and ice cream followed
by an evening with the TV remote. (For more than a dozen years he prepared most of his own meals, but he always considered cooking a chore,
rather than a creative pleasure.)

Shortly after Nan's funeral, Bill began joining us regularly for a
home-cooked dinner, usually on a weekday. After dinner we often
played high-spirited games of Rummikub, a game that generally follows the rules of gin rummy but is played with cubes on a table like
dominoes. Even though Bill reciprocated by periodically taking us to
dinner at a local restaurant, there was an unevenness about the arrangement. One of us always had to "invite" the other. We needed a
different system with no formalities.

Dinner and movies together on the weekends seemed like the obvious answer. But threesomes are not part of the natural social order.
Before 1992, each of us spent Saturday nights with our spouses and occasionally with other couples. Betty Nan and I had several unmarried
friends—as Bill and Nan did also—but as a rule of thumb we would
meet our single friends on weekday evenings, almost never on a Saturday night.

Still, for a dozen years the Bill–Betty Nan–Obe Saturday night
threesome seemed natural, appropriate, uncomplicated. Like everything else in my relationship with Bill, we approached it cautiously.
For several weeks each of us, for our own reasons, had doubts about
the feasibility of a regular Saturday night outing. But we soon bonded
as a threesome.

II.

The movie genres Bill and I enjoyed most were farcical, slapstick comedies and tense, violent thrillers, particularly those with war themes. Betty Nan shared our taste—to a point. She did not find our preferences offensive, but she thought we should also see situation comedies and musicals with some regularity. Since we were a threesome of equals, every third movie was "Betty Nan's kind."

Many of the war movies we particularly liked were R-rated. (Violent, gory pictures get that rating almost automatically.) Some gutter language and nudity often goes along with the R rating, but this did not bother us. However, we never saw films that included explicit sex scenes. Betty Nan found it awkward—"unpleasant" may be a more accurate word—to be seen with two adult males at a movie that included such content.

On its surface it may appear inconsistent, even strange, that two intellectuals who had read widely in twentieth-century fiction and drama judged films by a different standard than they used for books or plays. We read and enjoyed literary criticism, but with movies we almost never sought more erudite commentary than standard newspaper reviews, and usually only the *Washington Post*'s. More important than the *Post*'s commentary and criticism was the fact that it published accurate plot summaries. Movies played an important role in our lives, but it was limited and specific. We knew what we liked and what we liked rarely won critical acclaim. On Saturdays we sought only escapist entertainment.

When reviewers dismissively described a film as "farcical," Bill and I read further. Excellent. Farcical movies usually made us laugh out loud. The criterion by which we distinguished "farce" from "comedy" was personal, idiosyncratic. While we enjoyed both genres, we especially delighted in farce. "Comedy," as we thought of the word, had an intellectual component. The laughs depended on wit, words, manners and subtle contretemps. "Farce" gave the audience comic fulfillment by using ridiculous situations, inappropriate clothing, mistaken identities and outlandish personalities to ridicule manners, dignity, status and pomposity.

Oscar Wilde, Noël Coward, Philip Barry and Neil Simon wrote memorable comedies. The performers in farces are more memorable than the writers: Charlie Chaplin, Bob Hope, the Marx Brothers, Jackie Gleason, W. C. Fields and Abbott and Costello had all enlivened many happy hours in our youths. They were the gold standard by which we measured contemporary farce. During the first four years of the twenty-first century, we saw at least half a dozen movies that fit this bill: *Old School*, *The Whole Nine Yards*, *Dodgeball*, *The Royal Tenenbaums*, *My Big Fat Greek Wedding* and *Starsky & Hutch*. Regardless of how the critics judged them, they worked for us.

Two film genres that we avoided were special-effects movies like *Star Wars* and *The Lord of the Rings* and self-righteous, "preachy" ones like *Paper Clips* and *Erin Brockovich*. Our inability to enjoy most special-effects films was probably age related, just like our inability to respond to the music our children couldn't get enough of. We skipped "preachy" movies because we resented spending our Saturday nights watching thinly masked inspirational sermons, sociology lectures and cautionary tales.

III.

BILL WAS HOSPITALIZED at least twice for major back surgery during the fourteen years between his appointment to the Court and our first meeting in 1986. His spinal problems were never resolved. Several times during our friendship, he spent one or two nights in the hospital seeking relief from his recurrent back pain.

His spinal malady affected our selection of movies—as it did almost everything he did. After sitting in one position for about a half hour, he had to stand, walk a few steps and stretch, as he did often while hearing oral arguments at the Supreme Court. If he had an aisle seat in a cineplex with stadium seating, he could usually stand up and stretch unobtrusively. We always arrived at movie theaters well before the lights went down so that Bill was sure to get an aisle seat. Early arrival at the theater also allowed Bill and me fifteen or twenty minutes of idle chatter and to review the past week's happenings and/or gossip. Bill's back problem precluded our seeing three-hour movies. Before that time had elapsed, he had to do more than stand up and stretch his back a little: he had to walk to the lobby two or three times, maybe more. This, of course, meant multiple interruptions during the feature. Bill had no interest in paying good money to see a film when he was certain he would miss vital segments of the story line. For this reason our threesome missed *Titanic, The Thin Red Line* and *Saving Private Ryan,* all award-winning movies in genres we enjoyed.

It was Bill's back problems that made us irregular patrons of the theater. Although we could have arranged to have aisle seats, playgoers are intolerant of members of the audience who stand up and stretch several times during the course of a performance, particularly a man measuring six feet two inches.

IV.

After Bill's death, the fact that he once saw *Old School*—a wacky, raunchy, slapstick farce—received unexpected media coverage. This came as a complete, almost shocking, surprise to me.

Old School was an uncomplicated, raucous film. It certainly was not the kind of movie that I anticipated would be mentioned from the pulpit in Washington's inspiring Roman Catholic Cathedral in the presence of the president of the United States and a cardinal of the

Holy Roman Church. But in an eloquent, emotion-freighted eulogy, Jim Rehnquist referred to his father's seeing *Old School* as evidence of his unaffected, well-rounded personality.

In many ways *Old School* was a sequel to the 1978 comedy classic *Animal House,* a film that the three of us had seen separately—and enjoyed. A simple plotline delivered an evening of laughs, and that was good enough for us. *Old School*'s tagline, "All the fun of college, none of the education," was accurate. Three thirtysomething buddies had reached the point in life where they had to choose between living as responsible adults with wives, homes and steady jobs . . . or reverting to their carefree, prankish days as fraternity boys. In turn, they tried to embrace the best of both worlds—without enrolling in a college or leaving suburbia, they would behave like uninhibited adolescents.

Bill and I both read Desson Howe's review in the *Washington Post.* He wrote:

> "Old School" is an extremely funny and, of course, socially unredeemable comedy . . . in terms of sheer belly-laugh count, this is the one . . . it is even (dare I say?) charming in some places. Those passing moments are thanks to Will Ferrell, who . . . doffs his clothes and, quite literally, takes his nudity on the road . . . as he is trucking down Main Street, his wife pulls up in a car next to him. Feeling no pain, he expresses no shock at all. He hops in nonchalantly, negotiating for space next to his wife's shocked girlfriends and asks, "Honey, do you think KFC's still open?"

The review failed to say that by most definitions *Old School* was raunchy. Within the performing arts world, "raunchy" has a precise meaning: it describes actions and content that are usually both lewd and crude but not pornographic. A raunchy movie includes many scenes with sexual innuendo and leering references to body parts, but no episodes with steamy seductions, kinky confessions or passionate lovemaking. *Old School*'s most memorable moments were a semi-nude wrestling scene where the participants (including a ninety-year-old toothless man and two bare-breasted young women) were smeared with K-Y Jelly, and a silly college class where fully clothed fraternity members received instruction in advanced sex technique.

Later that evening, at a local Italian restaurant, Betty Nan ridiculed her male companions' movie choice. Did we knowingly select a low-brow raunchy film? Or did the *Washington Post* mislead us? she asked. Our too-loud laughter was sophomoric and embarrassing, she added. Next time we picked a movie, she hoped it would be something more memorable.

But Bill never forgot that evening. The following week, he proudly told his law clerks that he had seen *Old School*. Several of them had seen it the same weekend. They were impressed that he and his respectable friends were willing to see an *Animal House*–type picture with few, if any, redeeming social or intellectual attributes. They even went as far as to congratulate him on his youthful approach to entertainment. He enjoyed that and gleefully relayed their comments to me.

Bill's pleasure in seeing *Old School* even made the scholarly, stodgy *George Washington University Law Review*, a publishing venue where comedies are rarely, if ever, discussed. In an issue chiefly devoted to a "Symposium on the Legacy of the Rehnquist Court," Courtney Gilligan, a George Washington University Law School graduate and a Rehnquist law clerk in 2003–04, wrote: "When we were discussing the new *Batman* movie, Chief Justice Rehnquist told me he had no interest in seeing *Batman*, but that he had just seen *Old School*, and thought it was a hoot."

A few days after Bill's funeral, the *Daily Pennsylvanian*, the University of Pennsylvania's student newspaper, interviewed Dana Rehnquist (an alumnus of Sharon High School) about her grandfather. She explained that he was a man who easily bridged generational gaps. The *Daily Pennsylvanian*'s lead paragraphs said: "College freshman Dana Rehnquist was on her way to dinner with her brother and grandfather one night a few years back when her grandfather, a big movie buff, announced that he had just seen a 'really raunchy' film.

He loved it so much, he said, that even when his disgusted friends wanted to get up in the middle and leave, he ordered them to stay put. The Chief Justice of the Supreme Court, it turns out, was professing his admiration for the frat house film, *Old School*."

V.

WAR MOVIES WERE probably Bill's and my favorite genre: we rarely missed a new one. We attributed much of our enthusiasm for war movies to our years as teenage soldiers. While the quirks of fortune gave both of us assignments where our valor and bravery were never put to the test, each of us had close friends and classmates who had been maimed or killed in action. We did not think our generation was the "greatest," but we did think we understood war better than younger generations.

Similar experiences as wartime soldiers was an important component of our relationship. But it was based on more specific things than just having been part of the great army that won World War II. One of the more important things we shared was that for more than half of our military careers we had been privates, the lowest rank in the most hierarchically structured organization within the American democracy. We were constantly reminded that we were the lowest of the low.

At Camp Picket, privates like me were required to polish the shoes and make the beds of the training sergeants who lived with us. In an earlier era we would have also emptied their chamber pots. On my nineteenth birthday, my parents visited me in Williamsburg, Virginia, and planned a celebratory dinner at the Williamsburg Inn, a top-level hotel. But we were unceremoniously turned away at the hotel's door because members of my low caste were not allowed in the restaurant or lobby.

Bill and I were emotionally, intellectually and socially ill equipped to spend our years between ages eighteen and twenty at the bottom level of a rigid caste system, and the experience left a mark.

VI.

BILL ENJOYED TELLING our mutual friends about our lowbrow movie tastes. The usual response was surprise, maybe wonderment. This, in turn, led to unfreighted, nonpolitical, sometimes intellectual conversation. We both took pleasure in explaining that our tastes were not as gross or unsophisticated as many of our contemporaries thought.

Occasionally when we were discussing—and justifying—our movie tastes in social company, Bill or I explained that almost all of the great dramas that had survived for centuries, or even millennia, are full of violence. The ancients considered brutal killings on stage essential components of drama. The most memorable soliloquies in *Hamlet* and *Macbeth* would probably not have enthralled audiences, Elizabethan or modern, if they had not been rendered dramatic by violent acts immediately preceding and/or following. The most violent scenes in Shakespeare are likely the most memorable.

I know of no modern movie that is as remorselessly cruel as *King Lear*. No contemporary producer would film a scene like the one in which Cornwall gouges out the eyes of Gloucester, an opponent in a political dispute. While a guest in Gloucester's house, Cornwall has his host tied down in a chair and then proceeds to blind him with his thumbs. As Cornwall finishes the second eye, he screams the play's most memorable line, "Out, vile jelly!" while his victim sobs and wails in agony.

Many Elizabethan and classical dramas had scenes of domestic violence onstage that would almost certainly be taboo by today's standards. Shakespeare's *Othello* savagely smothers his wife, Desdemona, with a pillow in her bed during a lengthy scene. Othello lifts the pillow periodically so that she can weepingly protest her innocence of the infidelity he believes he is avenging. But he ignores her screaming pleas. After each protestation he violently replaces the pillow until she eventually suffocates—at center stage.

VII.

In 1996, our threesome strayed from our agreement to avoid movies lasting three hours or more. Notwithstanding its length, Bill wanted to see *Nixon*, Oliver Stone's polemical film starring Anthony Hopkins. The movie was controversial from the moment it went into production. Juxtaposing the names of Richard Nixon and Oliver Stone made that inevitable. Most reviewers said it so demonized the thirty-seventh president that it diminished some of the more important anticonservative points Stone was trying to make.

We went to see *Nixon* knowing full well that it was propaganda, but we were still curious. Bill may have been Nixon's most important appointment; he was certainly his most lasting. Bill's attendance at the film would probably have been considered newsworthy. But he made no effort to conceal it. The three of us, quite publicly waited our turn in the ticket line at the Cineplex Odeon Shirlington.

Oliver Stone was well known for directing hard-hitting, message-driven, liberal-left movies. He had won two Academy Awards for anti-Vietnam war films (*Platoon* and *Born on the Fourth of July*). *Nixon* was actually an attack on the growing conservative movement in the United States, rather than a biography or cinematic analysis of Nixon's character. The dour, moody Richard Nixon was an easy target for an anticonservative movie, while Barry Goldwater and Ronald Reagan, who played far more important roles in the conservative movement's ascendancy, were charming men with sunny dispositions and upbeat personas. By 1995, when the film was released, Goldwater and Reagan were widely viewed as visionary men of integrity, while Nixon was still seen as a devious, smarmy man who had resigned from the presidency in disgrace.

We thought Oliver Stone's *Nixon* would be a straightforward hatchet job. We got what we expected—a polemical movie—except that we were also surprised to find *Nixon* dull and tedious. Whatever reservations we had going in, we were prepared for a gripping, tense drama. Oliver Stone was a first-class talent whose pacifist movies we had enjoyed, even though we had not fully agreed with them.

Although Bill was not mentioned in the movie, there were several nongenerous—albeit general—comments about Nixon's Supreme Court selections. Professional historians, even those who shared the film's bleak view of Richard Nixon, noted its many inaccuracies. Several were obvious. One that was particularly annoying was the statement that Nixon had appointed three Supreme Court justices; he actually appointed four: Warren Burger, Harry Blackmun, Lewis Powell and William Rehnquist. The error certainly did not hurt Bill or the film's story line, but it did adversely affect Stone's credibility. It was the kind of gaffe that should have been picked up by a low-level fact checker.

The filmmaker's sloppy research did not bother Bill. But it deeply offended Stephen Ambrose, the noted historian and Nixon biographer. "[Oliver Stone] feels free not merely to conjecture, but also to invent scenes that never happened, to give one man's words to another, and to assign Nixon posts that he never held," Ambrose explained in a book on Stone's cinematic achievements. "He wants to change the country and points to the Nixon presidency as proof of the need for radical political action. In that sense, it matters greatly that he has distorted the past." Bill did not think Stone should be held to the standards of a true historian, particularly since *Nixon* was not promoted as a documentary. He believed it should be judged as a polemic, a genre that includes hyperbole. In *Hustler Magazine, Inc. v. Falwell,* Bill wrote a majority opinion defending the legitimacy of hyperbole as part of political satire.

Bill had no personal feelings for Nixon. He only met him one-on-one once, and that meeting was impersonal, tantamount to a job interview. It took place shortly after he knew he was on Nixon's "short list" for the Supreme Court nomination. The president asked questions and Bill gave carefully crafted answers. That was the extent of it.

Even though Richard Nixon had named him to a coveted life-tenured job, Bill declined an invitation to travel on Air Force One to Nixon's funeral in California in April 1994. He believed it was appropriate and proper for former Nixon cabinet officers like Henry Kissinger, George Shultz and James Schlesinger to attend. They had shared his confidences and discussed public policy ideas with him. But Bill had never been a colleague or confidant. Nixon's other three Supreme Court appointees (Burger, Blackmun and Powell) were all alive at the time. They all chose to watch the proceedings on TV.

VIII.

In 1997 WE made an exception to our no-preachy-movies guideline. We went to see *Amistad*, Steven Spielberg's horrors-of-slavery epic starring Anthony Hopkins, Morgan Freeman and Matthew McConaughey—and, most importantly, retired justice Harry Blackmun in a cameo role. It was the only time we attended a movie where we knew one of the actors.

Before accepting Steven Spielberg's invitation to play the part of Justice Joseph Story (an associate justice of the Supreme Court that heard the *Amistad* case in 1841), Justice Blackmun wrote Bill a formal note to determine if he had any objections. Bill, had none. As a matter of fact, he was impressed with his colleague's wage rate: Justice Blackmun was paid $540 a day, the Screen Actors Guild minimum for actors with small speaking parts. Blackmun spoke three lines and was paid for two days' work, plus travel expenses to the site of the filming. If he had lived long enough to retire in good health, I believe Bill would have enjoyed playing a bit part in a movie, particularly that of a judge.

Amistad's story is gripping: it was the name of a slave ship carrying contraband human cargo from Spain to Cuba. In graphic detail, Spielberg creatively portrayed the cruelty that prevailed on slave ships; the most dramatic scene involved throwing overboard several dozen slaves chained to rocks when it was feared that a British warship might seize the vessel. En route, the slaves mounted a successful revolt that resulted in the slaughter of the ship's crew. Without the murdered officers' navigational skills, the slave-manned ship sailed aimlessly for several weeks until it ran out of provisions. Adrift and close to starvation, the slaves surrendered themselves to a merchant ship located off the coast of Connecticut.

Several years of legal wrangling ensued after the fifty-three surviving slaves were put ashore in New Haven, Connecticut. The case was finally resolved by the United States Supreme Court, where John Quincy Adams, the former president, represented the slaves and their abolitionist patrons. His speech before the Supreme Court was the movie's high point: "If this be civil war," Adams said in his final argument, "let it come. And if it does, may it be the last battle of the American Revolution."

At dinner following the movie, Bill said he suspected Adams's speech was not authentic. Supreme Court arguments in the early nineteenth century, he observed, were constructed differently than the dialogue in Spielberg's movie. His suspicions led him to ask the Supreme Court librarian to look up the oral arguments and briefs from the 1841 *Amistad* case. He discovered that there was no record of Adams's speech.

This was unusual. Before the advent of modern stenography, lawyers were expected to submit copies of their arguments to the Supreme Court clerk so they could be made part of the official record. Cases were sometimes kept "open" for years while the clerk waited for all the lawyers to make "corrections" to their speeches so they could become part of the permanent record. In the official record of the *Amistad* case there is a notation that President Adams never sent the Supreme Court the text of his peroration, despite repeated requests. Indeed, the clerk in 1841 noted that the record would be considered "complete" without Adams's speech. According to Bill, the "complete" notation indicated that the clerk had believed Adams's speech was unimportant; if the clerk had thought otherwise, he would have noted that the record was "incomplete."

IX.

REGULAR VISITS TO a cineplex (approximately fifteen times a year) by the same threesome, followed by two hours or more of relaxed conversation over food and drink, means that over the years we talked together about good and evil, right and wrong, bravery and cowardice, in varied ways that would be difficult—virtually impossible—for sophisticated adults in most other circumstances. When we started going to the movies together on a regular basis in 1992, we sought uncomplicated escape and easy companionship, nothing more. But we got a lot more.

TWELVE

HISTORIAN

I.

HISTORIAN WAS BILL'S second vocation. It was not his avocation or his hobby. Regardless of how crowded his schedule was, he always made time to work on his history books—and, to my knowledge, he never missed a publisher's deadline. He considered himself a pro, and he was one. In shopping-mall bookstores, periodical ads and book expos, his books were promoted in direct competition with works by bestselling authors. Law school libraries routinely added his books to their reference collections.

While reviewers rarely ignored the author's name, most judged Bill's books on the basis of their historical and literary merit. Newspaper and magazine criticism followed a pattern. Reviewers who focused on a book's authorship were usually critical. Those who focused on a book's content usually found it a worthy addition to the American history genre. While Bill rarely read news reports or editorial commentary about his judicial decisions or Supreme Court activities, he carefully read reviews of his books. The harshest criticisms that I read came from law school professors. Every time a new Rehnquist book was published, at least one prominent professor tried to diminish it with words like "shallow," "superficial," "lowbrow" or "chatty." All of these words were appropriate when applied to certain parts of each book. But they did not describe any of his books when they were considered as complete entities.

Bill's history-writing style was more like that of a journalist than an academic or a lawyer. While he usually wrote simple, declarative sentences, he regularly interposed artful constructs that tended to make his prose style sprightly. As a former political speechwriter, he understood that maintaining reader interest—and enjoyment—was the first challenge of someone writing for a mass audience.

All of Bill's books are properly classified as "popular history." The target audience was thoughtful people without special knowledge of legal theory or American history, the kind of people who have liberal arts college degrees, buy nonfiction bestsellers and never forget to vote. In the preface to one of his books he explains that the main job of his primary editor (his daughter Nancy Spears) was "to make me sound less like a lawyer." Then he added, "And I hope she has succeeded."

II.

WHEN BILL'S FOUR books are viewed as a single entity, the work of one man over a period of less than two decades, a unifying theme is apparent. All were concerned with important but little-known aspects of the United States legal system. They reflected the author's understanding and constant awareness of the close relationship between legal systems and political process. He always found contemporary relevance in specific historic events. It was the skill with which he tied the past to the present—and the future—that made his books exceptional.

Only well-documented situations interested Bill: the impeachment trials of Supreme Court Justice Samuel Chase and President Andrew

Johnson; the suspension of habeas corpus by Abraham Lincoln during the Civil War; the internment of Japanese-Americans during World War II; and the presidential election of 1876 when the popular-vote loser became the winner because of the vote of one Supreme Court justice. As a researcher, he discovered very few new facts. While he studied original documents and read books by contemporary observers, he had neither the time nor the inclination to seek out and pore over aggregations of incidental data. He was not interested in hairsplitting and minutiae. After extensive reading and study of original sources, he arrived at insightful and creative conclusions about the significance of events long past.

Bill approached his historian job like a judge. He viewed historical facts as evidence—and he treated evidence respectfully. He was always careful not to tamper with it. Yet, part of a historian's job, like a judge's, is to look beyond the evidence itself. Bill looked for context, the environment in which the evidence was created and the character and motivations of those who created it. He, like Winston Churchill, Theodore Roosevelt and Leon Trotsky, was a professional historian who had also made much history.

Better than many academic historians, Bill understood that while new books are published almost annually about George Washington, Abraham Lincoln, Julius Caesar and the Peloponnesian Wars, those that are considered worthy of review are rarely based on previously unknown minutiae. Those that prevail in the marketplace and win plaudits from critics—and some new entries always do —combine fresh insights and perspectives with superior organizational and writing skills.

III.

BILL'S FIRST BOOK, *The Supreme Court: How It Was, How It Is,* was published by William Morrow & Co. in 1987, with a revised edition published by Alfred A. Knopf in 2001. It was his most successful book, both critically and commercially.

Although more than two-thirds of the book is devoted to Supreme Court history (analysis of famous and transforming cases, plus sketches of interesting and influential justices), the remaining third is likely the more interesting. It is part memoir and part a nuts-and-bolts guidebook to Supreme Court operations. Each section is personal and quirky—including his selection of the most significant cases and the most interesting justices—and tells a great deal about the author as well as about the Supreme Court.

Much of the memoir portion deals with Bill's experience in 1952–53 as a law clerk to Justice Robert H. Jackson, a New Deal superstar and the chief prosecutor at the Nuremberg war crimes tribunal, which condemned Nazi Germany's wartime leaders to the gallows. He was awed by the Supreme Court Building the day he first walked up the marble steps as a young law clerk reporting for work, and that feeling of awe never left him. Although moved by the place and its importance, he was not a shy, unobtrusive law clerk who labored diligently and rarely left the chambers of the justice for whom he worked. He got to know all of the justices. Justice Felix Frankfurter who, as a Harvard professor, was one of the chief architects of the New Deal before President Roosevelt appointed him to the Supreme Court, became a personal friend. Thirty-five years later, Bill took pride in recalling that the justice attended his engagement reception and urged him to become active in right-wing politics.

The book's historical section reviews noteworthy cases from the Court's earliest years (shortly after the Constitutional Convention) until 1956, a date with no historic significance. Bill selected the year because that is when Justice William Brennan was appointed to the Court. Everyone serving on the Court when the book was written (1986) was appointed after Justice Brennan, and Bill did not want to comment on cases in which any of his colleagues had participated.

Bill's detailed description of the "justices conference," at which cases are decided and the writing of opinions is assigned, was probably the book's high point. Lawyers, judges, scholars, journalists and law school faculties had long been curious about what happened at the supersecret—and vastly important—Supreme Court justices conference. Few top-level government functions not connected with intelligence gathering or national security are as hidden from public scrutiny.

Bill's book described the conference's operation for the first time. Nobody attends the conference except justices. A marshal stands guard at the door to make sure that there are no intruders or eavesdroppers. According to Bill's book *The Supreme Court: How It Was, How It Is*, the justices conference is more of a ritualized, intellectual exercise than a freewheeling discussion among longtime colleagues and professional peers. At the conference, where the chief justice presides, each justice states his or her position on a particular case once—and only once. Justices speak in seniority order, and the junior justices rarely make significant additions to the process because their position on a particular case has usually been fully explained by a more senior justice. The youngest justice (in terms of seniority) serves as secretary and keeps score. Bill was ambivalent about the justices conference. It was efficient, fair and orderly, and he admired that. But it was also without spontaneity, which at times he found frustrating. Important new ideas were sometimes missed because they developed in a particular justice's mind while various legal positions were being explained—and the justice had already spoken.

The 2001 revised edition of *The Supreme Court: How It Was, How It Is* was reviewed as a "new" book in several newspapers. Two new chapters were added, "The New Deal Court" and "The Warren Court." The first addition covered an important and contentious period in the Court's history. The Warren Court's story was compelling, and by 2001 every member had died. Therefore Bill felt comfortable commenting on it. He wrote admiringly of Chief Justice Earl Warren's political skills and his leadership when he made a personal project of securing a unanimous decision (without any separate concurring opinions) in *Brown v. Board of Education*. Although the justices were deeply divided in conference, all signed the final decision after being subjected to a master politician's charm. The only person ever elected governor of California three times, Warren came to the Court with heavy credentials as a politician but only limited ones as a legal scholar. He was convinced that if the *Brown v. Board of Education* decision led to civil unrest and violence (as happened), it was important that the Supreme Court appear firm and united. The chapter concludes with an analysis of the controversy over Chief Justice Warren's successor in which Bill discusses the limits on ethical and appropriate conduct by justices.

While Bill never owned a desktop PC or a laptop, he learned something about spell-check in 1987, long before most Americans had computers in their homes. *The Supreme Court: How It Was, How It Is* was copyedited and fact-checked at many levels by its publisher, William Morrow & Co. At the printer it was checked one last time by a computer program similar to spell-check. The printer's computer program made a change—one that it was programmed to do—in Bill's discussion of the appointment of Bushrod Washington (George Washington's nephew) to the Supreme Court in 1798 by John Adams. The computer program assumed the date reference was an error and changed it to 1978. The mistake was not corrected until the book went into its second printing several years later. When I told Bill about the small date error I had picked up in his book, he told me he had already discovered it himself. He then added that he often used it as a test. When people flattered him about his book, he often told them about the error created by the computer. The reaction usually told him whether they had read the whole book or just the first and last chapters.

IV.

Bill's second book, *Grand Inquests: The Historic Impeachments of Justice Samuel Chase and President Andrew Johnson,* was published in 1992, also by William Morrow & Co. I comment on it at length in Chapter Five ("Impeachment").

In this book, Bill tells how the article of the Constitution that authorizes Congress to remove from office members of the executive and judicial branches through the impeachment process gives the legislative branch the potential to destabilize the government. Nothing but the randomness of the human condition can explain why in 1991 Bill felt that a once-in-a-century event like a presidential impeachment was important enough to write a book about—and then seven years later he became a central figure at the United States's second presidential impeachment trial, 131 years after the first.

V.

In 1997, approximately one year before the publication of Bill's third book, *All the Laws but One: Civil Liberties in Wartime,* Bill changed his second vocation's behind-the-scenes infrastructure. Before his death in 1980, Justice William O. Douglas, a prolific author, introduced Bill to his literary agent, Robbie Lantz. Lantz, whose author clients included Lillian Hellman, James Baldwin and Carson McCullers, sold Bill's first two books to William Morrow & Co. and also advised him on the arcana of the New York book publishing scene. But Lantz's main interest was showbiz, where he represented marquee stars like Bette Davis, Elizabeth Taylor, Richard Burton, Yul Brynner, Myrna Loy and Liv Ullmann. His glitter world approach to historical writing did not fully mesh with Bill.

After approximately ten years' experience in the literary marketplace, Bill decided that a public figure like the chief justice of the United States, who was also a sophisticated lawyer and an established author, did not need a literary agent—and he could save the ten percent fee he paid Lantz. Patricia Hass, a Washington-based editor at Alfred A. Knopf, whom he met at a party at the home of Justice Byron White, replaced Lisa Drew as his editor and took over any agent functions he was unable to handle himself.

VI.

All the Laws but One: Civil Liberties in Wartime, Bill's third book, reviews the severe limitations that have been imposed on civil liberties during wars by Abraham Lincoln, Woodrow Wilson and Franklin D. Roosevelt, all generally perceived as champions of personal liberty. A book about how iconic figures wrestled with profound conflicts of ethics and principles of governance should have been a bestseller. But it flopped in the marketplace.

In 1998 most book-reading Americans considered the notion remote that an American president would have to face the dilemmas inherent in reconciling democratic principles and the exigencies of war. However, the flow of history made Bill's third book, like its immediate predecessor (*Grand Inquests*), timely shortly after its release date, in 2001, terrorists flew fully-fueled airplanes into the World Trade Center in New York and the Pentagon in Virginia.

All the Laws but One begins with a review of the circumstances that led President Abraham Lincoln during the Civil War to suspend habeas corpus, a basic right guaranteed by the Constitution: the right of a person who has been arrested to face his accuser and to know the exact nature of the crime he is alleged to have committed. It also discusses at length the internment of Japanese-Americans during World War II.

I believe it is Bill's empathy with elected representatives—those who must hastily make practical decisions that may seriously compromise basic freedoms—that makes the book particularly insightful. He acknowledges that in times of war, when nationhood itself may be at stake, the abridgment of freedom is sometimes appropriate. But, on the other hand, he is critical of wartime presidents who curtailed personal liberty more than necessary in the guise of national defense.

Many of the civil liberties issues raised by the war on terror are similar to those that Bill discussed in *All the Laws but One*. In April 2004, six years after the publication of his book, and 140 years after President Lincoln suspended habeas corpus, Bill presided over the Supreme Court when it heard oral arguments in *Rasul v. Bush*, possibly the most important habeas corpus case since the Civil War. At issue was the right of "enemy combatant" prisoners captured in the Afghanistan war and incarcerated at Guantánamo Bay, Cuba, to file writs of habeas corpus and to hear in open court the specific crime for which they were being held. While a majority of the Supreme Court held that the prisoners had a right to petition for habeas corpus during incarceration at Guantánamo Bay, Bill was one of three dissenters.

All the Laws but One's final chapter has a Latin title, *"Inter Arma Silent Leges,"* that Bill translated: "In time of war, the laws are silent." After discussing more than a dozen specific situations in three administrations, Bill explored whether a constitutional system of government can survive the threats to a nation's sovereignty that exist only in times of war. Wartime presidents and peacetime presidents behave differently, he concluded, regardless of their political orientation or party affiliation. And he believed this was inevitable. None responded to war's dangers and demands exactly as they themselves had anticipated.

"It is neither desirable nor is it remotely likely," Bill concluded, "that civil liberty will occupy as favored a position in wartime as it does in peacetime. . . . The laws will not be silent in time of war, but they will speak with a somewhat different voice."

VII.

Bill's last book, *Centennial Crisis: The Disputed Election of 1876*, was published by Knopf a few months before his thyroid cancer surgery. It discusses the circumstances that led to a Supreme Court justice playing a major role in bringing 1876's presidential election's conflict to closure. In Chapter Six ("Disputed Election"), I explain how Bill used the story of the presidential election of 1876 to partially explain his and his colleagues' actions in November and December of 2000.

While Bill's second and third books became timely and significant a few years after their release, *Centennial Crisis* became timely in midcourse—while he was writing it. The prologue and epilogue, which relate the election of 1876 and the election of 2000 to each other, were not included in the book's original outline that he submitted to his publisher. The flow of history made all of his books timely and tended to prove his belief in the contemporary relevance of his historical studies.

VIII.

Bill developed a no-cost method of doing prepublication market research for his books. His "focus groups" were mostly lawyers, judges and law school students, the people who attended his speeches. They unknowingly tested new chapters in his books. For the first few minutes of his speeches, he talked about the topic assigned to him, the history of the institution that was hosting him or the anniversary he was helping to commemorate. Then he would explain that he had been doing some fascinating historic research that he thought his audience would also find interesting. He then read the chapters he had most recently completed in his work in progress. Audience responses told him which sections were particularly interesting and which ones were confusing or dull.

Notwithstanding his use of personal—and free—market research, half of Bill's four books were commercial losers. While he did not consider making money the most important measure of a book's success, it was one he valued and respected. He was disappointed with himself if a book's first-year sales did not cover his advance. As he saw it, when book royalties did not cover his advance, he was being subsidized by his publisher. And he certainly did not enjoy being subsidized—by anybody.

Only his first book, *The Supreme Court: How It Was, How It Is,* was a commercial success from the beginning. It sold well in bookstores as well as on university campuses and in the Supreme Court's bookshop, which is operated by—and for the profit of—the Supreme Court Historical Society. Although it became a required text at several law schools, his annual royalty checks rarely, if ever, exceeded four figures.

Bill's 1992 book about impeachments, *Grand Inquests,* also earned a small profit. It was salvaged from failure by Bill Clinton's impeachment seven years after its original publication. The 1998 paperback reissue of *Grand Inquests* sold briskly during the few months when the Clinton impeachment—and Bill's central role as the Senate's presiding officer—was front page news.

IX.

Even after illness overtook him, Bill never considered giving up his second job. He enjoyed researching and writing history for mass audiences. If health problems ever forced him to resign as chief justice, he planned to continue his work as a historian.

At the time of his surgery, he was researching ideas and themes for his next book. While he had not settled on a particular historical event or an overarching theme, one of the areas he was considering was military justice and courts-martial procedure. It was another important area of the law that is outside the mainstream and that he believed was fraught with the potential for abuse—like impeachments, a ticking legal time bomb.

One of the historic incidents he was considering for the new book was the 1876 massacre of General George A. Custer and his entire cavalry garrison of more than two hundred United States soldiers by a raiding party of Sioux, Lakota and Cheyenne Indians. A special court of inquiry convened by President Rutherford B. Hayes in 1879 reviewed conflicting stories as to why Custer's troops had been ambushed and murdered, but it was unable to come to a clear conclusion. There were no courts-martial, although many questions were raised about the conduct of nearby troops, including charges of repeated atrocities against the Indians that may have incited the massacre. Before the presidential court of inquiry began its deliberation, several military tribunals and state inquiry commissions had arrived at varying—and conflicting—conclusions.

X.

ONLY TWO CHIEF justices have written books during their incumbency: John Marshall, who wrote a five-volume biography of George Washington, his wartime commander; and William Rehnquist. Both men wrote history on two levels: while fastidiously chronicling the details of interesting personalities and events, they discussed important ideas about government and the law under the historical study rubric. Marshall wrote about the principles and virtues of the dying Federalist Party, under whose banner he had been elected to Congress and been appointed secretary of state. Bill chose to write about anomalous legal-political situations that tended to prove the fragility of America's constitutional system.

THIRTEEN

COMINGS AND GOINGS

I.

BILL WAS OFTEN described as reclusive, withdrawn and antisocial. I believe this was incorrect. I attribute much of this to the fact that he had few friends in the journalist community. He did not seek their company—or their kudos.

While Bill was not a glad-hander, he certainly enjoyed friends and parties. Whenever possible, he avoided the high-visibility, glitzy social events that journalists cover. Elected politicians are dependent on publicity: being seen at important media events, being photographed with the right people and, equally important, having their absence noted at controversial gatherings. But Bill had a life-tenured job. He had a small circle of good friends in Northern Virginia and Vermont, none of whom held important elected office nor, to my knowledge, were listed in Washington's Social Register. They were accomplished contemporaries. They could make conversation about a wide variety of subjects. Additionally, he played in regular bridge and poker games, which led to dinner and party invitations from within those groups. While Bill respected and sincerely liked his court colleagues, he only socialized with a few. The philosophical divide that split the justices when they voted on cases had nothing to do with those whose after-hours company he found most enjoyable.

II.

BILL'S AVAILABILITY FOR a movie one Saturday in mid-March was almost a sure thing. That was when The Gridiron Club of Washington held its annual dinner. Sponsored by a small club composed of sixty Washington correspondents who represented important newspapers (it has broadened its memberships since we began going to the movies regularly), the Gridiron dinner is a major Washington social event. The president and vice president often attend, and at least one Supreme Court justice usually does also. But during the last decades of his life, Bill skipped the event. He simply did not enjoy it. Since few quasi-official events are scheduled the night of The Gridiron Club dinner, he was almost always free to go to a movie on "Gridiron Saturday."

Bill thought the event was contrived; he felt it was so artificial that it demeaned the Washington press corps when it was supposed to enhance its prestige. While all male attendees are expected to wear white tie and tails, and foreign diplomats are expected to wear their medals and sashes, few of the female attendees are correspondingly couturier-garbed and bejeweled. Since men are rarely expected to wear white tie and tails at White House dinners or formal embassy parties, he considered it a bit of silly pomposity for a dinner sponsored by the working press corps.

Bill compared the evening's agenda to initiation night at a college fraternity: a staged "solemn ritual" is performed in a darkened room and fraternity brothers act out assigned roles. The Gridiron routine includes ceremonial pistol shots and speeches in a totally darkened ballroom, followed by formulaic, ghostwritten, humorous remarks by public officials. The evening concludes with musical skits that gently ridicule incumbent officeholders, in which the lead roles are usually sung by nonjournalist ringers.

Bill viewed the evening's bonhomie and camaraderie as manipulative showmanship. He acknowledged that the notion of setting aside an evening once a year—or possibly more often—when journalists and the public officials that they covered could socialize together was a good idea: a relaxed exchange of ideas over drinks and a good dinner would be useful. But a majority of the guests at the Gridiron dinners are neither officeholders nor members of the Washington press corps. They are publishers, CEOs, lobbyists, movie stars and assorted political types who have nothing to do with the evening's original intent. Fewer than one in five attendees is either a Gridiron Club member or a Washington officeholder.

III.

WHILE BILL SHUNNED the Gridiron Club dinner, he was never available for a movie on the last Saturday night in January when the Alfalfa Club held its annual dinner: that he looked forward to. He felt that the ambience at that event was unforced, relaxed. The members were friends or peers. Made up of two hundred leaders from government and business, plus a dozen or so high-profile media and sports figures, its dinners had a minimum of ceremonial posturing. Bill joined in 1978 and attended almost every year thereafter until he became ill. President George W. Bush is a third-generation member. His father, President George H. W. Bush, was an Alfalfa Club president, and James Baker served as club president while he was secretary of state.

Although the format for both dinners includes political jokes and music, the main difference between the event Bill enjoyed and the one he shunned was the attendee list. Most Alfalfa Club members held or had previously held government positions at or near the pinnacle of power. What they shared were successful careers and unique experiences. This allowed them to easily cross partisan and political divides. It contrasted with The Gridiron Club, whose stylized format was designed (probably unintentionally) to compensate for the fact that the journalist members had little in common with many of their guests.

During Nan's lifetime, the Rehnquists occasionally participated in special events that were arranged for them by the State Department or the White House protocol office. Nan enjoyed escorting the wives of foreign justices or attorneys general to museums, historic sites and suburban shopping malls. After her protracted illness and death, Bill wanted his social life to be invisible.

IV.

ONE OF BILL'S pet aversions from which he was unable to escape was standing in receiving lines at receptions. Whenever he was able to avoid one, he did. He found it an unpleasant duty for three reasons. First, standing in the same position, while shaking hundreds of extended hands, aggravated his ongoing spinal problems. Second, he did not enjoy going through a meaningless exercise with people he did not know. Third, when he recognized a friend in a receiving line, he resented being reduced to a trivial, quickie conversation with someone he knew and liked. He had two unpleasant experiences in receiving lines that strengthened his resolve to avoid them whenever possible.

One incident occurred in February 2004 at an event celebrating the University Club of Washington's centennial anniversary. (Bill was a longtime member of the club, used its indoor swimming pool regularly and had many friends there.) He and Ambassador William Howard Taft IV, the great-grandson of the tenth chief justice and the University Club of Washington's first president, were the main speakers at an anniversary salute, held in the National Geographic Society's auditorium. After their talks, the speakers greeted their fellow club members in an informal receiving line.

While shaking hands with an attractive, fashionably dressed young woman he did not know, he was suddenly embraced enthusiastically and kissed on the mouth while an accomplice took their picture. A few people stared, but the receiving line continued as if nothing had happened. (Observers likely assumed the young woman was a relative or the child of a friend.)

For some people, such an incident could be brushed aside and quickly forgotten. But for Bill, it was an assault on his sense of decorum. Even though it was carried off with such aplomb that nobody in the room was aware that anything out of the ordinary had occurred, Bill was so disturbed by it that he described it to me in detail on the phone a few evenings later. He was particularly bothered because the episode took place at *his* club.

A few years earlier, he had a similar experience in a receiving line—without the kiss—at a dinner of the Supreme Court Historical Society, another organization of which he was a longtime member. Although cameras are forbidden in the Supreme Court Building, where the event took place, one camera got past the metal detectors and security guards, and Bill had his picture taken while an unknown woman wrapped her arms around him affectionately.

These were isolated and unusual incidents. We live in a country of courteous people. A well-known and controversial public official can almost always enjoy a quiet dinner at a local restaurant without being harassed by political zealots or bothered by autograph seekers. When he was with us, Bill's privacy was never challenged, although I am sure lawyers and judiciary bureaucrats occasionally identified him. We always settled restaurant tabs in cash. If a server urged us to charge on a credit card, we assumed he or she was looking for an autograph. Once a restaurant proprietor asked Bill to autograph a menu and he graciously complied. But we never ate there again.

V.

BILL WAS DEFIANTLY open about his after-hours movements. He saw no reason to be furtive, taking pride in the fact that his personal life was above reproach. He did not care if his neighbors knew when he came and went; his home faced a main thoroughfare, and every weekday morning at 8:30 a.m. *promptly* a black Lincoln Town Car drove up in front of the house in clear view of all passers-by.

On weekends Bill's comings and goings were also easy to follow. When he was home his small brown Subaru Forester was parked in front of his house. Unlike many of his neighbors, his townhouse did not have a garage. When the Subaru was gone on a Saturday or Sunday, a potential threat easily could have parked in front of a neighbor's townhouse and awaited Bill's return. After he parked his car, Bill had to walk twenty to thirty feet along a poorly lit, unprotected sidewalk until he reached his townhouse.

Bill's address and telephone number were printed each year in the Washington Golf and Country Club's roster, which was distributed to the membership as well as to candidates for admission. If he requested it, the club would have been happy to print his name only. But he never requested it. Bill personally answered his doorbell and telephone. I urged him to have caller ID installed in his phone, but he declined until his final illness, and then health care professionals answered his home phone.

Despite possible security issues, Bill approached Halloween and its trick-or-treat ritual with gusto. He always answered his doorbell himself and entered into animated conversation with neighborhood children and their parents. He got many more visitors than his immediate neighbors—and he was well aware of it. It was known in the larger Arlington community that he greeted trick-or-treaters personally. Parents wanted to give their children a special Halloween experience: making small talk with the chief justice of the United States.

Although I never accompanied him abroad, he reported that on many visits to distant lands, even for pleasure, the host government insisted on providing him with a 24/7 security detail. As a gracious guest, he accepted his host's courtesies, even though he considered it intrusive and unnecessary.

When someone asked Bill why he did not have a bodyguard or a security detail, his response usually had two parts. The first was historical: in the course of two centuries, only twice did someone attempted to assassinate a Supreme Court justice. The first incident had nothing to do with the Supreme Court. In 1889, Associate Justice Stephen J. Field, who had been chief justice of California before his federal appointment, was shot in a California railroad station by another former chief justice of California with whom he had a long-simmering feud. It is doubtful if any kind of security procedure could have prevented two former state chief justices from getting into close proximity with each other, even though one carried a pistol. The second involved shots fired into an empty room by an anonymous gunman. Shortly after Justice Harry Blackmun (author of the majority opinion in *Roe v. Wade*) came home one blustery evening in March 1985, several shots were fired into the living room window of his Arlington apartment when he was in another room. There is reason to believe that the gunman—who was never apprehended—was more interested in scaring the justice than in killing him.

The second, and more important reason, was that Bill felt that a security guard would compromise his privacy and probably could not defeat a well-planned assassination anyway. Constant surveillance would have altered his lifestyle and accomplished little or nothing. More security would be a waste—and Bill hated waste.

VI.

AFTER NAN'S DEATH, Bill and his divorced daughter, Jan, who also lived in Arlington, gave several joint parties. Regardless of whether a Bill-and-Jan party was a casual backyard get-together or a black-tie dinner, the guests were half his, half hers. The guest list was truly diverse. One-half of the attendees were the same age as the other half's children. Some guests were important and prestigious; others were just beginning their careers. This atypical Washington mix of age and status meant that their parties were rarely stuffy or hierarchically structured.

The close proximity of Jan and her two daughters, Natalie and Claire, gave Bill many of the joys of being part of a family after Nan's death. For all three generations it was an uncomplicated relationship. A trial lawyer with experience both as a government prosecutor and with large law firms, Jan served as inspector general of the Department of Health and Human Services during President George W. Bush's first term. She was her father's date at many formal state dinners and embassy events. Bill occasionally attended Natalie's and Claire's soccer games as well as their Bible classes after Sunday worship at the Lutheran Church of the Redeemer in nearby McLean. He taught both girls to play chess, usually at Sunday afternoon tutorials (after the end of football season). But he failed to spark their interest in remembering and reciting poetry. For a while he offered a monetary reward to whoever learned to recite one new poem by Sunday after church, when they would be tested. But they refused to take the bait. He attributed his failure to the fact that rote memorization is held in low regard by most twenty-first-century educators. But another contributing factor was that Bill did not understand how much money it takes to incentivize a teenager in the Washington suburbs, where babysitters earn ten dollars an hour.

While most Bill-and-Jan parties were relaxed, casual affairs with small sandwiches, cakes and drinks on Bill's patio, in June 2002 they hosted an elegant black-tie dinner in the Supreme Court Building. They said the only reason for the party was to reciprocate for the many times they both had been invited out in the ten years since Nan's death. There were approximately fifty guests, split about evenly between friends of the host and friends of the hostess. The formal invitation had a gold embossed seal of the Supreme Court of the United States at the top and began, "The Chief Justice and Janet Rehnquist request . . ."

Bill's touch made the event relaxed. Immediately after dinner he amused his guests with humorous anecdotes about his predecessors, whose portraits lined the room. His easy familiarity with their personal lives made me think I was listening to one of England's royal dukes proudly explaining the origins of his family's coat of arms and its armorial standard.

After Bill's irreverent tour through Supreme Court history, the guests moved to another room that was arranged like a theater. There we were entertained by a glass harpist who had previously played with the National Symphony Orchestra. A glass harp is a collection of approximately seventy-five glass jars of different sizes that have been filled to varying heights with liquid. A glass harpist creates both complex and simple music by moving his wet fingers among the jars. After the harpist had played several pieces of complicated classical music, Bill suggested he play some familiar songs. Within minutes a classical concert had become a lively sing-along with the host as maestro. Since the harpist was a Scot, the sing-along began with "The Bonnie, Bonnie Banks of Loch Lomond," and continued with "My Bonnie Lies over the Ocean." Popular American show tunes followed. Then the maestro led his guests in "My Country 'Tis of Thee" and "God Bless America." They all got the clue: it was closing time.

VII.

IN THE SPRING of 1997, Bill and Jan invited me to what looked like a routine Sunday afternoon get-together on Bill's patio. Dress was to be casual and the invitation was simple. I assumed it would be similar to the several that had preceded it. Bill's guest list would include all the "usual suspects," plus a few of his Supreme Court colleagues. Jan's guests would be perky, young professionals who were not particularly awed by Bill or his friends. Soon after arriving, I noticed that there was one person standing near Bill who seemed to be the center of attention. After ten or fifteen minutes of cocktail conversation, I, like the rest of the guests, came to understand that the party had a special purpose: to introduce Bill's friends to Marilyn Bollinger.

A trim, attractive divorcée in her early sixties, Marilyn and her then husband, an accountant, had been across-the-street neighbors of the Rehnquists in Phoenix. In addition to neighborly, casual barbecue evenings together, the two couples worked together as volunteers in Barry Goldwater's presidential campaign in 1964. Bill and Marilyn reconnected at a party given by mutual friends while he was teaching his annual Supreme Court history course at The University of Arizona James E. Rogers College of Law in Tucson.

Marilyn's dress and style were understated and assured. Those same two words could be used to describe Bill. To meet his friends in a casual patio setting, she wore an ankle-length denim skirt, a simple white blouse, low-heeled moccasin-type shoes and Arizona Indian jewelry. Her short hair had a vibrant brownish hue tinged with gray.

As a young woman Marilyn had traveled around the world with her father, a mining engineer who worked for various international copper mining and smelting companies. Although born in the United States, she had graduated from high school in Australia and then returned to America to attend the University of Arizona, where she received a master's degree in psychology. Before she retired and moved to Tucson in the early 1990s, she had two successful careers: for almost twenty years she was a high school teacher in Yuma, Arizona, and Las Vegas, then she worked for a decade as a geriatric nurse.

When I first met Marilyn, she was working on her third career. She was one of the proprietors of an unusual and interesting business. Several times a year, she and a partner took a group of approximately a dozen middle-age women to southern France or western Ireland, where they rented a house for two weeks. In the mornings the women played golf together. In the afternoons they visited painters, potters and weavers. After a few rounds of cocktails together in the house that Marilyn and her colleague rented for them, they had dinner at a country inn with a simple menu. They avoided big cities, large museums, fancy hotels and four-star restaurants. While the trips were promoted only by word of mouth, she and her partner took four to six groups to Europe each year. They operated with a waiting list.

Over the years I was often asked if Bill was serious about his "lady friend from Arizona." If I had known the answer, I would *not* have shared the information. But I did not know. Betty Nan and I twice shared the movie dates with Bill and Marilyn, the only times he thought two couples would be preferable to our usual Saturday night threesome. While over the years Bill's name was linked in the press with several women, some of whom he dated, none except Marilyn shared movie dates with us. Marilyn died of cancer in 2001, approximately four years after the party where I met her. Bill stayed in touch with her throughout her illness, and a condolence letter from him was read at a memorial service.

At different times, two widows, longtime friends of Bill, suggested to me that it would be more natural if occasionally we went to the movies as two couples instead of always as a threesome. While neither woman was involved with him romantically, he knew them well and enjoyed their company. They were almost always invited to his parties. They both proposed that they pay for their own movie tickets and dinner and park their cars at our home. Since we lived farther from Arlington's movie theaters than Bill, we usually picked him up on the way. This arrangement would make it a Dutch treat evening instead of a date. By parking at our house, he would be spared from awkward good-night rituals on his doorstep or hers. But each time I told him about the inquiry, the answer was the same: "No."

VIII.

Bill enjoyed exchanging gifts with his friends and family—but only as long as the gift was not costly and the giver had invested some time and effort in it. For his eightieth birthday I gave him a 1924 silver dollar to carry in his pocket for good luck. (In the autumn of 2008 a similar coin was offered for sale for $7.50 by an online numismatist.) For his sixty-fifth I had a World War I–era tennis picture that I clipped from a magazine put in a simple frame. For his seventieth it was a can of tennis balls.

Every Christmas, Bill gave Betty Nan and me a poinsettia. He always personally delivered a carefully wrapped plant. He would phone in advance and arrange a time over a December weekend when he could deliver his Christmas gift. He believed a Christmas gift without a holiday visit was an incomplete gesture. (In the days when we played our poetry game after tennis, several times we found use for a line in James Russell Lowell's *The Vision of Sir Launfal:* "For the gift without the giver is bare . . .")

We reciprocated each holiday season by delivering our holiday gifts at a set time and staying afterward for a yuletide visit. Until 2004 our gift was always a box of homemade cookies. In 2004, when his tracheotomy tube precluded normal eating, we reversed roles: we brought him a poinsettia plus a vibrating Gillette razor. After thanking us, he said he was not sure if he would ever be able to use the razor. He might return it at a later date. Radiation treatments had killed his facial hair, and he did not believe it would ever grow back.

The movie threesome at Obe's seventy-fifth birthday party.

IX.

FESTIVE PARTIES ATTENDED by twenty to thirty guests celebrated Bill's sixty-fifth, seventieth and eightieth birthdays. The first was organized by Nan; the invitation read, "Fun and Games at Nan and Bill's." Although she had cake, candles and singing, the invitation did not indicate that it was a birthday party for the host's sixty-fifth.

Bill's two big birthday parties after he became a widower were elegant but low-key affairs at the residences of ambassadors from friendly nations. His seventieth was at the residence of the ambassador of Austria, and his eightieth was held at the residence of the ambassador of

Sweden. The ambassadors from both countries were personal friends of his. Over the years he had visited their countries several times, delivered talks to legal and academic groups and hosted events for local dignitaries at the United States embassies in Vienna and Stockholm.

At the casual Bill-and-Nan sixty-fifth birthday party, the games were competitive (Rehnquist style), with Pictionary being the main event. Pictionary is similar to charades. It is also played with teams. In charades, one team member selects one thing from a prepared list, usually a list of books, movies or TV shows. Then, on the basis of pantomime acting, the person who made the selection tries to convey to teammates the title of the book, movie or TV show. In Pictionary, one team member draws a card from a deck and then draws a picture of an object (person, animal or thing) to explain to his teammates the word description that is on the card. In both games all play is under time pressure.

In most Pictionary games, the player doing the drawing uses a small tablet that is passed among fellow team members. But at Bill's birthday party the pictures were drawn on large sheets mounted on an easel in the middle of the living room. Several of the players had no drawing skill or sense of proportion. Some guests were embarrassed by their artistic awkwardness. This led to raucous laughter and friendly jabs about talent and particularly to the lack of proportion when depicting the difference between male and female zoo animals as well as historic personages.

Sandra O'Connor captained one Pictionary team and I led the other. The game broke up somewhat earlier than the host and hostess had anticipated. Justice O'Connor accused my team of taking too much time between turns, cheating on the clock. She demanded that we be penalized or the game suspended. My teammates in turn said that her team was guilty of other time clock infractions. The timekeeper, the wife of another justice, refused to get involved. Justice O'Connor then tried unsuccessfully to persuade one of the several professional judges present (including the host) to rule on the dispute. When none of the judges in the room agreed to get involved in the dispute, she quit on behalf of her team. While she made a few comments about talented artists and no-guts judges, everybody was relieved when an awkward situation ended. At the end of the evening, each guest received a uniquely Rehnquist party favor: a jar of Nan's homemade jam.

Only while driving home did I fully realize that earlier in the evening I had watched Justice O'Connor demonstrate her well-known social acumen. I had not paid attention to the fact that some of Bill and Nan's guests were becoming slightly distressed at being forced to demonstrate their artistic ineptitude. But Justice O'Connor did. When it became apparent to her that several of Bill's friends were not fully enjoying his birthday party, she contrived an excuse to break up the game.

X.

Official government events, particularly those held at the Supreme Court, are usually somber and serious. The stately, historic building, with its high ceilings and omnipresent uniformed guards, makes almost any festive celebration sited there a little more stuffy and formal than the same event would be in a different environment. There is one exception, however: Inauguration Day. For the families and friends of justices, inaugurations are special.

Each justice's guest list is limited to eight or ten, depending on whether the justice and his or her spouse elect to have lunch after the swearing-in ceremony with Congress or with their family and friends in the Supreme Court Building. We were two of Bill's ten guests for the 1992, 1996, 2000 and 2004 inaugurations. All the events were similar, except in 2004, when Bill could not personally play host to his guests.

Festivities begin at 9:00 a.m. with a continental breakfast for the justices and their guests. The breakfast has the feeling of a pre–

football game tailgate party, except there is no alcohol. The justices and their spouses, children and guests are all dressed in outlandish garb. They are prepared to sit for several hours in blustery subfreezing weather. A roaring fire crackles at one end of the elegantly paneled public conference room where the breakfast is held, and multiple TV sets situated around the room allow guests to check what their favorite TV chatterer is saying about the upcoming event. (Of course, the Weather Channel has the most viewers.) It is one of the few Washington social events that takes place in a federal building—and that is paid for by the government—where there are no congressmen, lobbyists or journalists present.

At the luncheon following the inauguration ceremony, tables for ten are set up, one for each justice, plus one for each retired justice and one for the Supreme Court's chief administrative officer. About half the justices elect to eat with their guests. But Bill had no choice. By long-established custom, the chief justice joined the president's table at the Capitol, along with the speaker of the House and the president pro-tem of the Senate and, of course, their spouses.

The preinaugural breakfast was Bill's kind of social event. It was relaxed and casual, but not boisterous or noisy. Serious people were sharing a historic event in an environment of legitimate camaraderie and bonhomie. He had known many of his colleagues' guests and most of their families for a long time. The mood was upbeat, and he made the most of it. Although he was not technically the host, he acted as if he were. He went from table to table and greeted old friends, particularly the widows of deceased colleagues, who were always invited to the Supreme Court's inaugural festivities.

When the justices and their guests gathered again at the luncheon following the swearing-in ceremony and the inaugural address, they had changed into standard business attire. Guests were advised to bring with them a small suitcase so they could change clothes after the ceremony. After the luncheon, each justice's guests did their own thing. Many went on to other parties in the Capitol or along the parade route. Some went home. Others remained in the Supreme Court reception rooms and watched the parade on large TV screens.

On January 20, 2005, Bill's table was without a host. His guests, most of whom had been at previous inaugurals, wandered about aimlessly at the breakfast. Although Bill's colleagues were as gracious and welcoming as ever—probably more so—I still felt a bit like an intruder, an uninvited guest, when my host was not there to greet me.

XI.

SINCE BILL WANTED to be anonymous and unnoticed on the weekends, he understood that standing in line occasionally at movie theaters and restaurants went with the territory. Better than many public figures—maybe most—he understood the difference between influence and celebrity, between power and privilege. Not wanting special treatment at supermarket checkouts or self service gas pumps was consistent with that understanding.

The "In Memoriam: William H. Rehnquist" issue of the *Harvard Law Review* included two short pieces that tell about this side of Bill's personality. James C. Duff, Bill's administrative assistant from 1996 to 2000 and currently director of the Administrative Office of the United States Courts, told the following story about how Bill enjoyed downplaying his own importance when he was away from the Supreme Court.

On a Sunday morning in New Orleans following a banquet speech the previous night, Bill walked from his hotel to the nearest Lutheran church. The minister there had a tradition of introducing visitors to the congregation.

"I see we have a visitor this morning," he said. "Would you mind standing and introducing yourself?"

"I'm Bill Rehnquist," he replied.

"Great," said the minister, "and where are you from, Bill?"

"I'm from Washington, D.C."

"And what do you do there, Bill?"

"I'm a government lawyer," he replied.

Chief Justice John Roberts's contribution to the *Harvard Law Review* included: "When strolling outside the Supreme Court with a law clerk to discuss a case, Chief Justice Rehnquist would often be stopped by visiting tourists, and asked to take their picture as they posed on the courthouse steps. He looked like the sort of approachable fellow who would be happy to oblige, and he always did. Many families around the country have a photograph of themselves in front of the Supreme Court, not knowing it was taken by someone who sat on the Court longer than all but six Justices."

The Journal of Supreme Court History published a remembrance by Noel J. Augustyn, Bill's administrative assistant from 1987 to 1989. Augustyn recalls that in preparation for a trip from Arlington to a conference in Charlottesville, Virginia (about 110 miles), Bill pulled up to a self-service gas station near his home and filled up his tank himself. When Augustyn asked what Bill thought the station owner would think of the chief justice pumping his own gas, Bill shrugged. "They don't know who I am, and if they did, they wouldn't care."

PART FOUR

FOURTEEN

DECLINE

I.

On Saturday, October 16, 2004, Bill informed me that he was going to have a small growth on his thyroid removed at the Bethesda Naval Hospital. He belittled his upcoming surgery. We made a movie date for November 7, three Saturdays forward. I accepted his casual attitude at face value. I reminded him that I, too, had had my thyroid removed fifteen years earlier and was back on the tennis court with him the following week.

Bill was not a devious man. He said what he believed. I am still convinced that at that time, three days before he entered the hospital, he was unaware of the seriousness of his condition.

Bill broke his news to me at Gaffney's Oyster & Ale House in Arlington as we were working on our betting card for the upcoming elections. Payoff would be on November 7, a few days after the election. Because of his throat problems, he decided to skip his after-dinner cigarette. Instead, we visited a Baskin-Robbins ice cream store in a nearby mall. Ice cream, we agreed, would soothe his sore throat. That this would be our last meal together did not cross my mind—even vaguely. I feel certain he did not think about it, either.

Earlier that morning, I had called him to review the Arlington movie listings. When he answered the phone he sounded hoarse. His voice had a strange rasp.

"You sound like you're in a tunnel," I said. "What's wrong?"

His answer was dismissive.

"Some thyroid problems," he explained. "It started about a week ago. It's not a big deal. I'll give you the details at dinner."

The timbre of Bill's voice had changed rapidly, but his speech was otherwise unaffected. After a few minutes of conversation, I became accustomed to the fact that his voice was different and paid no further attention to his condition.

Two weeks earlier I had attended his eightieth birthday celebration at the Swedish ambassador's residence. It was an elegant, relaxed affair for two dozen good friends, most of whom knew each other. After dinner, Ambassador Jan Eliasson proposed a toast to his fellow Swedes' long life and continued good health. Bill's response was clever and funny: it included jokes about Swedes, along with some self-ridicule about his own diminished ardor. His voice was perfect then.

The rapid deterioration of his speech, coupled with the thyroid growth diagnosis, might have tipped off a trained physician that he faced big troubles ahead. But I missed it, and I believe Bill did also. A factor in his casual approach toward the "small growth" on his thyroid gland was that he was aware of the fact that his thyroid did not function optimally. Through the years he had had thyroid function tests and took a daily dose of Synthroid, a synthetic thyroid supplement.

II.

WHEN THE NEWSPAPERS said that Bill was recuperating after his operation at his "suburban Virginia home," it created the comforting image of genteel, elegant surroundings. But the reality was different.

Following his surgery, Bill was too weak to climb the eight steps leading to his front door, so he lived in the basement of his Arlington townhouse. This area included a tiny bedroom and a former recreation room with a wet bar and calendar-type art on the walls. While he greeted his friends, reviewed briefs, watched TV and slept in his townhouse, he never again sat at his dining room table, slept in his own bed, ate meals prepared in his kitchen or entertained family and friends in his tastefully decorated living room.

Only with this arrangement could he continue to live in his own home. The basement recreation room in which Bill spent almost all of his waking hours opened onto a patio that allowed wheelchair access. The room was converted into a parlor–office–TV room. It was furnished with a large recliner in front of a TV (where he spent most of his last days), an old sofa, a card table and assorted chairs. The adjacent small room where he slept did not have a bathroom en suite. Before his illness, the basement recreation room had been used to host card games and to greet guests going to parties in the patio. During his convalescence, the wet bar facilitated the work of the medical professionals who cared for him and lived in the rest of the house.

An invalid's life on North Glebe Road in Arlington was slumming compared with the Eisenhower Suite at Walter Reed Army Medical Center, where Bill had been confined for several days in 2002 after ruptured ligaments in his leg were surgically repaired there.

Ike and Mamie Eisenhower were a military couple who had lived most of their adult lives in government housing. Their medical problems, great and small, had been treated in military hospitals. It was natural, therefore, that they would want to give some of their prized possessions to a suite in an Army hospital reserved for the use of general officers and a limited number of other officials at the top of the federal hierarchy. They replaced several pieces of government-issue furniture with antiques from their home in Gettysburg, Pennsylvania. They also donated original works of art to which they were personally attached. One wall was decorated with an oil portrait of Winston Churchill painted by Ike from a photograph of his wartime comrade-in-arms.

After the completion of his original thyroid surgery at Bethesda Naval Hospital, Bill was invited to convalesce there in a similar suite reserved for the use of admirals. Skilled medical services would have been available around the clock, but he preferred to be in his own home and sleep in his own basement without a retinue of obsequious attendants. Bill's unstylish, utilitarian home on North Glebe Road reflected his personality and tastes. Home was where things were familiar, convenient, useful and comfortable—and, most important, *his*.

III.

TO FULLY COMPREHEND the environment in which Bill spent almost a year, it is necessary to describe some of the outward manifestations of his malady. He could no longer sustain himself. He needed health care professionals nearby at all times. From the day before his surgery until his death, no morsel of food crossed his lips. As if he were a baby, care providers fed him at set times each day. Artificial feeding for an adult is a complicated and distasteful procedure. Pureed food is pumped directly into the stomach.

To give him the pleasurable sensation of taste, I started bringing him lollipops when I first visited him in early November 2004. Then other friends brought him the same. After a few months he said he no longer enjoyed them. Sensing taste without simultaneously chewing, swallowing and smelling had become more tantalizing than gratifying.

From top to bottom, his weight loss became apparent. His face became gaunt and jowly. The skin below his chin, on either side of the tracheotomy tube, hung like a rooster's wattles. He moved his belt buckle in a notch every few weeks. When the waist in a pair of trousers is four to five inches too wide, their ill fit tells a story in loud and clear tones. He was wasting away—rapidly.

Even in his weakened state, Bill's innate sense of courtesy did not desert him. When Betty Nan came down the stairs to his basement home, Bill always stood up to greet her, regardless of his weakened state or how difficult it was to hold up his pants. She was a woman: for him, standing when a woman entered a room was almost reflexive. It was the same way if a woman entered an elevator and he was wearing a hat: he immediately uncovered his head.

The tracheotomy tube was an unpleasant appurtenance for visitors as well as for the patient. It accumulated moisture at its stub end when he spoke, and he was constantly wiping it with a tissue. During the early months after his surgery, there were additional tubes and devices protruding from his neck. I never inquired about their purpose, but I do know that he found talking around the "contraptions" (his word) in his throat annoying and awkward, even if it was not actually painful. After the "contraptions" made talking on the telephone difficult, he gave up answering his home phone himself. Still, up until the end, one of his few pleasures was taking a call if it contained a morsel of gossip or a news tidbit he might have missed.

IV.

In mid-November 2004, three weeks after his surgery, I began visiting Bill regularly with a set routine. The ground rules for my visits were set by his daughter Jan. They were simple and I observed them fastidiously. I was to come to the house on Sundays, approximately fifteen minutes before a Washington Redskins football game. This would allow a little time for gossip and guy talk before the game. At kickoff time he would turn on the TV and we would then watch one quarter of the game together, but never more. If either of us had something to say, we would wait until a commercial break, when Bill muted the TV.

With this arrangement, Bill had company for almost an hour, but he did not have to sustain a lengthy conversation. We continued this routine until the end of the football season. Many weeks I brought him clippings from *People*, *Sports Illustrated*, the *Economist*, the *New Republic* and *National Review*, all of which I subscribed to and none of which he read regularly. It was another way of communicating in a manner that did not require him to take part in a lengthy conversation.

V.

DURING BILL'S WORST days in the winter of 2004–05, when chemotherapy and/or radiation treatments made him feel weak and miserable, he pushed himself to keep up with his job. It meant reading and thinking through heavy, complex legal documents. It also meant discussing them intelligently with his clerks and colleagues.

His law clerks, secretary and chief of staff came to his townhouse basement on a regular basis. They reviewed with him transcripts, briefs (many of which he had read before his illness), court management questions and his colleagues' positions and opinions. Even though he found it painful to talk or write, he dictated his view on pending cases, as well as letters and memos related to his job as the federal judiciary's CEO. This allowed him to participate in the Court's work long before he was well enough to be driven to the Supreme Court Building and take his proper place at the center of the bench.

Bill loved his job—and "love" is the correct word. He approached it with diligence and gusto as well as affection. While duty was undoubtedly a factor in his forcing himself to work hard during the bleak, melancholy months following his surgery, probably more important was the fact that labor on court-related tasks was almost the only thing that brought joy into an otherwise dismal existence.

Once over luncheon at the Two Quail Restaurant shortly before our sixty-fifth birthdays, Bill had laconically asked if I realized that in two weeks he would be a true anomaly: he would be a federal bureaucrat who was working for free. At sixty-five he was eligible to retire with a full (100 percent) pension for life plus health insurance, an office, a secretary and certain other amenities. Therefore, he did not earn one dollar more by working every day than he would have if he had retired.

The chief justice of the United States has a vast array of duties and responsibilities outside the Supreme Court that are virtually unknown to the general public. Most important is his role as the chief executive officer of the entire federal judiciary, in which capacity he is responsible for a six-billion-dollar budget and nearly thirty thousand employees. During his very first weeks out of the hospital, when his social life was limited to watching one quarter of a football game with me and visiting with one or two other friends, he met on a regular basis with Sally M. Rider, whose title was administrative assistant but who served as his chief of staff. A lawyer-administrator, she particularly helped with matters that required his attention as the CEO of the federal courts system. Rider received a brief moment of national recognition when she was shown on TV walking behind Bill at the edge of the inauguration platform just before he administered the oath of office to President George W. Bush on January 20, 2005. This was the first time he'd been seen in public since his operation three months earlier.

VI.

DURING THE FIRST months of 2005, I visited Bill regularly for five to fifteen minutes on weekday evenings in addition to Sunday afternoons. Even though they were casual why-don't-you-drop-by-tomorrow visits, they had to be carefully coordinated because his early evening hours were usually occupied with medical procedures, some of which left him debilitated.

It was during one of our brief early-evening visits in the spring of 2005 that I inadvertently learned that he had taken a subtle but unambiguous position in support of the Vietnam War in 1973. During a rambling discussion of politics, I mentioned that as a print journalist I was fascinated by the fact that in an era when most candidates seem fixated on the importance of TV exposure, many respected analysts had credited a blockbuster book with a major role—possibly the decisive one—in George W. Bush's surprise victory the previous November. In *Unfit for Command,* a Texas lawyer and a Harvard-trained psychologist said that John Kerry had lied about his combat record in Vietnam and, possibly more important, that some of his 1970s work as a peace activist may have been treasonous. The anti-Kerry polemic sold nearly one million copies, many in battleground states where the GOP's victory margin was narrow.

To my shock and surprise, Bill said that he had read *Unfit for Command.* One of its authors, John E. O'Neill, had personally inscribed a copy to him. O'Neill was a bright, interesting man who Bill considered a friend. He took his writings seriously. In 1973–74 he had been one of Bill's law clerks. They had kept in touch. Bill knew the names of the law firms he had practiced with in Texas. He even knew that he had recently given one of his kidneys to his ill wife.

I was nonplussed. When I followed up by asking Bill what he thought of O'Neill's book, he was dismissive but certainly not critical.

"Nothing much new there," Bill said. "John's been obsessed with Kerry's duplicitousness since I first met him. It's part of his religion. He's always been convinced Kerry was a traitor."

O'Neill came to Bill's chambers with a different record than any other clerk he hired. Probably no Supreme Court law clerk in the past half century began his tenure with a similar résumé. O'Neill was a poster boy for pro-war veterans groups during the bitter national political debate over America's continuing involvement in the Vietnam War.

The son of an admiral, O'Neill had graduated from the Naval Academy near the top of his class. He had served valorously in Vietnam before attending The University of Texas School of Law, where he graduated first in his class. His credentials were impeccable. But that did not make him unique. In the early 1970s, there were several other Supreme Court clerks who had won medals for bravery in Vietnam. After their discharge they had attended prestigious law schools from which they graduated with high honors. What made O'Neill different—and Bill's hiring of him significant—was his pre-clerkship notoriety.

A year before his clerkship began, O'Neill had a private but well-publicized meeting at the White House with President Nixon and Secretary of State Henry Kissinger. The meeting had been covered on all network news programs as well as in lengthy articles in the *New York Times* and the *Washington Post*. As a decorated veteran who supported the war, he made a platform appearance at the 1972 Republican National Convention a few months before he began his clerkship. A year earlier he had debated John Kerry, who at that time headed a large antiwar veterans group, on Dick Cavett's nationwide late night TV show on NBC.

Even though John O'Neill was indisputably smart, qualified and talented, he carried baggage. He was well known and controversial. He had been an active participant in an unresolved political debate. Bill selected him from a pool of several hundred 1970, 1971 and 1972 law school graduates whose grades put them at or near the top of their class, none of whom was well known or controversial. I can find no explanation for Bill's choosing O'Neill as one of his law clerks in 1973 except to make a personal statement in support of the Vietnam War and to make it in his preferred way: by indirection.

VII.

Until the very end, movies were an important escape for Bill. Our movie threesome began watching DVDs in his basement in the spring of 2005. Our favorite genres did not change, but since current films that were playing at local cineplexes were not available on DVD, the video rental catalogue became our movie guide. Bill's deteriorating health made it difficult for him to watch a film for more than an hour and a half. A film's length became our first, and controlling, consideration. This limited our options. But it also may have improved the quality of the films we saw. We were forced to rent "oldies but goodies."

By definition, classic films, like classic literature, music and art, have survived time's rigorous process of natural selection. In the 1940s and 1950s, feature-length movies were usually shorter than they are today: moviegoers wanted the same two to two and a half hours of entertainment, but along with a star-studded feature they were usually shown a newsreel, a cartoon and a humorous "short."

Renting vintage movies required a new selection routine. I reviewed the video catalogue at our home. Then I faxed Bill a list of classic films. He faxed back several selections to compensate for the fact that the video rental stores usually had only one copy of each title in stock and our first choices might not be available. One list was also supposed to cover several movie dates.

During the spring of 2005 we watched *The Petrified Forest* with Humphrey Bogart and Bette Davis; *Coogan's Bluff* with Clint Eastwood and Lee J. Cobb; and *The 39 Steps*, an Alfred Hitchcock thriller. All three had unlikable main characters, guns, violence, taut dialogue and first-rate acting. They had no social message or moral theme. Their sole objective was to evoke a mood. And they succeeded: for ninety minutes we forgot our travails.

We also saw *My Favorite Wife* with Cary Grant and Irene Dunne, a wacky, pre–World War II farce about a man who remarries after his wife is presumed lost in a shipwreck. Shortly after the wedding, the presumed-dead wife appears on the scene. She says that she spent seven years on a South Seas island with a handsome man with whom she had a dependent, affectionate and close—but always celibate—relationship. It was *Old School* for an earlier generation: belly laughs, unsubtle sexual jokes, implausible social situations, husbands and wives who seemed to enjoy embarrassing each other and hilarious mistaken identities. But pre–World War II raunchy farces included no profanity, no detailed discussions of sex acts, no toilet talk, no nudity—just plenty of innuendo, smirks, leers and body language.

We also regularly viewed made-for-TV World War II documentaries. They easily met both our time and our content requirements. Then in late spring the female member of our team spoke up for adding a few musicals to our repertoire. Since most musicals on DVD last substantially longer than ninety minutes, we agreed to split the time and watch a musical on two successive Saturday afternoons. One of our choices was Rodgers and Hammerstein's *South Pacific*. It had a World War II story line and its lilting, catchy lyrics were familiar. We enjoyed the first half of the DVD in early July. It was a nostalgic, fun afternoon.

VIII.

WE WERE ABOUT to start the second half of *South Pacific* when Bill told me that the end was near. It was between 2:00 and 2:30 on Saturday, July 30, 2005. The statement was straightforward, factual. There were no clever circumlocutions, just a simple statement.

As always, before we began the DVD, I asked Bill, "What's the latest on your health?"

He responded matter-of-factly, almost casually. It was as if I had asked about the weather or the previous night's Nationals baseball game.

"They discovered the growth is coming back," he said. "I am going off chemo. It's not doing much good."

He had just said, *I am going to die shortly. I have fought hard. But I have lost.* He was giving up chemotherapy, the side effects of which he found agonizing and debilitating. I was at a loss for words.

After a few seconds of awkward silence, I asked, "Does that mean that contraption in your throat [the tracheotomy tube] won't be coming out this summer?" He had expressed the hope that, if the chemotherapy was successful, the tube would be removed before the Court reconvened in October.

"Never," he replied.

That was it. Further talk about his health was pointless—and unwelcome.

Before we got Bill's news, *South Pacific* had seemed an ideal movie choice. Even though he could no longer sing along, he enjoyed hearing the familiar Rodgers and Hammerstein tunes. But now it was totally inappropriate. Still, we went through with the afternoon's agenda as planned. I wanted to go home, but Bill's matter-of-fact attitude made that impossible. "A Cockeyed Optimist" and "Happy Talk," with their cheerful, upbeat lyrics, made me cringe. After the movie ended, we chatted. Instead of agreeing that *South Pacific* was a poor movie choice for that day, we talked about how the idyllic scenery seemed out of place in a war story and how Ensign Nellie Forbush in a real battle zone would not have been allowed to flounce around in short shorts. Next time we agreed we would watch a classic crime film.

But, of course, there was no next time.

When Betty Nan and I finally got up to leave, all three of us were at a loss. It was an awkward moment. Articulate people became tongue-tied.

Neither "Good luck" nor "Good-bye" seemed appropriate.

Finally, Bill suggested I call during the week to discuss our next movie selection. Maybe it was time for another made-for-TV war documentary.

I agreed.

Then the three of us shook hands—silently.

IX.

BILL'S MATTER-OF-FACT DEMEANOR and terse statements could not hide his disappointment. He had fought valiantly and painfully. But he had failed. For six months—since the completion of his radiation regime around New Year's—he had believed that chemotherapy, with its myriad unpleasant side effects, would pay off. I feel certain that he believed his tracheotomy tube would be removed during the summer and that by October he would be a whole person once again.

At the conclusion of his radiation regimen in early January, Bill had reported that his cancer had been killed. He had read many of the gloomy prognoses that were reported in the newspapers and on TV, but he believed he was among the lucky few who had beaten the odds. He was proud of himself. He had approached his chemotherapy treatments optimistically. If successful, chemotherapy would shrink the dead growth so that it could be surgically excised.

I do not in any way doubt that Bill believed what he told me. Self-delusion was not part of his character. He would not have lied to me repeatedly. Every time I visited him or whenever we talked on the phone, I asked about his health. He expected it. Much of the chemotherapy was unpleasant and debilitating, and it required a few overnights in the hospital. He talked candidly about the chemo's side effects. But his long-term outlook was always upbeat—until the end of July.

X.

THE LAST TIME Bill and I visited was on August 19, 2005. Both of us knew there would not be many more visits, if any. Still, there were no maudlin musings. We enjoyed a half hour of talk: sports, salacious gossip about a mutual friend, politics, clippings and the program of The Mont Pelerin Society meeting in Iceland, for which I was leaving the next day.

In the three weeks since Bill had shared the news of his death sentence, we had talked on the phone often but he had discouraged visits. When I visited him on August 19, he had visibly deteriorated. His voice was much weaker. His body seemed to have shrunken. For the first time he had to use a walker to shuffle from his lounge chair to the bathroom, a distance of less than twenty feet. Previously he had walked to the bathroom unaided.

He was still up to reading portions of magazine articles, particularly offbeat ones about politics and sports. I brought with me current issues of *Sports Illustrated* and the *American Spectator*. I brought the latter because it included an article about politics by Conrad Black, the British-Canadian press magnate. I knew Bill admired Black's FDR biography. He once described it as one of the few 1,200-page books that he had read that would not have been improved if a good editor had cut it in half.

We talked mostly about the upcoming Mont Pelerin Society meeting in Reykjavik. When I showed him the program, he commented on the names of several of the speakers with whose writings he was familiar. He also picked up on the title of a paper by Mart Laar, a former prime minister of Estonia and a Hayek disciple. Laar's talk about how in a single decade Estonia had been transformed from a tiny Soviet republic into a booming capitalist, free-market exemplar was entitled, "The Road *from* Serfdom." For Bill and me this was full circle, and we both recognized it.

A shared interest in Friedrich Hayek's philosophy had helped establish the strong bond between us. The Estonian politician's clever play on the title of the Hayek book that had had such a profound effect on both of us made us laugh a little during an otherwise dour final visit.

I checked the time: a half hour had elapsed. I pointed at my watch.

Bill nodded in agreement. We both knew this might be our last visit together. Still, we pretended there would be more times when we could chat about politics, ideas, friends, literature, family, sports.

Neither of us wanted to say good-bye.

That would have been too final.

Bill's last words to me were "Be sure to send me a postcard from Reykjavik."

I did send the postcard. It told about the Estonian politician's paper, "The Road *from* Serfdom."

But it arrived the day after his death.

XI.

NEWS OF BILL'S death on September 3 did not come as a surprise. I had known that the end was near. Yet, that Saturday night was very special for me. It will not be forgotten.

When I returned home after seeing a movie with another couple, I learned I had received two phone calls earlier in the evening: one from Nancy Spears, Bill's daughter, and one from Janet Tramonte, his secretary. The two calls were separated by less than twenty minutes. Neither woman left a message. Their names were enough. They wanted me to learn the sad news from them before I heard it on TV or read it in the newspaper.

I found it ironic—symbolic as well—that Bill's family and staff could not inform me of his passing in a timely way because Betty Nan and I were at the movies with another couple. Since our movie-date threesome had seen almost all the films I wanted to see, we had rarely gone to the movies with other couples before Bill's illness.

Later that evening, when the cable news channels began broadcasting video clips of Bill's life and career, their superficiality and tediousness brought home to me how little the world knew about my friend.

They made me aware of how fortunate I had been to have enjoyed a long friendship with a multifaceted, unusual man who brought out the best in me.

I knew that sharing memories is one of the ways we keep from losing them. It is probably the best way. That night, when my mind was flooded with memories of our nineteen-year friendship, I began to consider whether the time had come for me to share some of my Bill Rehnquist experiences and recollections. It was only a fleeting thought on that Saturday night in September 2005. But it was one that did not go away.

During the ensuing months I thought, and rethought, about whether it would be worthwhile for me to share my memories with contemporaries, as well as scholars and historians for whom Bill Rehnquist was an important personage, but not a real person. On that night—and during the days and months that followed—I decided that I had a duty to tell the world about his many hidden sides.

FIFTEEN

REQUIEM

I.

BILL'S FUNERAL ON September 7, 2005, was as unusual and unique as he was. It is unlikely that anyone present had ever attended a similar ceremony. It opened with a simple welcoming talk by a prince of the Holy Roman Church, splendid and regal in his scarlet robe, sash and biretta. Immediately following his brief remarks, Theodore Cardinal McCarrick, archbishop of Washington, became virtually invisible when he turned over Washington's grand Roman Catholic cathedral to three Lutheran pastors from small suburban churches. The Protestant clerics conducted a Lutheran service titled "Celebration and Commitment" in a Roman Catholic shrine dedicated to the celebration of Masses. It was the first and only time the cathedral was the site of a Lutheran prayer service according to diocese records.

The incongruity between the cathedral's grandeur and the Lutheran rite's simplicity made the event unforgettable. The cathedral was built to awe. It seats two thousand in its main sanctuary, plus several hundred more in side chapels. A thirty-five-foot mosaic of Saint Matthew, the patron saint of civil servants, looks down benignly on all worshippers. The cathedral's splendor is apparent outside as well as inside. Its 190-foot dome towers over its neighborhood, where the maximum allowable building height is 110 feet.

The casket that lay before the cathedral's elaborate and majestic altar was a simple, unpainted pine box, the kind that is usually used to bury paupers, criminals who die in prison and Orthodox Jews. While family members and friends often deliver eulogies at funerals, at Bill's there were only "remembrances," including one by the president of the United States. Bill, who used words carefully and respected others who did, would have appreciated the fact that at his funeral there were no formal addresses that praised and honored him (eulogies) or expressions of sorrow and lamentation that mourned his passing (elegies), only simple, colloquial, nostalgic—and often amusing—talks (remembrances).

The cathedral's elegant grandeur could not change the mood of the service or the mourners. The mourners were there to celebrate the long life of a warmhearted, private man who cherished family and friendships. The importance of William Rehnquist's public office dictated that his funeral be held in a vast, elegant cathedral. The ceremony's simplicity contrasted starkly with the venue's grandeur. Few if any members of the congregation had previously witnessed a cathedral ceremony where a Roman Catholic cardinal wearing the stunning vestments of his high office played the modest role of a host welcoming guests to his home.

II.

TWO OF THE Lutheran pastors regularly officiated at the McLean, Virginia, church where Bill worshipped every Sunday. The third officiated at the Bethesda, Maryland, church where he worshipped regularly while his wife Nan was alive. The white-robed, bareheaded Protestant clerics who conducted the Lutheran rite were the ministers at suburban churches. Within the Lutheran Church's clerical hierarchy, they were near the bottom. They conducted their weekly rites in young community churches with pleasant but unimposing structures and more youth activities than funerals.

Bill enjoyed working in a pillared, carpeted, marble hall designed to awe. But he also enjoyed being an anonymous suburbanite far from Washington's glitz. President Bush spoke eloquently on behalf of the country Bill loved and served. While his was the only remembrance that was not personal, it still reflected warmth, familiarity and respect. All of the other speakers were frank, candid and often entertaining. They presented unaffected, from-the-heart reminiscences that were intended for a congregation of family, friends, admirers and colleagues. There were no lofty exhortations for divine blessings.

The funeral was typically Bill: hearty laughter and somber scripture readings, formulaic supplications and sentimental nostalgia. The president and vice president one row in front of law clerks, old friends and anonymous admirers. The talks were punctuated with elegiac organ chords. Even patriotism had a prominent part in the order of service. After the remembrances of President Bush and Justice O'Connor, but before the family remembrances, the congregation rose to sing all verses of "America the Beautiful."

Possibly the most poignant remembrance was the last. It was delivered by Bill's granddaughter Natalie (Nan Rehnquist's given name) Lynch, who lived nearby, attended church with him on Sundays and shared at least one evening meal with him each week. Natalie read a letter she had written to him during the summer when they both knew the end was near. He suggested that she read it at his funeral. It told how in a relaxed, giving way he had created a lasting bond with a teenage girl. She also related how her grandfather enjoyed bologna, jelly and mayonnaise sandwiches and tried to encourage his grandchildren to develop good memories, offering a shiny quarter to anyone who could recite the capitals of all fifty states.

Even President Bush embraced the neighborhood church mood. As Andy Stewart (Justice Potter Stewart's widow) was leaving the church with the Supreme Court justices and their wives, President Bush, an old family friend, left his pew and walked across the center aisle to kiss her (Justice Stewart had administered the vice presidential oath to George H. W. Bush in 1980 and 1984).

No tickets or special credentials were required for admittance to the cathedral. A relatively small section near the altar was roped off for justices, family, close friends, former clerks and federal judges. Senators and congressmen were seated on a first-come, first-seated basis, just like Lutheran Church of the Redeemer parishioners and Arlington neighbors.

III.

My PERSONAL RESPONSE to the masterfully staged funeral was disappointment. It was an unusual, eloquent, memorable event. The varied and diverse musical selections reflected the sophisticated tastes of the man whose life was being celebrated. Still, I did not find the service uplifting.

While I was unfamiliar with the liturgy of both the Roman Catholic Church and the Evangelical Lutheran Church, I was still fascinated by the cultural clash between the bare-bones Lutheran ritual and the cathedral's grandeur and opulence. Throughout the service, I kept looking back and forth from the cathedral's large and beautiful artifacts to the cardinal in his regal vestments to the president and the vice president seated in the front row next to the flag-draped pine box. I was observing superficialities because my emotional self was somewhere else.

My thoughts were on happy times I had shared with my friend Bill, on death's finality. The religious service was formal and impersonal— and grief-laden meditation is always personal and solitary. The contemplation of death, like death itself, is lonely.

The feeling of loneliness was heightened by the fact that I was separated from Betty Nan shortly before "the procession." We were sitting at the end of the fourth or fifth row unobtrusively holding hands when a young man in a black suit with a "button" in his right ear tapped Betty Nan on the shoulder. "Follow me," he said. He escorted her to a seat a few rows distant. Then a similarly garbed young man took her place next to me.

When the president attends an event such as this, Secret Service agents occupy most of the aisle seats. I understood and respected this. Still, I did not expect to find myself squeezed between an on-duty agent and a complete stranger at Bill's funeral.

IV.

ALL OF BILL'S friends were aware of his obsession with punctuality. Within the Supreme Court Building or socially, a "meeting time" was precisely described by the position of two hands on a clock. This applied equally to movie dates, parties, judicial conferences and Smithsonian board of regents meetings.

Still, Bill's own funeral began fifteen minutes late. At ten minutes past the scheduled starting time, Mike Tramonte, the husband of Bill's longtime secretary, who was seated in front of me, held up his arm and pointed at his watch. "You can tell he's upstairs," Mike said. "If he was here, this show would be rolling along by now."

V.

LOW-KEY FUNERALS WERE the Rehnquist way. When Bill's wife, Nan, died in 1991, her funeral was conducted in the suburban Emmanuel Lutheran Church. It was a simple religious rite devoid of personal remembrances or special music. There was no indication that it was the funeral of a prominent person, except that there were two reserved sections near the front of the church. As mourners entered the church, uniformed security guards from the Supreme Court discreetly checked their clipboards to determine in what section an invited guest should be seated. Emmanuel Lutheran's pastor, the Reverend Jan P. Locking-bill, who was one of the three Lutheran clergymen who officiated at Bill's funeral, conducted the entire service at Nan's.

Visitation, the night before Nan's funeral, was held in a second-floor parlor of Joseph Gawler's Sons funeral home in northwest Washington. The Rehnquist family greeted friends in an unostentatious, commercial undertaking establishment with a large neon sign on the front lawn.

While the funeral home had been notified in advance, and Secret Service men were hidden throughout the building, visitors were unaware of their presence (at least, I did not recognize them) until sirens signaled that President George H. W. Bush and his wife, Barbara, were approaching. Conversations were interrupted and visitors were quickly ushered into a nearby parlor, where Secret Service personnel maintained surveillance while the president and his wife visited with the Rehnquist family. While the Bush family was paying its respects to the Rehnquist family, all traffic on the streets near the Gawler's funeral home was diverted, and no cars were allowed in or out of the funeral parlor's parking lot.

VI.

THE LOCAL WASHINGTON newspapers praised Washington's Theodore Cardinal McCarrick for his generosity and ecumenicism in allowing the Roman Catholic Church's sacred cathedral to be used for a Protestant service conducted by Lutheran ministers. But within the church's vast hierarchy as well as within the Washington Diocese's leadership, there were dissenters. Some felt strongly. They said it was a desecration. More than a century earlier the cathedral had been consecrated to the service of the Holy Roman Church, they said. To use its altar for a religious service other than a Mass was contrary to the purpose for which it was built and specifically dedicated.

Although this aspect of the event was glossed over in the secular press, the Catholic News Service thought it important enough to distribute to its clients a detailed analysis of the underlying issues. "Both the Code of Canon Law and the Directory for the Application of Principles have provisions that give a local bishop authority to allow services of other faiths in Catholic churches," it explained. "While Catholic churches are generally reserved for Catholic worship the local bishop may decide to allow their use by other faiths."

While there was never an attempt to establish a quid pro quo between the use of the cathedral and Bill's decisions as a Supreme Court justice, many editors of Catholic newspapers juxtaposed the cathedral story with paragraphs praising Bill's dissents in *Roe v. Wade* in 1973 and in *Planned Parenthood v. Casey* in 1992. No member of the Supreme Court had a more consistent anti-abortion record than Bill.

VII.

THE REHNQUIST FUNERAL was the second to be conducted for a Supreme Court justice in the Cathedral of St. Matthew the Apostle, and it was by far the less controversial of the two. Justice William Brennan's 1997 funeral Mass, which was celebrated in the same cathedral, caused a loud furor. Justice Brennan, a lifelong Roman Catholic parishioner, had voted with the majority in *Roe v. Wade*.

Many prominent Catholics, both laymen and clergy, believed Justice Brennan had sinned and was unworthy of one of the Church's highest honors: a requiem Mass in a cathedral. Several groups petitioned the Church's hierarchy to deny him final sacraments. Others felt that, even if he were granted his church's final rites, it was inappropriate to honor him in the sacred, grand and prestigious Cathedral of St. Matthew. In the end, a requiem Mass was celebrated for Justice Brennan in the cathedral. But, while President Clinton eulogized Justice Brennan, the religious service was conducted by two young priests and a monsignor. The fact that neither a cardinal nor a bishop participated was interpreted by many as a not-too-subtle statement by the Catholic Church's leadership.

While the requiem Mass was being celebrated in the cathedral, the anti-abortion group Rescue America staged a protest rally on the street in front. The demonstrators issued a press release that claimed that a Catholic church was "desecrated" when it honored "a man who was a key figure in expanding abortion rights in America."

Many Catholic editors wrote critical editorials. "Justice Brennan was a Catholic, but he fell prey to the worst heresy of our secularist age: the errant belief that Catholic citizens should somehow 'separate out' their faith from their public service . . ." the *Arlington Catholic Herald* in suburban Washington said. "While he should be commended for his passionate opposition to racism and sexism, he must also be exposed for his complicity in the most brutal decision in all of American jurisprudence."

VIII.

THE POST-FUNERAL RECEPTION in the Supreme Court Building was a casual, relaxed, wine–and–hors d'oeuvres social event, little more. It had neither the somber mood of a gathering of mourners nor the gaiety of a party. Its only connection with the funeral was that the same people were present and the socializing was taking place in the building where the dead man had gone to work for three decades. For two hours no family member was present. There was no guest book to sign, no receiving line. Only a few justices were present. Most of them drifted off before the family made its first appearance.

For former Rehnquist law clerks, the reception was like the last reunion of a military unit. Over the years the law clerks had gone their different ways, but like nostalgic former warriors they were drawn together by a profound experience that had demanded their best and altered their lives. They would always share a Bill Rehnquist experience. Without Bill in attendance, future reunions, if any, would be sterile and likely dull. Since their service spanned the thirty-three years Bill served on the Court, most were not even contemporaries. Several of Bill's earliest clerks had already retired, while the youngest ones were testing what parts of the profession most appealed to them.

All former clerks had been notified of Bill's death on Sunday, September 4. They came from all over the world to pay their final respects and to visit with each other for what would likely be the last time. Thirty-one had served as pallbearers. After the reception they returned to their respective homes. The bond which held them together was broken.

When the family finally arrived after participating in graveside rites at Arlington National Cemetery, they entered unobtrusively through a back door and did not attempt to form a receiving line. The main attractions at the reception were chief justice designate John Roberts (Bill's clerk in 1980–81) and his wife, Jane. Mourners waited in line to chat with them. Incumbent justices and family members received far less attention. His presence gave the event an upbeat, "The king is dead, long live the king" mood.

IX.

Burial in Arlington National Cemetery was appropriate for the Rehnquists. Nan had been buried there in 1991 beneath a stone Bill had selected and designed. Bill had spent almost half of his eighty years in his country's service, including three years on active duty in the Army Air Corps during World War II.

For most Americans, any reference to Arlington National Cemetery conjures up images of military pomp and ceremony: riderless horses with reversed boots, muffled drums, ancient caissons, honor guards with fixed bayonets, and fife-and-drum corps in Revolutionary War uniforms. But that is only a tiny part of one of America's great institutions. Buried beneath row on row of simple markers are the remains of more than three hundred thousand soldiers and sailors who achieved no great distinction in life, whose names and whose families are long forgotten, but who wished to join a final bivouac of men and women who had served their country with devotion and pride.

The shortest route from Bill's home in Northern Virginia to his chambers passes by Arlington National Cemetery. It was part of his life for several minutes every workday. It was a familiar place. It was an important landmark in his home community. Bill had attended burial services there often, for contemporaries and neighbors as well as Supreme Court colleagues. But he never viewed Arlington National Cemetery as a grand monument to noble warriors and glorious victories. Rather, it was a very large country churchyard that served the needs of a large, patriotic community, of which he was a part.

While all honorably discharged veterans and their spouses are eligible for burial in Arlington National Cemetery, nonveterans can be buried there only after receiving a special waiver from the president or the secretary of the Army. Only slightly more than three hundred waivers have been granted since the Department of the Army began keeping records. Eight of those have been issued for Supreme Court justices and their spouses: William O. Douglas, Thurgood Marshall, Harry Blackmun and Warren Burger, none of whom had served in the military.

Before 1982 only three Supreme Court justices were buried in Arlington National Cemetery, none of whom required waivers: Oliver Wendell Holmes Jr., a battle-wounded Civil War hero; Hugo Black, a World War I artillery captain; and William Howard Taft, a former commander in chief and a former secretary of war. But eight out of the eleven justices who have died since 1982 have been buried there. (Half were veterans.) Neither cemetery nor court officials can explain why almost three-fourths of the justices who have died in the past twenty-five years have wanted to be buried in Arlington National Cemetery, while almost none of their predecessors did.

For almost a century, since the dedication of the Tomb of the Unknowns in 1921, Arlington National Cemetery has been one of Washington's most popular visitor venues. The Tomb of the Unknowns was dedicated to the memory of the thousands of American soldiers whose remains could not be identified in the midst of battlefield carnage. Since its dedication, it has been guarded around the clock every day by specially trained soldiers who are members of the United States Army's "Old Guard." Although visitors have always been fascinated by the precise marching of the Old Guard and the tomb's stark but splendid simplicity, interest in the cemetery skyrocketed after the well-publicized burials of John and Robert Kennedy there. It currently attracts more than 7 million visitors annually.

For Bill, Arlington National Cemetery was a natural. He lived in Arlington, and the cemetery was part of his local community. But most important, love of country defined his life, and he belonged in a community of patriots.

AFTERWORD

I.

My contribution to Bill Rehnquist's portrait is now complete. A treasured friendship has been brought to a close.

The act of closure has also been an act of opening. The small details aggregated here have opened to public view little-known but significant facets of Bill's personality and character. I have embraced the portraitist's technique of selection. While it may appear random at times, that is appropriate. Much of life itself is random. Therefore, in the end, it enhances understanding.

It is difficult to establish a clear linkage between a public official's personal life and his work, between his values and his actions, between his quirks and his writings. The linkage is almost always obscure. Often it is actually hidden. Yet, it is real and substantive, important and abiding. Frequently a friend's memoir is better able to show the linkage than a learned narrative. Still, this book is not about the profession of judging or its consequences. It is about a man who earned his living as a judge, a yarn in which the protagonist was a judge.

All biographical writing includes a subjective, personal component. It is inescapable. While the subjective component can be distortive, revisionist, perverse or just plain dishonest, it more often adds to a biography's legitimacy, as I believe it does here. On the rare occasions when friendship and truth seemed to be at odds, I have served truth for friendship's sake.

I have portrayed a man of high character who was honest, disciplined, dedicated to his profession and his country—and very smart. Still, he, like all of us, had personality quirks. They were interesting and revealing. Many were funny. A few were annoying. Some he joked about with friends and family. None were manifestations of deep character flaws. Depiction of the subject's blemishes is an essential part of portraiture.

II.

BEFORE BILL WAS buried, President Bush had named his successor. At the apex of government, succession had been timely, orderly and seamless. Still, Bill's death created a great void at the Supreme Court. The old order had passed. John Roberts, the new chief justice, brought with him the perspectives and insights of a new generation. He was born in 1955, the same year as Bill's son, Jim, a decade after the end of World War II.

While the succession at the Supreme Court was smooth, the change was profound. Bill's perspective could not be replicated. The knowledge and life experiences he brought to the job were his—and his alone. His outlook was unique to his generation, to his time in history.

Bill and I shared a generational perspective. Like most boys who graduated from high school in 1942, while still teenagers we had already acquired a deep-seated and personal understanding of the power of government. And we dreaded it. We knew that shortly after our eighteenth birthdays the government of the United States of America, the government of the democracy that we loved, could take away our liberty. We knew that after a few months training, a low-level military bureaucrat could send us on a new assignment. It might be for more training. But it also might be to some contested barricade where our deaths were likely, probably inevitable. This youthful experience with government power in the United States affected our thinking the rest of our lives. Understanding this is part of fathoming Bill.

III.

IN DIVERSE CIRCUMSTANCES I have shown Bill's dislike of ostentation. He often referred to himself as a public servant. It was a description he liked. He understood that a servant, public or private, had a master. His master was the people of the United States of America. He was secure in the knowledge that he was empowered by the Constitution of the United States. He could be removed from office only by impeachment. He did not need to be reassured about his importance— by anybody. It allowed him to bring extraordinary energy and focus to his work without the need to seek prominent friendships, high-level associations or a social circle that would bolster his ego.

IV.

THE THIRD ANNIVERSARY of Bill's death has now passed. I am happy that this task has been completed on a timely basis. With each turn of a calendar page, memories become more blurred, more remote. This is the way of life. Still, a great, gaping void remains. Even if its outlines have become blurred, its dimensions have not diminished.

My feeling of loss—like my portrait of my friend—is best described through superficialities. When aggregated, they tell a story. I go to the movies less often now than when Bill was alive. I have not found a luncheon companion with whom I can play memory games. I never drop rhymes or quotations into dinner conversations because I fear looking like a smart aleck. This year I watched the World Series alone.

There is no incentive to read a book promptly so I can discuss it before a movie starts, or at lunch, or on the phone; I therefore read fewer books. While many of my friends can discuss politics intelligently, none have Bill's knowledge and informed understanding of political history, process and people. Each time I chat with someone who is supposed to have a unique understanding of the electoral process, I long for Bill.

V.

After death, it is all metaphysical. There are no events, no experiences, no conversations, no jokes. There are only abstractions: mourning, nostalgia, melancholia.

My friendship with Bill grew out of a shared respect for poetry's capacity to evoke profound feelings, to give unity and meaning to the transcendental, to help people fathom life's mysteries. It is appropriate, therefore, to share these lines from a contemporary elegy:

> The dead abide, as grief knows.
> We are what we have lost.

ACKNOWLEDGMENTS

ATTEMPTING TO EXPLAIN and fathom the character of a historic figure who was also a dear friend has been daunting. Yet, the task has also been fulfilling and enjoyable. To a large extent this is attributable to the wise and good-humored advice and encouragement I have received from loyal friends and family. I have received editorial guidance from experienced editors who were familiar with the techniques of historians and biographers, from professionals who had worked in the chambers of the chief justice and the Administrative Office of the United States Courts, from published authors who understood the art and craft of writing books and from well-read friends.

Jim Sadkovich, who edited my last book, *Soldiering for Freedom*, at the Texas A&M University Press, helped me visualize how a disconnected series of essays could be organized into a narrative. Steve Strasser, a friend and former *Newsweek* editor, helped me to understand a memoir's structure and purpose. I discussed matters involving law, taste, protocol and privacy—as well as stylish writing—with Sally M. Rider, director of the Rehnquist Center at The University of Arizona James E. Rogers College of Law and Bill's chief of staff from 2000 until his death; David A. Sellers, assistant director of the Administrative Office of the United States Courts; and Thomas McGough, a partner in ReedSmith, an international law firm, who was Bill's 1979–80 law clerk. Richard Rahn, Leslie D. Simon and my daughter Roni Obermayer Atnipp are published authors and excellent writers. They critiqued my book in terms of its viability in the literary marketplace. Charles McKittrick and Ted Peyser reviewed the completed manuscript the week before I submitted it to the publisher. My talented friends, each in his or her own way, challenged my assumptions, and helped me to see my work with perspective. The importance of their contribution and the depth of my appreciation cannot be overstated. Still, none rewrote as much as a complete paragraph. No part of this book has been ghostwritten.

Putting pen to paper is only one part of writing a book. Other friends have given me invaluable help in other areas. Some have talked with me about strategies, history, relationships, biases and the United States legal system; others have helped me to make contacts; and others contributed special skills as artists and photographers. Each has helped in a special and unique way. To all I am deeply grateful. This group includes Scott Boseley, Marji Ross, Al Leeds, Herbert and Jeanne Hansell, James Heller, Arthur S. Obermayer, Richard Weintraub, Bob Madani, Alfred Regnery, Grayson Hanes, Malinda Waughtal, David Swanson, Joyce Barnathan, Samantha Solleveld, Jerry and Laurie Feinberg, Robert Hormats and Mary Lenn Dixon.

I am a journalist who typed his own stories on a daily basis for many years, but I never felt that I wrote as well at a keyboard as I did with a ballpoint pen on a ruled pad. Therefore, this entire work has been written in longhand. My scrawl has been deciphered by Cathy Wilson, who has been my secretary and office assistant for fifteen years. I acknowledge with gratitude her devotion and her ability to deal with my many idiosyncrasies.

Research for this book has been done in public and university libraries, newspaper and institutional archives, public record rooms and on the internet. In all of this I have been assisted by Regina A. Lee of Wickliffe, Ohio, and Barbara van Woerken and Beth Shankle, research librarians at the National Press Club's Eric Friedheim National Journalism Library in Washington, D.C. All three are bright and resourceful young women who understand that successful researchers must be both creative and diligent.

I have resisted the temptation to stay in touch with the Rehnquist family. Since Bill's funeral I have no had contact with them. (I chatted briefly in 2006 with Janet Rehnquist at a mutual friend's retirement party.) If I had solicited their opinions, plumbed their memories or allowed them to review my manuscript, I would have produced a vastly different book. This is not a book of consensus. It is a personal memoir buttressed by extensive research into public records, books and periodicals.

Ed Schlesinger, who edited this book at Pocket Books, has a deep understanding of what makes narrative flow and what makes a book interesting. He has taught me much.

My agent, Sam Fleishman of Literary Artists Representatives, has become a friend as well as a business colleague. In addition to representing me as a literary agent, he has counseled me on other matters, both financial and intellectual. He is very smart.

Ever since our wedding in 1955, Betty Nan and I have faced all of life's challenges and adventures together. We are a happy team. Her enduring and abiding love is what makes each day on life's journey a joy. In the development of this particular book she played a special role. And my gratitude goes beyond that of an author to a loyal, devoted and perceptive spouse. Bill was Betty Nan's friend as well as mine. They liked and respected each other. If they had not, Bill's relationship with me would not have flourished as it did.

Arlington, Virginia
April 2009

NOTES AND SOURCES

PREFACE

Dartmouth College Green Book for the Class of 1946, Volume XXXII, Hanover, NH, 1942 (freshman annual of the class of 1946; Herman J. Obermayer and James Heller are classmates).

Hustler Magazine, Inc. and Larry G. Flynt v. Jerry Falwell, U.S. Supreme Court, 485 U.S. 46 (1988).

Internet: "Gage Academy of Art, Seattle, Thomas Loepp"; Thomas Loepp promotional literature.

Justice: The Memoirs of Attorney General Richard G. Kleindienst by Richard G. Kleindienst, Jamison Books, Ottawa, IL, 1985.

New Orleans Times Picayune, "Miss Levy Weds Mr. Obermayer," New Orleans, LA, June 29, 1955.

Presidential Proclamation, Office of White House Press Secretary, September 4, 2005 (ordering that the flags on all federal buildings be flown at half-staff).

Ralph Waldo Emerson, Essays & Lectures, The Library of America, New York, 1983, p. 339 ("Friendship").

Roe v. Wade, U.S. Supreme Court, 410 U.S. 113 (1973).

San Diego Union, "Ceremonies, Large Receptions of Summer's Most-Feted Brides," San Diego, CA, August 30, 1953, p. D-1.

San Diego Union, "San Diego Obituaries," San Diego, CA, September 9, 1962, p. A-16 (Dr. Harold D. Cornell).

Shorewood (WI) High School Yearbook 1942.

Soldiering for Freedom: A GI's Account of World War II by Herman J. Obermayer, Texas A&M University Press, College Station, TX, 2005.

The Rehnquist Choice: The Untold Story of the Nixon Appointee That Redefined the Supreme Court by John W. Dean, Simon & Schuster, New York, 2001.

The Road to Serfdom by Friedrich A. Hayek, The University of Chicago Press, Chicago, IL, 1944.

The Washington Post, Washington, D.C., October 20, 1991 (Natalie Rehnquist Dead).

Who's Who in America 2004, Marquis Who's Who, New Providence, NJ.

CHAPTER ONE

A History of Washington Golf and Country Club: A Century of Tradition 1894–1994, Arlington, VA, 1994 (presidents who have belonged to the club).

A. Linwood Holton was governor of Virginia 1970 to 1974. He was the first Republican governor of Virginia since Reconstruction.

Alice's Adventures in Wonderland by Lewis Carroll, London, 1865.

Booknotes, "The Supreme Court," Interview with Brian Lamb (C-SPAN), Washington, D.C., April 10, 2001.

Economic Affairs, "Looking Back at the Condensed Version *(Reader's Digest)* of *The Road to Serfdom* After Sixty Years" by John Blundell, Oxford, England, March 2004.

"Elegy Written in a Country Churchyard" by Thomas Gray, London, 1751 (*The Oxford Book of English Verse: 1250–1900*, edited by Arthur Quillen Couch, Oxford University Press, Oxford, England, 1900).

Grand Rapids Press, "Neighbors Liked Visits From 'Bill,' " Grand Rapids, MI, September 5, 2005 (Jean Lauren, Rehnquist's sister, was marketing executive in Grand Rapids).

National Personnel Records Center, St. Louis, MO. "Soldier's Qualifications Card—William Hubbs Rehnquist."

Oklahoma! "Oh, What a Beautiful Morning" by Richard Rodgers and Oscar Hammerstein II, New York, 1943.

Porgy and Bess, "It Ain't Necessarily So" by George and Ira Gershwin, New York, 1935.

Reflections on Ice-Breaking by Ogden Nash, 1924.

1776 by David McCullough, Simon & Schuster, New York, 2005.

Showboat, "Ol' Man River" by Oscar Hammerstein II and Jerome Kern, adapted from a novel by Edna Ferber, 1929.

South Pacific, "You've Got to Be Carefully Taught" by Richard Rodgers and Oscar Hammerstein II, adapted from James A. Michener's *Tales of the South Pacific*, New York, 1949.

Thatcher's People: An Insider's Account of the Politics, the Power, and the Personalities by John Ranelagh, HarperCollins, London, 1991.

The Bible, Psalm 23 (Old Testament).

"The Deserted Village" by Oliver Goldsmith, London, 1770.

The Downing Street Years by Margaret Thatcher, HarperCollins, New York, 1993, pp. 12–13.

The Road to Serfdom by Friedrich A. Hayek, The University of Chicago Press, Chicago, IL, 1944.

Virginia House of Burgesses, Williamsburg, VA, March 23, 1775 (Patrick Henry).

Washington Post, "Bechtel to Move Jobs to Frederick County," May 15, 1998, p. B-3.

"We Shall Overcome," theme song of the Civil Rights movement in America in the 1950s and 1960s. It was adapted from a traditional gospel hymn.

CHAPTER TWO

Berlin Evening Journal, Berlin, WI, June 7, 1877; November 14, 1877; September 1, 1891; April 7, 1900; June 17, 1911; June 19, 1911; November 24, 1952 (various articles about Margery Peck Rehnquist's family).

Census of the United States, Reports of Population; Race Breakdown, Milwaukee, Shorewood, 1930, 1940, Wisconsin Historical Society.

Fifteenth and Sixteenth Census of the United States, Reports of Population, Racial Makeup, Milwaukee.

Fox Point-Bayside-River Hills Herald, "Supreme Moment: Chief Justice Gives Mom a Courtly Birthday Bash," East Berlin, WI, May 7, 1987 (Margery P. Rehnquist, AAUW).

Images of America: Shorewood, Wisconsin, Shorewood Historical Society, Arcadia Publishing, Chicago, 2000.

Images of America: West Milwaukee, West Milwaukee Historical Society, Arcadia Publishing, Chicago, 2005.

Internet: www.andyhardyfilms.com (Andy Hardy fans home page).

Internet: www.hellomilwaukee.com/census (demographic characteristics of Milwaukee).

Internet: www.kenyon.edu (Kenyon College).

Internet: www.kenyonreview.org *(Kenyon Review).*

Internet: www.roadsideamerica.com (Ripon, Wisconsin, birthplace of the Republican Party).

Internet: www.shorewoodschools.org/sch.; www.shorewoodhistory.org/history (Shorewood High School).

Internet: www.spwi.org (Victor Berger and Socialist Party in Milwaukee).

Milwaukee Journal, "Member North Shore Republican Organization," Milwaukee, WI, December 24, 1971 (William B. Rehnquist).

Milwaukee Sentinel, "Rehnquist Dies, Father of Justice," Milwaukee, WI, July 13, 1973 (William B. Rehnquist obituary).

Milwaukee Sentinel, "Rehnquist's Mother Dies," Milwaukee, WI, September 26, 1988.

New York Times, "La Follette Death Ends Era in West, Hope for Progressive Comeback Diminishes—Party Once Was Supreme Power in State," February 26, 1953.

Presidential Election Results, Milwaukee Board of Elections Commission, Milwaukee, Shorewood, 1932, 1936, 1940, Wisconsin Historical Society.

Shorewood Class of 1942 Reunion Booklet (1980). Robert Brachman described himself as "President of Henri's Foods Products, manufacturers of dressings for salads" (where he had been employed thirty years). In the 1991 yearbook, he said he had been retired for five years.

University of Wisconsin, Academic Transcript, Margery Anne Peck, Class of 1918.

University of Wisconsin, Milwaukee, Division of Archives and Special Collections, UNW Libraries, Golda Meir Library, Milwaukee, WI (City Club of Milwaukee, minutes, correspondence, brochures, etc.).

CHAPTER THREE

Arizona Daily Star, "Richard K. Kleindienst, Watergate Figure, Dies at 76," Tucson, AZ, February 4, 2000.

Arizona Election Results 1952, 1956, 1960, 1964, 1968, Arizona Secretary of State, Phoenix.

Arizona Politicians: The Noble and the Notorious by James W. Johnson, University of Arizona Press, Tucson, AZ, 2002, pp. 177–183.

Arizona Republic, Phoenix, AZ, September 21, 1963; October 11, 1963; October 12, 1963; February 11, 1964; July 16, 1964; July 20, 1964 (Kitchel and Kleindienst lead Goldwater presidential campaign).

Barry Goldwater by Robert Allen Goldberg, Yale University, New Haven, CT, 1995, pp. 127, 143, 144, 256.

Before the Storm: Barry Goldwater and the Unmaking of the American Consensus by Rick Pearlstein, Farrar, Straus & Giroux (Hill & Wang), New York, 2001, pp. 363, 418, 424, 461 and 511.

Flying High: Remembering Barry Goldwater by William F. Buckley, Jr., Basic Books, New York, 2008, p. 135.

History of the Class of 1930 Yale College, New Haven, CT.

History of the Class of 1930 Yale College—Twenty Year Yearbook, 1950, New Haven, CT.

In April 1947 Friedrich Hayek convened thirty-six scholars, historians and philosophers from around the world who shared an interest in free market economics and classical liberalism. Hayek believed these concepts were becoming extinct in Europe following World War II. The group met at Mont Pelerin, Switzerland. They formed a society which was to meet at regular intervals to discuss the future of classical liberalism. Among those attending that initial meeting were Ludwig Erhard (future chancellor of West Germany) and two Americans who later won Nobel Prizes in economic science (Milton Friedman and George Stigler). Hayek also won a Nobel Prize in economic science.

Independent: A Biography of Lewis W. Douglas by Robert Paul Browder and Thomas G. Smith, Alfred A. Knopf, New York, 1986.

Internet: www.phoenix.gov/citagov/history.

Justice: The Memoirs of Attorney General Richard Kleindienst by Richard G. Kleindienst, Jamison Books, Ottawa, IL, 1985.

Martindale-Hubbell Law Directory, Martindale-Hubbell, Inc., Summit, NJ (listing of lawyers and law firms in Phoenix, AZ, 1954 to 1968).

Minneapolis Morning Tribune, Minneapolis, MN, July 12, 1952 (Warren Burger's role in switching Harold Stassen votes to Dwight Eisenhower at 1952 Republican Convention).

The Arizona Republic, "Denison Kitchel, Adviser to Goldwater Campaign," Phoenix, AZ, October 23, 2002 (obituary).

The Arizona Republic, "Naomi Douglas Kitchel," Phoenix, AZ, April 2, 2004 (paid funeral notice).

The Glorious Disaster: Barry Goldwater's Presidential Campaign and the Origins of the Conservative Movement by J. William Middendorf II, Basic Books, New York, 2006.

The Making of the President 1964 by Theodore H. White, Athenaeum Publishers, New York, 1965.

The Mont Pelerin Society met in Reykjavik, Iceland, August 21–24, 2005. Papers were delivered under the general rubric "Liberty and Property in the Twenty-first Century."

The Rehnquist Choice: The Untold Story of the Nixon Appointee That Redefined the Supreme Court by John W. Dean, Simon & Schuster, New York, 2001.

The Supreme Court: How It Was, How It Is by William H. Rehnquist, William Morrow & Company, Inc., New York, 1987; revised edition, Alfred A. Knopf, New York, 2001.

Time, "The Head Honcho," July 17, 1964.

Time, "Kleindienst Steps Up," February 28, 1972.

Touring the Upper East Side: Walks in Five Historic Districts, New York Landmarks Conservancy, 1995 (Colony Club).

What Happened to Goldwater? The Inside Story of the 1964 Republican Campaign by Steven Shadegg, Holt, Rinehart and Winston, New York, 1965.

Yale College '92 Class Book, New Haven, CT (William Lloyd Kitchel, father; James E. Wheeler, uncle).

CHAPTER FOUR

Arlington County Official Election Results, 1980 to 2004, The Electoral Board and Office of Voter Registration (precinct results).

Arlington County Profile 2005, FAQ, Department of Community Planning Housing & Development.

Arlington County (VA) Central Library, "Grand Opening," December 12, 1992.

Arlington County, Virginia: A Modern History by Sherman Pratt, Book Crafters, Chelsea, MI, 1997.

Arlington Heritage: Vignettes of a Virginia County by Eleanor Lee Templeman, published by the author, 1959.

Citizen, Arlington County, Virginia, Fall 1992 (library dedication).

District of Columbia: A Bicentennial History by Daniel L. Lewis, Norton, NY, 1976.

Hearings Before the Senate Committee on the Judiciary on the Nomination of Justice William Hubbs Rehnquist to Be Chief Justice of the United States, July 29, 30, 31 and August 1, 1986. Senate Hearing pp. 99–1067. Senator Patrick Leahy, p. 265.

Internet: www.citydata.com/city/Greensboro-VT; www.greensboro.gov office.com (Greensboro, VT, description and data).

Internet: www.mountainviewcountryclubvt.com (Mountain View Country Club, Greensboro, VT).

Internet: www.oha.alexandriava.gov/bhrc (slave markets in Alexandria, VA).

New York Times, "Rehnquist Hearing Turns Town to Deed Pondering," August 2, 1986.

Old Dominion Citizens' Association Neighborhood Conservation Plan, March 2002 ("The Birches" history).

Planning Research and Analysis Team: Rock Spring Data; XLS, XLS, Arlington County Planning Division.

Princeton Connection: A Century of Princetonians in Greensboro, Vermont by John C. Stone II (Greetings and Reflections Project of Princeton University's 250th Anniversary Celebration), Princeton, NJ, 1996, 1998.

Promotion brochure, Highland Lodge and Caspian Lake, Greensboro, VT.

Racial Composition of Arlington, Virginia, 1990 and 2000, Bureau of Census, U.S. Department of Commerce, Washington, D.C.

Washington Post, "Surreal Estate," January 20, 2006, p. C-3 (sale of Rehnquist townhouse).

Time, "Through the Wringer," August 11, 1986.

Washington Prime Properties LLC sales brochure. Includes full description of the Rehnquist townhome in Arlington, VA, October 2005.

CHAPTER FIVE

Arizona Daily Star, Tuscon, AZ, April 10, 1964; April 28, 1964; April 29, 1964; May 2, 1964; May 7, 1964; May 13, 1964; May 14, 1964; May 15, 1964; May 19, 1964; May 21, 1964; May 22, 1964; May 26, 1964; May 27, 1964; May 29, 1964; June 4, 1964; June 6, 1964; June 9, 1964; June 17, 1964 (articles in which William Rehnquist's name appeared during the impeachment trial before the Arizona Senate).

Arizona Republic, Phoenix, AZ, (reference to Rehnquist role in 1964 impeachment trial). February 20, 1964; February 27, 1964; April 11, 1964; April 21, 1964; October 22, 1971.

Essay on Warren Hastings by Thomas Babington Macaulay (edited by Joseph Villiers-Denney), University Press of the Pacific, San Francisco, CA, 2002.

Grand Inquests: The Historic Impeachments of Justice Samuel Chase and President Andrew Johnson by William H. Rehnquist, William Morrow & Company, Inc., New York, 1992.

Jesse Addison Udall Manuscript Collection (MS 311), University of Arizona, Tucson, AZ.

The Senate voted 59–41 on February 9, 1999, in favor of opening to the press its deliberations during the "verdict stage" of the Bill Clinton impeachment trial. The motion failed because it required 67 votes to change a Senate rule. The rule affecting deliberations on an impeachment verdict have been part of the Senate rules since the nineteenth century.

CHAPTER SIX

Breaking the Deadlock: The 2000 Election, the Constitution and the Court by Richard A. Posner, Princeton University Press, Princeton, NJ, 2001.

Centennial Crisis: The Disputed Election of 1876 by William H. Rehnquist, Alfred A. Knopf, New York, 2004, pp. 5–6, 119, 220–48.

Harvard Law Review, "The Supreme Court 2000 Term, Comment: *Bush v. Gore* and Its Disguises: Freeing *Bush v. Gore* from Its Hall of Mirrors" by Laurence H. Tribe, Vol. 115, 2001, pp. 297–98.

New York Times, November 7 to December 13, 2000 (general coverage of election dispute).

Supreme Injustice: How the High Court Hijacked Election 2000 by Alan M. Dershowitz, Oxford University Press, 2001.

The Longest Night: Polemics and Perspective on Election 2000, edited by Arthur J. Jacobson and Michael Rosenfeld, University of California Press, Los Angeles, CA, 2002.

The Votes that Counted: How the Court Decided the 2000 Presidential Election by Howard Gilman, University of Chicago Press, Chicago, 2001.

Too Close to Call: The Thirty-Six-Day Battle to Decide the 2000 Election by Jeffrey Toobin, Random House, New York, 2001.

Washington Post, November 7 to December 13, 2000 (general coverage of election dispute).

Washington Post, "The Nominee: For Mukasey, Some Questions about (His) Security," October 16, 2007.

CHAPTER SEVEN

A Social Statement on the Death Penalty, Evangelical Lutheran Church of America, September 19, 1991.

Board of Education of Kiryas Joel Village School District vs. Louis Grumet, U.S. Supreme Court, 512 U.S. 687 (1994).

City of Boerne vs. P. F. Flores, Archbishop of San Antonio, U.S. Supreme Court, 521 U.S. 507 (1997).

Collected Poems of T. S. Eliot, 1909–1935, "Ash Wednesday," Harcourt Brace & Company, New York, 1936, p. 109.

Correspondence. Regina A. Lee and Susan Gibbs, Director of Communications, Archdiocese of Washington, D.C. (list of presidents and Supreme Court justices who attended the Red Mass since 1990).

Internet: www.johncarrollsociety.org (history of the John Carroll Society, purpose and events of the Society).

Internet: The Huffington Post, Alan M. Dershowitz, September 4, 2005.

Passover Haggadah: Obermayer Family Seder. During the years when William Rehnquist attended the Obermayer Family Seder, the service followed a special family Haggadah written/compiled for the exclusive use of the Obermayer family. (A Haggadah is a special prayer book for the first nights of Passover.)

Plymouth United Church of Christ Records, University of Wisconsin Milwaukee, Division of Archives and Special Collections, UWM Libraries, Golda Meier Library, Milwaukee, WI (Rehnquist family activities at Plymouth Church, United Church of Christ 1925–54).

Reformed Jewish Voice of New York, 2007 (opposition to the death penalty).

Religious Action Center of Reformed Judaism Press Release: "The Largest Jewish Organization Calls Supreme Court Ruling a Devastating Blow to Religious Liberty" (Rabbi David Saperstein, director, said, "Today's decision in Flores will go down in history with Dred Scott . . . among the worse mistakes this court has ever made"), June 25, 1997.

Supreme Injustice: How the High Court Hijacked Election 2000 by Alan M. Dershowitz, Oxford University Press, New York, 2001, p. 243.

United Church of Christ News, "William H. Rehnquist 80 was UCC During Supreme Court Summer Break," September 6, 2005.

CHAPTER EIGHT

Concord Monitor, Concord, NH, July 1, 1976 (Justice Souter's comments on New Hampshire's statute authorizing cameras in courtrooms. Souter was New Hampshire's attorney general at the time).

Hustler Magazine, Inc. and Larry C. Flynt v. Jerry Falwell, U.S. Supreme Court, 485 U.S. 46 (1988).

Masson v. New Yorker Magazine, Inc., U.S. Supreme Court, 501 U.S. 496 (1991).

Milkovich v. Lorain Journal Co., U.S. Supreme Court, 474 U.S. 1 (1990).

Miracle at Philadelphia: The Story of the Constitutional Convention, May to September 1787 by Catherine Drinker Bowen, Little, Brown & Co., Boston, MA, 1966.

Nation, "Courting Libel," New York, November 22, 1990.

Senate Judiciary Committee Testimony by Justice David H. Souter, March 26, 1996 (subcommittee on budget).

Thomas Nast (1840–1902) was the chief political cartoonist for *Harper's Weekly* from 1862 to 1886. During that period he played a major role in bringing down the political machine of William Magear Tweed in New York.

Understanding Media: The Extensions of Man, Marshall McLuhan, McGraw Hill, New York, 1964, Chapter 24.

Washington Post, "Rehnquist Eulogies Look Beyond Bench" by Charles Lane, September 18, 2005, p. A-3.

Washington Post, "Rehnquist Solves Riddle," July 12, 1999.

Washington Journalism Review, "*New Yorker* Libel Case Threatens the Press" by Lyle Denniston, March 1991.

CHAPTER NINE

A Dictionary of the English Language, in Which the Words Are Deduced from Their Originals and Demonstrated in Their Different Significations by Examples from the Best Writers by Dr. Samuel Johnson, London, 1755.

Frankly Just Between Us: My Life Conducting Frank Sinatra Music by Vincent Falcone and Bob Popyk, Milwaukee, WI, 2005 (Sinatra dressing rooms had to be supplied with a carton of cigarettes).

His Way: The Unauthorized Biography of Frank Sinatra by Kitty Kelly, Bantam Press, 1986 (Sinatra smoked before concerts and recordings).

Internet: www.endocrineweb.com/caana (anaplastic cancer: the least common thyroid cancer).

Internet: www.henryrosner.org/Caruso/museum (Enrico Caruso's addiction to cigarettes).

Internet: www.ratical.org/radfiation/CNR/PBC/Chap9 (1924–44 radiation policy at Massachusetts Eye and Ear Infirmary, Boston).

Internet: si.edu/aboutregents (chief justice is a Smithsonian Regent by statute).

New York Times, "Extended Absence of Chief Justice Hints at More Serious Cancer Than He First Indicated," November 2, 2004.

New York Times, "Prognosis Depends on Which Type of Cancer He Has" by Linda Greenhouse and Katharine Q. Seelye, October 26, 2004, p. 1 ("Smoking is Not a Risk Factor for Thyroid Cancer").

New York Times, " 'Rehnquist Treated for Thyroid Cancer,' Supreme Court Says," October 26, 2004, p. 1.

Radiation Research, "Thyroid Cancer after Exposure to External Radiation: A Final Analysis of Seven Studies," Radiation Research Society, March 1995 (Vol. 141, No. 5), p. 275.

Washington Post, "Rehnquist Has Surgery for Cancer in Thyroid," Washington, D.C., October 26, 2004, p. 1.

Washington Post, "Rehnquist's Illness Forces Absence: Chief Justice's Treatment Suggests Thyroid Cancer at Its Most Serious," November 2, 2004, p. 1.

University of Maryland Faculty/Staff Directory, College Park, MD, 1990–91, 1991–92, 1992–93 (Obermayer adjunct journalism professor).

CHAPTER TEN

Harvard Law Review, "In Memoriam William H. Rehnquist," Chief Justice John G. Roberts Jr., Vol. 119, No. 1, November 2005, p. 2.

Internet: www.foxnews.com/story0,2933,168676.00.html (Nancy Spears's eulogy mentions betting).

Internet: *Slate,* "Tennis and Top Buttons: Remembering William H. Rehnquist" by Richard W. Garnett, September 4, 2005.

Inventory for William H. Rehnquist's Estate, Office of the Clerk of the Circuit Court, Arlington County, Virginia, filed May 5, 2006.

Legal Times, Washington, D.C., September 13, 2005 (David Leitch and R. Ted Cruz discuss Chief Justice Rehnquist's enjoyment of betting).

New York Times, "Eulogies for Rehnquist Recall a Man of Many Interests," September 8, 2005, p. 16 (reference to betting at Rehnquist funeral).

PS: Political Science and Politics (The American Political Science Association), Washington, D.C., October 2004, pp. 839–42.

"Rehnquist Buried at Arlington," Cox News Service, September 8, 2005 (Nancy Spears's eulogy mentions betting).

"Remarks by Associate Justice Sandra Day O'Connor, Funeral Service for William Hubbs Rehnquist, Chief Justice of the United States, September 7, 2005" (Supreme Court document).

Rudy Boschwitz (1930–) United States senator from Minnesota 1979–91, ambassador to the United Nations Human Rights Commission, 2005.

The Charlie Rose Show: A Conversation with Chief Justice William Rehnquist, March 12, 2004.

CHAPTER ELEVEN

Amistad (1997) starring Morgan Freeman, Anthony Hopkins and Matthew McConaughey. MPAA Rating: R for some scenes of strong, brutal violence and some related nudity.

Becoming Justice Blackmun: Harry Blackmun's Supreme Court Journey by Linda Greenhouse, Time Books, Henry Holt Company, New York, 2005, p. 247 (Justice Blackmun acts in *Amistad*).

Daily Pennsylvanian, "A Grandfather's Legacy of Law, Humor and Love," University of Pennsylvania, Philadelphia, PA, September 12, 2005 ("Old School").

George Washington Law Review, "Symposium on the Legacy of the Rehnquist Court Brings Together Legal Experts, Scholars, Judges, Students, Faculty, Alumni, and Media," October 28, 2005 (Courtney Gilligan, "Old School").

King Lear by William Shakespeare, Act III, Scene 7.

Nixon (1995) starring Anthony Hopkins, Joan Allen and Powers Boothe. MPAA Rating: R for language.

Old School (2003) starring Luke Wilson, Will Ferrell and Vince Vaughn. MPAA Rating: R for some strong sexual content, nudity and language.

The Motion Picture Association of America's film-rating system is used to rate a film's thematic and content suitability for certain audiences. R (Restricted): Attendance by persons under 17 requires an accompanying parent or adult guardian. May contain very strong language or strong sexual content/innuendo, explicit nudity, violence and gore, or drug use content. *The Tragedy of Othello, Moor of Venice* by William Shakespeare, Act V, Scene 2.

CHAPTER TWELVE

All the Laws but One: Civil Liberties in Wartime by William H. Rehnquist, Alfred A. Knopf, New York, 1998.

General George Armstrong Custer, a Civil War hero, was massacred along with all of his troops by Sioux, Cheyenne and Dakota Indians in the Battle of Little Bighorn, Montana, June 25, 1876. Inconclusive official investigations into the circumstances surrounding the event were made by various inquiry commissions appointed by federal, state and military authorities.

Grand Inquests: The Historic Impeachments of Justice Samuel Chase and President Andrew Johnson by William H. Rehnquist, William Morrow & Company, Inc., New York, 1992.

National Personnel Records Center, St. Louis, MO, "Soldier's Qualification Card: William Hubbs Rehnquist."

Shafiq Basul, et al. v. George W. Bush, et al., U.S. Supreme Court, 542 U.S. 466 (2004).

The Supreme Court Historical Society, Washington, D.C., operates the gift shop in the Supreme Court Building. Rehnquist books were offered for sale there.

The Supreme Court: How It Was, How It Is by William H. Rehnquist, William Morrow & Company, Inc., New York, 1987; revised edition, Alfred A. Knopf, New York, 2001.

CHAPTER THIRTEEN

Arizona Republic, "Marilyn D. Downey" (paid funeral notice), Phoenix, AZ, July 10, 2001 (Marilyn Bollinger legally retook her maiden name in 1999).

Harvard Law Review, "In Memoriam William H. Rehnquist" by James C. Duff (Administrative Assistant [Chief of Staff], 1996–2000), p. 16, Vol. 119, No. 1, November 2005.

Journal of Supreme Court History Society, "The Chief I Knew" by Noel J. Augustyn, Vol. 31, No. 1 (2006).

Journal of Supreme Court History Society, "The Story of the Attempted Assassination of Justice Field by a former associate on the Supreme Court of California," Vol. 30, No. 2 (2005).

New York Times, "Shot Fired Through Window of Blackmun Home," March 5, 1985.

The Alfalfa Club was founded in Washington, D.C., in 1913. There are approximately two hundred members.

The Vision of Sir Launfal by James Russell Lowell, Houghton, Mifflin, New York, 1848.

CHAPTER FOURTEEN

American Spectator, "George W. Bush, FDR, and History: Franklin Roosevelt's Biographer Assesses Our Consequential President" by Conrad Black, April 2005, p. 28.

New York Times, "Antiwar Veterans Are Labeled 'Irresponsible' by Rival Group," June 2, 1971 (John E. O'Neill and John Kerry publicly disagree about Vietnam War).

Program: Regional Meeting of the Mont Pelerin Society, The Hon. Mart Laar, former Prime Minister of Estonia, "Estonia: The Road *from* Serfdom," Reykjavik, Iceland, August 22, 2005.

Unfit for Command: Swift Boat Veterans Speak Out Against John Kerry by John E. O'Neill and Jerome R. Corsi, Regnery Publishing Company, Washington, D.C., 2004.

Washington Post, "2 Vets Assail Reports of Viet Butchery," June 7, 1971 (pro–Vietnam War statements by John O'Neill on CBS's *Face the Nation*).

CHAPTER FIFTEEN

Arlington Catholic Herald, "Justice Brennan and the Liberal Era: May They Rest in Peace," Arlington, VA, August 7, 1997.

Catholic News Service, "Lutheran Funeral in Catholic Cathedral; Unusual but Permitted," September 6, 2005.

Correspondence between Regina Ohlin and Susan Gibbs, Director of Communications, Archdiocese of Washington, D.C., December 22, 2006–March 2, 2007 (videotaping of Rehnquist funeral by Archdiocese of Washington).

Funeral Program: "A Service of Celebration and Commitment to God of the Life of William Hubbs Rehnquist Chief Justice of the United States: 1924–2005," Wednesday, September 7, 2005.

Funeral Program: "The Memorial Service for Natalie Cornell Rehnquist: 1929–1991," Emmanuel Lutheran Church, Bethesda, MD, October 22, 1991.

Internet: Slate, "Arlington National Cemetery; Dying to Get In? Here's How," December 13, 1997.

Internet: www.arlingtoncemetery.org/historical ("Historic Facts About Arlington National Cemetery").

New York Times, "Eulogies for Rehnquist Recall a Man of Many Interests," September 8, 2005, p. 16.

New York Times, "Yale Society Resists Peeks into Its Crypt," November 4, 1988 (Justice Potter Stewart administered oath of office to Vice President George H. W. Bush in 1980 and 1984).

New York Times, "With Gentle Humor, Brennan Is Buried," July 30, 1997.

Washington Post, "Rehnquist Eulogies Look Beyond Bench; Chief Was a Family Man and a Tennis Fanatic," September 8, 2005, p. 3.

AFTERWORD

Collected Poems 1957–1982, Wendell Berry, Farrar, Straus & Giroux, New York, 1982, p. 240.

PERMISSIONS

INDEX

Note: Page numbers in italics refer to illustrations.

Printed in the United States
By Bookmasters